ADVANCE PRAISE FOR
ANGELA SANTOMERO AND *PRESCHOOL CLUES*

"Angela is carrying on Fred's legacy with her work in children's media—a modern-day Fred Rogers."

—Joanne Rogers

"Angela Santomero is a bigger showrunner than Vince Gilligan, David Milch, and Judd Apatow combined—to a kid. The creator of *Blue's Clues*, *Super Why!*, *Creative Galaxy*—and yes, *Daniel Tiger's Neighborhood*—is the driving force behind the best educational programming for children."

—Fatherly.com

"*Preschool Clues* will be required reading in every course about child development, and it will be on every kid TV producer's bedside table, but more importantly it brings great and fun parenting insights from the eyes of a thoughtful, child-centered, famous TV producer. Angela has watched more preschoolers react, learn, change, and laugh from interactions with TV."

—Gerry Laybourne, media entrepreneur,
cofounder of Katapult, cofounder of Oxygen Media,
and president/leader of the team that created Nickelodeon

"Leave it to the genius behind *Blue's Clues* and *Daniel Tiger's Neighborhood*, Angela Santomero, to translate her knowledge of child development research into the ultimate parenting book. It includes guiding principles and hundreds of easy and fun everyday activities parents and teachers can use to raise children to be thoughtful, caring, and truly engaged learners!"

—Ellen Galinsky, author of *Mind in the Making:*
The Seven Essential Life Skills Every Child Needs

"Angela Santomero reveals the elements that make her shows both entertaining and educational, and clues parents to do the same in their everyday moments with young children."

—Joanna Faber and Julie King, authors of
How to Talk So Little Kids Will Listen

"Children are active and children are curious. Angela Santomero, who has harnessed their curiosity with brilliant children's television, has brought her creative instincts and solid developmental science to bear on how we can join and parent children in their world, which so seamlessly spans the physical and the digital. With this active, verb-driven, warm, and humorous guide, she offers clues to understanding and enjoying our young children while directing their endless energy toward their best selves.

—Michael Rich, M.D., The Mediatrician, and director of the Center on
Media and Child Health (CMCH), Boston Children's Hospital

"In this practical and research-based guide, Santomero, *Blue's Clues* cocreator and creator of *Daniel Tiger's Neighborhood* and other children's TV shows, helps parents of preschoolers understand how to use media effectively and age appropriately. . . . Parents will find plenty of fresh ideas for raising "smart, inspired, and engaged" preschoolers in this wise and enthusiastic text."

—*Publisher's Weekly*

"Fans of *Blue's Clues* and Santomero's other popular children's shows will enjoy her practical advice and conversational tone. Educators and parents will likely find a takeaway or two in this breezy, informative read."

—*Library Journal*

PRESCHOOL CLUES

Raising Smart, Inspired, and
Engaged Kids in a Screen-Filled World

ANGELA C. SANTOMERO, M.A.
with Deborah Reber

TOUCHSTONE
New York London Toronto Sydney New Delhi

Touchstone
An Imprint of Simon & Schuster, Inc.
1230 Avenue of the Americas
New York, NY 10020

First Touchstone trade paperback edition April 2018

TOUCHSTONE and colophon are registered trademarks
of Simon & Schuster, Inc.

For information about special discounts for bulk purchases,
please contact Simon & Schuster Special Sales at 1-866-506-1949
or business@simonandschuster.com.

The Simon & Schuster Speakers Bureau can bring authors to your live event. For more
information or to book an event, contact the Simon & Schuster Speakers Bureau at
1-866-248-3049 or visit our website at www.simonspeakers.com.

Interior design by Jill Putorti
Cover art: Santo Studios LLC
Photo by: William Taufic

Manufactured in the United States of America

10 9 8 7 6 5 4 3 2 1

Library of Congress Cataloging-in-Publication Data is available.

ISBN 978-1-5011-7433-9
ISBN 978-1-5011-7434-6 (ebook)

To Greg, Hope & Ella—when I was a preschooler and I played "house" I would dream you all up—but playing house for real is better than any dream. I love you more.

And to Fred Rogers—for being the premier influencer in the world of children's media—and my friend. I hope I've made you proud.

CONTENTS

CONTENTS

HELP, MODEL, OBSERVE

LAUGH, SING, CELEBRATE

FOREWORD

Every minute of a preschool child's life is of enormous value. What children encounter and learn during those minutes shapes the developing brain with lifelong consequences. Today's preschool children spend many of those minutes with screen media, especially television and other forms of video. Are these minutes well-spent? Decades of research have found that the answer is both yes and no.

As an example of the two sides of this answer, my colleagues and I studied more than 500 children's TV viewing during their preschool years (half the children were in Massachusetts and half in Kansas). We studied those same children more than twelve years later when they were near graduation from high school. Among other things, we obtained their high school transcripts. Those teens who watched mostly educational programming during the preschool years (at that time, mostly *Mister Rogers' Neighborhood* and *Sesame Street*) got better grades in high school English, math, and science, read more books outside of those assigned in school, and were less likely to endorse aggressive and violent solutions to social problems. A preschool TV diet rich in educational programs predicted good outcomes in high school. In contrast, those teens who had preschool television diets rich in violent action programs got poorer grades, and were more likely to endorse aggressive and violent behaviors.[1] Watching moderate amounts of television, by itself, was neither good nor bad. What mattered was *what* the children watched. In contrast to Marshall McLuhan's famous dictum, "the medium is message," we concluded that the "message is the message." A nutritious TV diet fosters healthy development; a junk TV diet does the opposite.

The foremost chef for nutritious preschool television is Angela Santomero. Her creations include *Blue's Clues, Super Why!,* and *Daniel Tiger's Neighborhood,* among others. In this book she reveals the secret sauce that induces kids to watch and learn and come back for more. Why was *Blue's Clues* the first preschool program to consistently invite audience participation? How does that help kids learn? What is the thinking behind creating the Clues and the Notebook, and why is Blue a girl? What are the behind-the-scenes decisions concerning pacing, repetition, and kids' emotional responses to the programs? How do Angela and her crew know that kids will like and learn from a program before it is aired? Here are the answers to these and many more questions.

I met Angela in the early 1990s when she was a young research coordinator at Nickelodeon. The company had successful programs for older kids, but was then trying to develop a new lineup of preschool programs. Because I was one of only a few developmental scientists who studied how children watch and understand television, I was invited to provide advice on the creation of these new programs. I agreed when the company said that the programs would be designed to be beneficial and educational for preschoolers. I was also pleased that the programs would not be interrupted by commercials. As we worked on programs such as *Gullah Gullah Island,* Angela would call me to take notes on my comments concerning program concepts and scripts. These calls always turned out to be much longer as Angela talked with me about research and her own ideas for children's programs. Over time, Angela began to develop more specific ideas for a program and pitched Nickelodeon on these ideas. To my delight, she systematically incorporated child development theory as well as my own and others' research findings concerning kids' TV viewing and comprehension. Underlying it all, she was inspired by her own memories of her preschool years watching *Mister Rogers' Neighborhood* and *Sesame Street.*

Eventually Angela was given the green light to develop a pilot for a new program tentatively called *Blue Prints*. Angela began to create what became a new age of preschool programming.[2] The show was different in many ways from good programs developed in previous decades. This was most obvious in the way it combined a live-action host character (initially Steve Burns) who lives in an animated world populated by an animated cast of characters. Nevertheless, every innovator takes advantage of earlier giants. Inspired by *Mister Rogers' Neighborhood,* Angela incorporated audience participation as an essential element of the program. Inspired by *Sesame Street,* Angela knew that the program, to be effective, must be based on foundational research (the accumulated knowledge and theory of child development research) and formative research specific to the program.

Finally, the big day came. The pilot episode of *Blue Prints* was finished, and it would be competitively tested against pilot episodes of several other programs. The pilots were shown to preschoolers and their attention and reactions were recorded. The results were clear; the children loved *Blue Prints*: They laughed, helped find Blue's Clues, yelled out the answers to thinking problems, and generally had a very good time. Testing showed that they learned important lessons taught in the pilot. When asked what the name of the show was, all the kids answered without hesitation, "Blue's Clues." The children gave the program its name.

Blue's Clues was chosen for broadcast. But there was a problem, it would be impossible in the time frame to have enough episodes completed to air a different episode every day. Episodes would have to be repeated daily, which would be a radical departure from usual practice. I brought the pilot home to see how my three-year-old daughter would like it and whether she would want to watch it more than once. She ended up watching it seventeen times by herself and with friends over about two weeks. Eventually, we did a study on repeated viewing. Not only did the children love watching the same episode five days in a row, their learning of ideas in the episode became much greater.[3]

Blue's Clues became a huge success and launched Angela Santomero's career as one of the foremost creators and producers of educational media for young children. Over time, her understanding of the audience has deepened, and all of the programs have been shown to have a real and positive impact. This may be why she has been able to have so many hit shows being telecast nationwide at the same time.

Blue's Clues changed the way young children watch television, forever destroying the myth that television is a "passive" medium. We did a study showing that experienced *Blue's Clues* viewers, compared to children who had not yet seen the show, were much more actively engaged in watching and participating than in other programs they had never previously seen.[4] The children had learned a new way of watching TV and preschool TV viewing would never be the same again. *Blue's Clues* and Angela have in fact inspired a new generation of television programs hoping to catch its interactive magic and engaged learning.

Every minute of a preschool child's life is important. Angela designs every second of every minute of her programs to maximize positive impact. In this book, she gives us the ingredients for a most nutritious preschool media diet enriched with numerous parenting insights.

Daniel R. Anderson, Ph.D.
Professor Emeritus of Psychological and Brain Sciences
University of Massachusetts Amherst

NOTE FROM THE AUTHOR

It was 1997 and I was seated at Fred Rogers' table at a Children and Media Conference. I might as well have been sitting with Justin Timberlake or Bruce Springsteen. This was the KING OF PRESCHOOL TELEVISION.

I couldn't believe it. I mean, I was that four-year-old who could not sit any closer to the television when *Mister Rogers' Neighborhood* was on. I talked to him through the TV. I believed him when he told me he was proud of me. I loved taking Trolley to the Neighborhood of Make-Believe only to return, once again, to hear Fred sing.

I had been talking a lot about Fred in the press lately, mostly about how I was inspired by him to co-create my own preschool show, *Blue's Clues*. I've always considered Fred my mentor from afar. In fact, as an eighth grader, while my classmates wrote about famous sports heroes or astronauts, I chose Fred Rogers as the subject of an essay paper about someone I looked up to, which is how I knew we had at least one thing in common—we both had a much younger sibling—and how I learned he had a master's degree in child developmental psychology. Now, all these years later, not only did we have the same graduate degrees—we also both went into media because we didn't like what was on television for preschoolers. I mean . . . the stars were aligned—and now we were going to have lunch together!

I couldn't eat as I sat at his table and quickly learned he was as kind and empathetic as his on-camera persona. He smiled. I smiled. Then, I finally got up the courage to walk over to his side of the table, crouch down next to him, and say hello. But instead, I said, "*I-just-wanted-you-to-know-the-whole-reason-I-went-into-children's-television-was-because-of-you!*" Smooth.

I paused to take a breath (or rather, gasp for air). Fred Rogers smiled, put his hand on my shoulder, and said, as if we had all the time in the world, "What is your name?"

I laughed as I told him my name, and we started our conversation all over again. As it happens, he still thought most children's television programs were missing the mark, but he did like my show, and recognized and appreciated its child development foundation. Overjoyed, I told him that our "Blue skidoo" was a transition device inspired by his Trolley. I told him that Steve talking directly to camera was because of how much I felt he had talked directly to me as a preschooler. Fred's smile broadened, and his eyes misted over. Then he said, looking right at *me*, "I'm so proud of you." And this time it wasn't through the television.

It was my turn to get misty-eyed.

GUILT: INTRODUCTION

When Katie gets home from picking up her kids from preschool, she's got exactly one hour to unload the groceries, transform a week's worth of leftovers into some sort of palatable meal, do a once-over of the living room so her book club can meet without risk of a Lego injury, and return two phone calls she couldn't get to while at the office.

So she throws together a healthy snack of apples and raisins, pulls out the beanbag chairs, and queues up a few episodes of her little ones' favorite show du jour, *Daniel Tiger's Neighborhood*. For forty-five minutes—almost an entire peaceful hour—Katie knows her kids are safe, happy, and hopefully even learning something. And she has the chance to catch her breath and do what she needs to do before the post-dinner/pre-bedtime madness ensues.

Yet while Katie is grateful for the break her children's media gives her, and she trusts that a kids' show on PBS can't be a *bad* thing, she can't help but feel uneasy, especially when that evening she reads yet another article in a Facebook parenting group espousing the "dangers of screen time" for kids. As parent after parent comments on the thread, judging those who stick their kids in front of the TV or bring devices with them to restaurants, the peace and calm Katie felt only hours earlier has suddenly been replaced by heavy doubt and guilt, and not for the first time.

Is Katie messing with her children's developing brains or turning them into passive little zombies? Is she a lazy mom who doesn't manage her time well enough? Should she have a better grasp on what her kids watch, when they watch it, and how it's impacting them? We live in a plugged-in, screen-filled world, and as a fierce advocate for the positive potential of media in kids' lives, I feel passionate about changing the discourse surrounding screen time to one that loses the shame and guilt and instead recognizes what a powerful tool high-quality programs for children can be, both for the young viewers *and* their caregivers.

When parents have the information that they need to make smart, informed choices about their children's media and understand how high-quality preschool programming powerfully resonates with, entertains, and teaches young viewers important social, emotional, and cognitive skills, they can feel confident using kids' media to their advantage and in a way that strengthens and supports their role as parents. An added bonus? They can do it guilt-free!

It's hard seeing parents like Katie lose confidence in how they're raising their kids because of a lack of awareness or clarity around the choices they're making about media. And I also know it can be overwhelming to know how to navigate all the options, not to mention make sense of sometimes conflicting research and recommendations. That's why I'm here to help.

After earning my master's degree in developmental psychology and instructional technology and media, creating some of the most successful educational preschool shows on television, and raising two girls who are now teenagers, I've come to know a few truths about kids and media:

- o Media can be an incredibly positive and powerful educational tool for preschoolers.
- o A preschooler's favorite shows are in reality some of their best friends and most influential teachers.
- o Kids' media can be a bonding experience that brings families together—to laugh, bond, and learn.
- o And most important, we can all lose the guilt. Because par-

ents can learn from their children's media too, especially when they know how to engage and interact with it.

My goal has always been to create media—on any screen—that will empower, challenge, and build the self-worth of preschoolers while making them laugh. Armed with research, years of working with kids, time I've spent in the preschool classroom, a passion for media, and the best team in children's media history, I have formulated the "recipe" for the most effective way to educate kids through media.

Blue's Clues, the first show I co-created at twenty-five years old with fellow co-creators Traci Paige Johnson and Todd Kessler, features a live-action host immersed in an animated world and the cutest blue puppy around. Who knew it would become one of the most successful preschool shows *ever*? Kids weren't only watching . . . they were learning. And we had the fan mail, ratings, and research to prove it.

Then I became a mom. And as a mom, I found myself doubting my parenting skills. I just wanted to *skidoo* right into my shows for guidance, as I poured everything I knew about kids' development into every script I wrote. I asked myself, *Should I be greeting my girls in the morning with, "Hi, out there, it's me, Mommy!" Should I sing whenever the mail comes? Should I spend twenty-two minutes figuring out what they want for snack? Where were my three clues for parenting?*

One night while at a book signing for my *Blue's Clues* books, a mom who also happened to be a teacher approached me and asked if I was raising my girls using the same philosophy that my shows are based on. She said she was utilizing the elements in her preschool classroom and was impressed with the results. I smiled and nodded, but inside I was thinking, *Am I practicing what I preach?* I knew in my heart that everything I know to be true about kids is the foundation of all of my shows. *But could I really look to my shows to help me be a better mom?* The answer was clear. *Absolutely.*

I've spent more than two decades creating and writing shows for kids that are based on the essential clues for healthy child development. In all my shows, I embed clues for respectful communication through the dialogue, playfulness through the animation, active engagement through taking time to Pause, and diffusing with humor as a conflict-resolution strategy, among many, many others.

Before having my own kids, I was creating shows for the kid in me. I was creating a make-believe world I wanted to live in. A world where I felt good about myself, a world that respected me for the smart kid I was, and a world that would want me to speak up and voice my point of view. In a sense, the make-believe, animated worlds I create for preschoolers are safe and happy places to play, explore, fail, try again, and learn.

As a mom and a kids' show creator, I knew my philosophy about kids—based on child development, education, and instructional television and media—were sprinkled throughout every show, from *Blue's Clues* on Nickelodeon and *Super Why!* and *Daniel Tiger's Neighborhood* on PBS to *Creative Galaxy* and *Wishenpoof* on Amazon. What I didn't realize was that my philosophy was so hidden that no one, except for a few people, like the teacher who was using them in her classroom, knew about them.

And the idea for this book was born.

I have teased apart my preschool shows and broken open the clues that are inside *all of them.* I've looked back at all the research that proves the success of using media to teach, influence, and inform. The mission for every one of my shows is to empower, challenge, and build the self-worth of preschoolers all while making them laugh. Inside this book I will show you exactly how to use that same philosophy in your everyday world.

By the time you're finished reading *Preschool Clues*, you'll not only understand exactly *what* your children are learning from the shows they watch and *why* their shows are so effective at communicating that learning—you'll know exactly *how* to apply that same tried and tested approach to the way you parent your kids, and with the same powerful results.

Watch, Learn, Know

WATCH

At seventeen, I was that babysitter in constant demand, but my first priority was always my three-year-old brother, Rob. He was (and still is) sweet and caring, and back then, a boy who was highly influenced by his two older sisters. He had a ton of empathy right from the start—he even worried about throwing a football for fear that the pointy edge would hurt the other person. He took his very first steps walking to me and constantly asked "Why" questions about everything as I read book after book to him (inspiration for *Super Why!*). I loved seeing how excited he would get when learning something new watching his favorite television shows.

One afternoon, he was watching a new show where the characters seemed to look right at him. They pointed to him and one by one they kicked at the air, and so did my three-year-old brother. In the course of watching the show, it was like my brother became part of the show—kicking at the TV, fighting "crime," and being celebrated for "beating the bad guys." And my brother loved it. I distinctly remember that moment, thinking about how amazing it was that these characters could get him to play with the television in this way. It reminded me of myself as a preschooler, interacting with Mister Rogers, but instead of kicking, I was *talking, thinking*, and *expressing my feelings*. And in that very moment—the same moment when my brother first discovered his favorite childhood TV show—I was sparked. I had my "a-ha!" moment. I wanted to create preschool TV that kids would love but would also make them interact . . . *without* kicking.

THE BIG QUESTION

Perhaps now would be a good time to address the elephant in the room, namely, the big question: *Should our preschoolers be watching television* or any screen at all? And if so, how much and what should they watch?* These are questions most parents consider at some point. And like all things with parenting, just about everyone has an opinion on the subject. Some parents opt for a TV-free home or severely limit media usage. Most of these parents have made the decision that TV is inherently bad for their children and believe watching it robs their children of time that could be spent engaged in imaginative or outdoor play.

If you're familiar with the Waldorf educational philosophy, you know that it strongly encourages keeping televisions out of the home and restricting children's interaction with computers. The Waldorf belief is that electronic media "seriously hamper[s] the development of the child's imagination—a faculty which is believed to be central to the healthy development of the individual."[1]

At the other side of the spectrum are homes where the TV is pretty much always on, essentially becoming the background and soundtrack to a child's life. Kids in these homes may end up watching upwards of five, six, or more hours of TV a day.[2]

Most families probably fall somewhere in the middle of these two extremes. According to a 2010 study by the Kaiser Family Foundation, kids ages eight to eighteen watch an average of four and a half hours of television per day, including content that's watched online, on devices, and on cell phones.[3] Four and a half hours . . . that's more than thirty-one hours of television content each week!

Regardless of where a child's TV screen time (programs viewed on screens such as TV, iPad, Kindle, etc.) usage falls on the spectrum, it doesn't change what's at the heart of the debate: *Is television for pre-*

---

* The way I see it, the words *television, media,* and *screens* are all interchangeable—content is content, no matter where you watch it!

schoolers inherently bad? I'm here to tell you once and for all: NO. (And because repetition is the key to learning, let me repeat that: *NO.*)

I firmly believe that all media is teaching our kids *something.*

ALL MEDIA IS EDUCATIONAL, BUT WHAT EXACTLY IS IT TEACHING?

The Food and Drug Administration (FDA) strictly regulates the way packaged food in the United States is labeled, making it relatively easy for conscious shoppers to choose products that align with their values and health goals. And while there are some regulations around kids' media—the 1990 Children's Television Act placed limits on the amount of advertising minutes in children's shows and demanded broadcasters prove their programs "served the educational and information needs of children"—we don't have much *transparency* as to what exactly constitutes an "educational program." In fact, *The Jetsons* was once ridiculously thought of as "educational" for space exploration. There's no easy way for viewers to understand the value of what they're watching and what exactly went into making it.

Much of the conversation regarding kids' media centers around screen time limits, and the American Academy of Pediatrics has been a highly vocal and visible contributor to the conversation, though it doesn't always get it right. In 1999, the AAP received a ton of backlash when it suggested that kids under the age of two should use no media at all, a recommendation that wasn't based in any real data or understanding of parents' lives. In 2015, the AAP retracted its statement, making new recommendations and guidelines for the different age spans of a preschool child, based on a fairly slim body of research.[4] However, the AAP remains firm that children under eighteen months should abstain from all screen time except for live interactive video such as FaceTime or Skype.

I agree that parents should avoid allowing their toddlers to engage in "solo media" or watching television by themselves. Studies point to poorer language skills and language delays in young toddlers if they're watching alone. I suspect these findings have to do with screen time replacing live interactions with caregivers. Similar results can be seen in studies that show a correlation between older kids who watch more television and poor reading levels. Here's another case where it's not necessarily the media that detracts from a child's ability to learn to read—it's that the *time spent* on media viewing takes away from time spent with books. Just like having an occasional sweet wouldn't replace all good food, media shouldn't replace the important activities like reading, free play, and live interactions that are so important for a preschooler's healthy development and growth. It's all about balance. In each of the "Clue" chapters, I'll be sharing with you my best suggestions for off-screen activities, both for you to engage in *with* your child and for them to enjoy on their own.

CONTENT IS KING

Today, the AAP suggests to limit screen use to one hour a day of high-quality programming for preschoolers ages two to five and points out that many of the apps and programs claiming to be educational are lacking. The AAP also provides an online tool for parents that acts as a guide to building a family media plan. I'm not here to push for a hard-and-fast rule with regards to screen time limits—I believe that parents should make the informed choices that work best for their family. More important than quantity is the *quality* of the educational media a parent chooses for their preschoolers. And that every hour of media be followed up at minimum with an hour of free play.

Co-Viewing Versus Involved Viewing

In addition to setting guidelines regarding screen time limits, the American Academy of Pediatrics has also pointed to the importance of the caregiver's role in media usage. The AAP's recommendation is that parents and caregivers "co-view with your children, help children understand what they are seeing, and help them apply what they learn to the world around them."[5]

In the same way that kids benefit socially and emotionally when their families regularly eat dinner together, talk, and play together, having a caregiver involved for any event or media interaction adds to the learning and enjoyment. In a study of *Sesame Street* episodes, preschoolers will verbalize more, play along, and retain and master concepts when a caregiver is present.[6] Having someone to ask questions when they don't understand something enhances preschoolers' learning.

While co-viewing every program with our preschoolers might be unrealistic, we *can* extend the definition to include *involved viewing* where we, as parents:

- o choose the high-quality media for our kids;
- o know what they are watching;
- o are involved by asking and answering questions and extending the learning before, during, or after the show is over.

We can and need to be *involved* in what media our kids consume the same way we are involved in what they eat. We need to know what the ingredients are in the shows and games that our kids are mesmerized by. We need to talk about the characters and the stories our preschoolers love—at any point in their day. We need to know how the media we choose for our preschoolers are affecting their brains, their morals, their values, and their beliefs.

As *involved viewers* of our kids' media, we are the gatekeepers. We are the ones who feed our preschoolers' brains by choosing what books they read, what activities they take part in, what toys and props they play with, and what media they consume. Just like we choose what foods we put into our cabinets and on the dinner table, we are active, informed, and involved consumers of our media. By being *involved viewers*, we are making informed, quality media choices for our preschoolers.

The Merits of Good, Quality Media

It's been proven time and time again that good, quality media can teach kids to read, gain kindergarten readiness skills, understand life lessons, and even foster kindness. Kids who were raised on a diet of good, quality media have expansive vocabularies, go to college, and score better on standardized tests than kids who didn't watch educational media.[7] It's also been proven that my recipe for curriculum-based "interactive" television, the kind of programming that elicits active participation from the home viewer, has strong educational merit.

As adults, we know that the media we consume influences pretty much everything in our lives—how we act, how we think, what we eat, what we do, where we go, what we aspire to, what's important, and what's funny. We are always learning from what we see and hear on TV, in movies, on our computer screens, on our iPads, in books, on phones, and on the radio. We even thought cigarettes were nothing to worry about until there was a ban on showing them in mainstream television shows and movies geared to kids and families! More important, our children are watching and learning right alongside us. The positive side of this is that as the technology grows, we can be increasingly savvy and choosy about our content.

Just as the food industry markets to kids so they'll want to consume cereals, fast foods, and other processed foods, there are millions of marketing dollars in play to get our children to watch television shows and play electronic games. With so much media around us and so much profit at stake, it's critical that we, as consumers, do our own due diligence to find high-quality shows that will support our kids' social, emotional, and intellectual development.

Food revolutionaries, such as author and food activist Michael Pollan and celebrity chef and healthy school lunch advocate Jamie Oliver, have helped reframe the way people think and talk about food—most important, how to ensure we are making informed food choices. In the same way, we need to make informed choices about the programs, games, and screens our kids interact with so that we, in turn, feed our kids good, quality content.

LEARN

Building Your Healthy Media Diet

WATCH TV, NOT TOO MUCH, MAKE IT INTERACTIVE AND EDUCATIONAL

Finding high-quality shows can take some effort because what we're looking to do is essentially create our own "healthy media diet," complete with lots of fresh, whole ingredients. We want to feed our kids high-quality programs and apps that spark their creativity and passion and enable them to learn as opposed to media that's nothing more than processed content with empty promises. So, how do we do that? Think of it as a screen time version of a healthy green smoothie. With a green smoothie, you've got the greens, the protein, and the sweets. With a high-quality preschool show, you've got education (the greens), interaction (the protein), and engagement (the sweets).

THE GREEN SMOOTHIE

1. Education (the greens): Just because a show *says* it's educational doesn't mean it is. As smart consumers, we need to dig deeper and ask questions to uncover a show's curriculum, teaching approach, and more.
2. Interaction (the protein): We want a show that allows children to participate, think, have a voice; that speaks to them with respect and sparks an interest or ignites a passion.
3. Engagement (the sweets): Effective, healthy media needs to be engaging and entertaining so kids will *want* to watch. No matter how good something is, if no one watches, no one will learn anything. Period.

Sure, there is no equivalent of a nutritional wrapper on the shows your children are watching. (Wouldn't it be great if there were?) But being a savvy media consumer doesn't have to be hard if you know what to look for and understand how to measure the "nutritional" value in your kids' media.

What follows is a detailed look at these three key ingredients for healthy media so you can create your own personal "Yes" list of media that is satisfying, nutritious, and beneficial all at the same time.

THE GREEN SMOOTHIE: INGREDIENT NUMBER 1: EDUCATION

Choosing good, quality programming is the foundation of a Healthy Media Diet. Don't worry—you don't have to have a PhD in educational psychology to discern what's really going on in the programs your kids are drawn to. But as smart consumers, we need to dig deeper and ask important questions. And, as the AAP said, we need to be able to distinguish between the shows that say they're educational but are lacking and the ones that really are.

I define good, quality educational media as *media with the intent to teach.* A quality show will marry a strong educational curriculum with the understanding of the visual medium of television, tell a preschool-appropriate story, and immerse viewers into the world to enhance mastery and spark change.

Here's a closer look at criteria worth exploring when determining a show's educational value.

A Strong Creator's Vision

A top-tier creator will have a vision built around a certain "need," a specific point of view and approach to address this need, and a sense of urgency about sharing it with the world. As parents, we're looking for strong visionary creators who respect our kids, don't talk down to them, understand their level of development, and want to spark their interest, whether it be math, science, imagination, or life lessons.

. . . .

VISIONARY CREATORS IN PRESCHOOL MEDIA

It's should be no surprise that in my book the best example of a visionary creator is Fred Rogers. As an example of his strong vision, Fred Rogers spoke to the United States Senate in 1969 to defend educational programming and to ensure funding for PBS. As the creator of *Mister Rogers' Neighborhood*, he said, "I give an expression of care every day to each child, to help him realize that he is unique. I end the program by saying, 'You've made this day a special day, by just your being you. There's no person in the whole world like you, and I like you, just the way you are.' And I feel that if we in public television can only make it clear that feelings are mentionable and manageable, we will have done a great service for mental health. I think that it's much more dramatic that two men could be working out their feelings of anger—much more dramatic than showing something of gunfire. I'm constantly concerned about what our children are seeing [on television], and for fifteen years I have tried in this country and Canada, to present what I feel is a meaningful expression of care." And that's when PBS got its first $20 million in funding.

Joan Ganz Cooney, a documentary producer, had a vision to change the world for children in poverty. She believed that "poor children were truly powerless, they are an absolutely mute minority." She wanted to create a show for preschoolers that would change their lives. She wanted her show to present "cognitive skills that children could learn while watching: letters, numbers, and reasoning skills." She submitted her idea to the federal government, the Ford Foundation, and the Carnegie Corporation, all of which agreed to fund her project. And in 1969, *Sesame Street* went on the air and has been positively impacting the lives of children ever since.[1]

. . . .

A Strong Curriculum

Good, quality educational media starts with the curriculum—a well thought out approach to how the learning will be conveyed. Without a curriculum, a show has no spine. A visionary creator needs her manifesto—her show "bible" that outlines the message and the approach to that message for writers, producers, and animators to follow to support her vision. According to renowned media researcher and authority Dr. Dan Anderson, calling something educational comes down to the merits of a curriculum as its foundation.

A show curriculum is a document created by or with a research professional that has broken down a show's educational goals and objectives into actionable steps that can then be brought into a writers' room and incorporated into each script. Different shows focus on different curricular areas, depending on the theme.

Of course, it's not enough to just *have* a curriculum. The approach to the curriculum is just as important—to extend the food metaphor, it's what takes a show from the television equivalent of fast food to a healthy meal composed of whole foods. All shows maintain different levels of these educational aspects in their scripts. *Sesame Street* began this groundbreaking approach in 1969 not only by having a strong curriculum but by also smartly incorporating it into every aspect of creating the show. *Sesame's* process to have curriculum advisors in the room with producers and writers is assurance that the curriculum is an important element in the show. The advisors have a seat at the table, literally.

In addition to having their curriculum advisors or researchers in the throes of the production process, the best educational shows also have episodes written with the curriculum as its spine. "Having the curriculum on the through-line" means that everything we do in an episode revolves around the curriculum (as opposed to just telling a story with a moral at the end). Though it's not a preschool show, a great example of a solid curriculum can be found in the Broadway smash *Hamilton.* The entire show is spelled out in the first lyric of the first song: "How does a bastard, orphan, son of a whore and a Scotsman, dropped in the middle of a forgotten spot in the Caribbean by providence impoverished, in squalor, grow up to be a hero and a scholar?" The curriculum is clear from the start: US history with a focus on Alexander Hamilton's impact on America. The curricular approach is immersing the audience in his time while revealing its relevance in our lives today.

As examples, here is a look at the different types of curriculums featured in each of my preschool shows:

Blue's Clues (Nick Jr.)
o Curriculum: *Kindergarten Readiness Skills* (Dr. Alice Wilder and Angela C. Santomero)
o Vision and Approach: Introducing everything preschoolers need to know before they enter kindergarten; approached through interactive games that are scaffolded (deliberately repeated) in levels of difficulty throughout the program.

Super Why! (PBS Kids)
o Curriculum: *Reading Skills* (Dr. Alice Wilder and Angela C. Santomero)
o Vision and Approach: Giving preschoolers the clues and skills to learn to read and love to read while using books as a resource for life. The curriculum is founded on skills the National Reading Panel deems critical for learning to read, and the approach is through scaffolded interactive games that focus on letter identification, word decoding, word encoding, and fluency.

Daniel Tiger's Neighborhood (PBS Kids)
o Curriculum: *Socio Emotional Skills* (The Fred Rogers Company; based on the work of Fred Rogers)
o Vision and Approach: Giving preschoolers and parents vocabulary to label their feelings and to provide actionable clues in the form of singable songs when dealing with life lessons such as disappointment, anger, sadness, making new friends, among others.

Creative Galaxy (Amazon Kids)
- Curriculum: *The Arts* (Dr. Alice Wilder)
- Vision and Approach: Giving preschoolers an understanding of how to solve problems by thinking outside the box and tapping into the power of art and creativity, while also introducing and fostering an appreciation for different art methods and the prominent art masters who used them.

Wishenpoof (Amazon Kids)
- Curriculum: *Executive Functioning Skills* (Dr. Alice Wilder; based on the work of Ellen Galinsky in her *The Mind in the Making: 7 Essential Skills*)
- Vision and Approach: Giving preschoolers a strong role model in lead character Bianca, who uses her gift of making wishes come true to help others and spread joy. In the process, she works to strengthen her own fledgling life skills and brings viewers along for the learning.

To learn more about the curricular foundation of your child's favorite shows, visit the websites for the network or channel it airs on, such as PBSkids.org, grownups.pbs.org, or check out Common Sense Media, which offers age-based reviews and commentary on all types of media. Interviews with the creators will also shed some insight.

Mastery

To label something as truly educational, we want to ensure that kids master the concepts in the program—to internalize the learning, make connections to their own world, and take the learning from the show to another level. We're not looking for them to parrot what they see on that specific episode or in that particular book. We're looking for that spark . . . that light-switch moment.

On our very first episode of *Blue's Clues*, we had preschoolers helping Steve put away groceries. Blue had knocked over the grocery bag and fruit had spilled out onto the counter. The kids at home were asked to help by looking at different foods, identifying the shapes, and labeling them. A simple shape game, we had a slice of cheese as a square, a graham cracker as a rectangle, and a bunch of grapes as a triangle. After Steve asked the question and Paused, kids at home were prompted to point to the shape he asked for. The shapes got progressively harder, as grapes are not necessarily thought of as a triangle. We scaffolded this game purposefully so we could have kids thinking more deeply about the task and start to master the concept behind it.

When screening this episode with a preschool class, one four-year-old girl jumped up after the show had ended, pointed to a light switch, and proclaimed, "That's a rectangle!" She then started a little preschool movement, and the entire class began to march around the room pointing to different objects and labeling their shapes. That little girl was sparked. *Blue's Clues* had helped her master the concept of shape recognition rather than just memory-based learning.

Research-Based

A good educational program will be drenched in research to ensure that the goals of the creator are met. Nothing makes me more incensed than having someone pitch a kids' show that's going to "change the world" and offer no proof. I've been working in kids' television long enough to tell you that not all shows are researched, even when they say they are. So as parents, we need to see who is behind the shows our little ones are watching and get clear on how much research is actually involved. I know your time is limited and you likely don't need more added to your plate, but when you consider the amount of time your child spends with their favorite shows and the characters in them, it only makes sense that you'd want to get to know them better so you can feel confident that the "relationship" is going to be a positive one for your child.

Research usually falls in one or more of the following categories:

Foundation in Research

Shows with a "foundation" in research are those where the creators themselves have a background in children and television research, have studied and immersed themselves in the research of their show, or have created their program with a curriculum in tow or a statement of purpose created by a researcher. It could also mean they are working in tandem with an educational advisor in the development of the program. For example, Joan Ganz Cooney conducted a formal study on using television as a medium to teach preschoolers *before* she created *Sesame Street*. During production, she did something that had never been done before in kids' TV—she gathered prominent educational researchers, writers, and producers and together they created an educational curriculum and guide for what *Sesame Street* would become.

Formative Research

Formative research is a phased process for ensuring each aspect of a program is meeting the needs as set forth by the creator and curriculum. For example, as we were developing *Blue's Clues*, I used my research chops to ensure my team and I, led by educational psychologist Dr. Alice Wilder, one of the key thinkers behind developing our groundbreaking research process, would paper-test each show, which meant bringing the script in a "storybook format" into schools to read to preschoolers. This method has become known as the first step of the formative research process in much of today's preschool television world. While *Sesame Street* brought episodes to preschoolers after the show was created, we stepped it up by testing shows through this formative research process. Then throughout the development of the pilot and the series, we would similarly test the show in various forms—paper and drawings, simple video storyboards, rough animation—and take children through the story and play the games with them. Our goal was and still is to see if it was interesting, if they were engaged, and, most important, how far we could push the educational content for them developmentally. At each stage, the researchers provide us with a data-filled memo of where and how we could develop the show to make it even more effective in these areas. This was groundbreaking in the world of children's television research as it had never been done before at this level. In his book *The Tipping Point*, Malcolm Gladwell cites this as one of the reasons that *Blue's Clues* is so "sticky."[2] I say that it's our secret sauce.

Summative and Longitudinal Research

While formative research is about ensuring the success and resonance of a show—or in our case, of each episode—summative and longitudinal research is conducted to confirm a program's effectiveness with a statistically significant sample of preschoolers. In the case of *Blue's Clues*, we use this type of research to determine the true learning and impact of our show in the lives of viewers.

YOUR HEALTHY MEDIA DIET: *EDUCATION*

Make a list of your preschooler's favorite programs and ask yourself:

- What are they learning? What are your kids taking away from their favorite shows? Remember: they are always learning something, whether a show is educational or not.
- How would you describe the creator's vision?
- What is the core curriculum of the show?

THE GREEN SMOOTHIE:
INGREDIENT NUMBER 2: INTERACTION

The second important ingredient of good, quality media for kids is the inclusion of some form of active participation or interactivity, meaning the show or app asks the home viewer to interact, participate, think, or has a call to action. We know that preschoolers want to be involved. They want to play. They want to help. They want to be asked questions. With the goal of educating kids through mastery, we want to see kids being immersed into our shows, fully engaged, and actively participating.

Some researchers have described watching television as a passive experience, labeling TV-viewing kids as "couch potatoes" who sit passively and watch whatever is on. Dr. Dan Anderson couldn't disagree more. Through his research we know that kids are active listeners, they are absorbing everything, and they are always learning.

There are many ways a preschool show can be interactive, but here are some clues for the kinds of things to look for when considering how your child is interacting with the shows they watch:

The Preschool Home Viewer Is a Main Character

I've always believed in including preschoolers in my scripts as actual characters in the series. Depending on the show, the "interactive" approach varies, but what's always the same is that the show assumes the preschooler is watching. We know, and acknowledge, they are there. This changes the way we script our shows, the way we storyboard the scenes, and the way we animate. Our characters address the viewers with the sole intention of eliciting a reaction. In the case of *Blue's Clues*, this interaction is "game show-esque" in nature as preschoolers are being asked direct questions. As a result, preschoolers aren't only *watching* the educational curriculum—they're *practicing* kindergarten readiness skills by playing along. In *Daniel Tiger's Neighborhood*, the interactive nature is more of an emotional bond, as Daniel talks directly to the home viewer to share his feelings, ask for help, and invite viewers to sing along with him. This emotional bond with Daniel fits right into the through-line of the social-emotional curriculum of the show and ensures kids at home feel for Daniel and want to learn the new strategy to help him, thus learning it for themselves as well.

Breaking the Fourth Wall

When choosing engaging, interactive content, look for a show that's designed to invite your preschooler into its world with curricular intent and purpose. One of the key ways to be interactive is when a character breaks the fourth wall by leaning in, looking directly at the camera, and talking to the viewer at home. The character is acknowledging the presence of the home viewer and respectfully communicating, actively listening, and seeming to affirm what they have to say. This interactive format is the key to preschoolers mastering the curriculum. Just as a hands-on science experiment leads to a deeper understanding of the science, using media as an interactive tool leads to a deeper understanding to maximize a preschooler's learning.

Fred Rogers was the first person to break the fourth wall and talk directly to the kids at home. He did this to impart his social and emotional curriculum and, as a result, kids felt as if Mister Rogers were a confidant and friend. In my shows, we break this fourth wall to help preschoolers learn how to think, not what to think, emotionally invest in and bond with our characters, and learn and practice life strategies.

Sparked to Play

To be high quality, a program doesn't have to overtly ask your preschooler to play along. It could also offer ways to extend the learning and play after the show is over. For instance, some shows include calls to action like suggesting viewers go outside to find objects in nature they can use to make a craft, as on *Creative Galaxy*, or the main character in *Tumble Leaf* suggesting kids go out and play. Shows can also spark kids to engage in other ways; for example, wanting to read the Curious George books after watching the series on TV or playing out a show dressed up as their favorite character.

YOUR HEALTHY MEDIA DIET: *INTERACTION*

Think of your preschooler's favorite shows:

- What is the role of your preschooler in the show?
- Does your child play along?
- Are they able to obtain mastery over the show's content?

THE GREEN SMOOTHIE:
INGREDIENT NUMBER 3: ENGAGEMENT

Engaging content is what makes a show sticky, relevant, funny, exciting, surprising, and different from anything else out there. The engagement tenet of a high-quality show will not only ensure the program remains memorable for a long time to come, but it will result in an enjoyable, connected, and positive experience. To identify shows that know how to engage your preschooler, look for programs that cause your child to lean in, get curious, and want to play. Here are some telltale signs of shows that incorporate this key ingredient:

Preschool-Relatable Storylines

It's important to understand whether or not a program, app, or movie is appropriate and relevant for where our child is socially, emotionally, and cognitively. In fact, even when a show is specifically marketed to preschoolers, it's still our job to understand whether or not it meets its mark and is truly age appropriate. While this is important for a number of reasons, from an educational perspective, when a program or story resonates with its target audience, the level of mastery will increase.

An example of a preschool-relatable storyline is an episode of *Daniel Tiger's Neighborhood* we created to explore the issue of separation anxiety. In the storyline, Daniel Tiger was feeling ambivalent about leaving his dad when it was time to be dropped off at preschool. Since our curriculum, based in Fred Rogers' work on social-emotional development, is to give preschoolers active strategies to help them with preschool-appropriate situations, we had Dad sing to Daniel "Grown-ups come back" as he gave him a hug. Daniel, on the verge of tears, sang it back to Dad, and we can see him visibly become calmer. He has this new nugget of information that helps him remember that it's going to be okay, because *grown-ups come back*.

Before we finalized the episode, we did in-house formative research led by Rachel Kalban, M.A., and tested it with a classroom of preschoolers, who, coincidentally, had just been dropped off by their parents and caregivers. And I'll never forget it—those preschoolers were mesmerized. They leaned into the TV. They looked at each other. Some even had tears in their eyes. And suddenly I was worried we were going to make a room full of three-year-olds cry (not a goal of mine!). But then I saw them smile as Daniel smiled and repeated the strategy. They interacted with Daniel Tiger for the rest of the episode, and we were later told they had sung the strategy throughout the day as they waited for their own grown-ups to come back. This response and high level of engagement showed us that we'd written a preschool age-appropriate story, and as a result, our educational message was more likely to be heard and mastered.

On the flip side, there is indisputable research showing a correlation between young children viewing certain media intended for older audiences and negative side effects. Putting our preschoolers in front of media not intended for them is akin to asking them to ride a bike before they're ready—it may lead to harm. One study conducted by Lillard and Peterson of the University of Virginia randomly assigned 60 four-year-olds to one of three groups: one that watched nine fast-paced minutes of a popular fantastical cartoon aimed at six- to eleven-year-olds; one that watched nine minutes of a slower-paced program featuring a typical preschool-aged boy; and a third group that was asked to draw for nine minutes with markers and crayons. Kids were then tested for executive functions, which are important skills related to planning, organizing, memory, and self-regulation. The preschoolers who watched nine minutes of the fantastical cartoon aimed at six- to eleven-year-olds scored significantly worse than the other preschoolers on skills including attention, working memory, problem solving, and delay of gratification, all skills that are associated with success in school.[3] Choosing appropriate shows for our preschoolers can make a huge difference in their development.

Good Use of Humor

In addition to featuring preschool-related storylines, a high-quality, engaging show is also funny, interesting, and participatory. We know we can't preach to an empty church. An audience has to *want* to watch a program in order to learn something, and the smart use of preschool-appropriate humor is a great way to achieve this. In fact, when a show is funny, interesting, and surprising, we know the stories and learning will stay with an audience that much longer.

As Dorothea Gillim, creator of vocabulary curriculum program *WordGirl* on PBS Kids, says, "Part of my mission is to make kids' television smart and funny. I feel as though we've lost some ground there, in an effort to make it more accessible. *WordGirl*'s focus is on great stories, characters, and animation. If all those elements are working, then you can hook a child who may come looking for laughs, but leave a little smarter."[4]

YOUR HEALTHY MEDIA DIET: *ENGAGEMENT*

Think of your preschooler's favorite shows and ask yourself the following questions:

- Are they engaging?
- Do they have preschool-relatable storylines? Are the stories positive?
- Do they employ a good use of humor?

AFTER THE SHOW IS OVER

Figure out or notice what about the show sparked your preschooler and offer an activity to extend the learning. What the activity is will depend on the show, but each of these types of activities will take the learning to new heights:

- Re-create a craft activity from the show or come up with your own.
- Draw the characters from the show.
- "Write" a new ending to the show.
- Bring out dress-up clothes to role-play and act out the stories.
- Find related books based on aspects of the show they found particularly funny or interesting.

. . . .

YOUR HEALTHY MEDIA DIET: *SELF-ASSESSMENT*

- How much TV are your kids watching per day?
- What are your kids gaining from the shows they are watching?
- What are your goals for your kids regarding the media they consume?
- What ingredients from the above list are the most important to you?
- Using the ingredients to help inform, what programs make your "Yes" list?
- What are some offline, extended activities you can regularly add into your routine?

YOUR HEALTHY MEDIA "YES" LIST

Here are three simple ways to practice involved viewing and design your own personal Healthy Media "Yes" List of shows and apps you feel good about feeding your kids. (Don't worry—I'll explain how to do that later in the book.)

o Be Involved: Research which shows are a match for your child's nature and developmental needs, have values you believe in as a family, and are good, quality shows. Watch at least one episode to understand the premise of the program. Read the reviews online.

Make a conscious decision about whether you deem the show appropriate for your kids to watch.

○ Ask the Questions: "What did Daniel Tiger do today?" "How did that make you feel?" "Has that ever happened to you?" Ask questions about the characters in the show the same way you would about your kids' friends at school. If your child wants to share, have them sing their favorite funny song or share an interesting game they just learned.

○ See the Spark: In the same way that you notice your child's love of jumping and take him to a playground with a mini-trampoline so he can jump to his heart's content, watch to see what sparks your child about the shows he or she is watching and find creative ways to extend the learning. Stay tuned for plenty of suggestions on how to do this in the Clue chapters.

KNOW

Laying the Groundwork to Inspire
Our Preschoolers to Learn and Grow

As is probably no surprise, the preschool years are perhaps my most favorite. And not just because these are the years when our kids truly find their voice, develop rich vocabularies and senses of humor, and start to show us glimpses of the amazing people they're going to become. No, the real reason I love the preschool years is because the years between ages two and five are undeniably the most important, most influential, and most critical in a child's life. When we *know* who our preschoolers are and what they are capable of, we can better influence and inspire them to learn and grow.

THE PRESCHOOL YEARS

In fact, the single most important factor in ensuring children become successful, productive, happy adults isn't the quality of their education or how high they score on an IQ or achievement test—it's what happens during a child's preschool years . . . *hands down*. This is a high-stakes game. Luckily, preschoolers are also the cutest and funniest human beings on the planet.

These little people are incredibly busy learning language, solving problems, thinking creatively, and figuring out how to get along with other people. And *how* they learn these things is determined by the level of stimulation they receive in the home between the ages of two and five. These years are the foundation for not only their tremendous social and emotional growth, but the educational foundation for kindergarten, elementary school, and beyond.

There is a *lot* going on in the brains and bodies of these young kids—they are so funny, full of life (and energy!), interesting and wise, innately helpful and empathetic, and just want to be heard and listened to. I like to think that if we do the hard work during these preschool years, the teenage years become that much easier.

UNIVERSAL TRUTHS OF PRESCHOOLERS

While preschoolers are different from one another in how they grow and develop, how quickly or slowly they go through the phases of development, and their learning styles, there are a number of aspects of child development that are universally the same:

○ All preschoolers play, in many different ways, to figure out their world.
○ All preschoolers need time to Pause. Pausing to let them think gives us amazing insight into who they are, what they know, and what interests them.
○ All preschoolers like to repeat. They learn through repetition, the more deliberate and purposeful the better.
○ All preschoolers imitate their parents as the "stars" of their show.
○ All preschoolers, universally, want to help—they are innately empathetic, and we can strengthen their empathy muscles through everyday activities.

PARENTS HOLD THE KEYS

Our role as parents is to be the "star" of our preschooler's favorite show—it's called "Real Life." We are their trusted guide—holding their hand literally and metaphorically as they figure out their way in the world, challenging them to jump higher and try something new, opening their eyes to new experiences, and helping them through hard times. Parents hold the keys to a preschooler's level of development—opening up the door to new opportunities, interesting adventures, games that build their cognitive abilities, and ideas that spark them. And above all, we have one incredibly magical tool in our notebook—*just being who we are.*

When we, as parents and caregivers, are involved, invested, engaged, and knowledgeable about our preschoolers' development, we can help to support them in a healthy, positive way. Research suggests the experience of a nurturing home environment could have a strong effect on brain development. Parents have a tremendous role in enabling children to develop their cognitive, social, and emotional skills by providing safe, predictable, stimulating, and responsive personal interactions. Everything parents do—feeding them, clothing them, keeping them safe, and teaching them age-appropriate skills like using the toilet, getting dressed, and catching a ball . . . even just talking to them—is shaping who they are.

At the same time, we're busy buying educational books and toys and supporting their learning to make sure our little sponges are on track cognitively and socially and are mastering concepts like colors, numbers, and letters, and adapting to behavior expectations. This is why I feel like a mama to all the preschoolers who watch my shows. And once my own kids hit the age group? Everything I did was elevated; I was determined, more than ever, to put easily replicated clues in our programs that preschoolers and their parents could use every day.

PRESCHOOL DEVELOPMENT

So, why are a child's earliest years so critical? Brain science tells the story: 80 percent of a child's brain development has occurred by the time she is three years old. Once she hits five, that figure is up to a whopping 90 percent. That means the bulk of a child's emotional and intellectual development has already been indelibly shaped by the time he's learning to do things like tie his shoes, ride a bike, and skip.

These are astonishing figures, and they speak to just how malleable and nimble a preschooler's brain is.

The Preschool Development Milestones

While preschoolers are defined as children between the ages of two and five, this age span is developmentally extremely wide, and the milestones they're going through are vast, as they are developing intellectual, physical, social, and emotional competencies all at once. It's a lot of work for them, and it's a lot of responsibility for us. By the time our little ones reach preschool, they have acquired control over their bodies, they can feed themselves, dress themselves, jump, run, show a preference for things, and have a strong will. These competencies are the manifestations of intelligence and personality. Understanding how preschoolers think, how they learn, and how they develop will empower us to nurture each area of our preschooler's development.

Cognitive Development

The notion of cognitive development originated with child development psychologist Jean Piaget who described in his Theory of Cognitive Development that children move through four different developmental "stages" as they grow, acquiring new abilities and skills at each stage.[1] The stages are: the Sensorimotor Stage, from birth to age two; the Preoperational Stage, from age two to about age seven; the Concrete Operational Stage, from ages seven to eleven; and the Formal Operational Stage, which begins in adolescence and spans into adulthood. According to Piaget, preschoolers have passed through the first stage, where much of what they learn is through picking up and manipulating objects and using their senses, and are now in the second, or Preoperational, stage. In this stage, Piaget believed that preschoolers make associations and learn about everything through play.

While Piaget's developmental stages are still recognized and subscribed to today by many researchers, new theories of cognitive development have emerged that show how much preschoolers are able to learn if taught in a play-based, preschool-appropriate way. Regardless of the particular theory or model of cognitive development one subscribes to, what's actually going on inside a preschooler's brain in terms of the new thinking and processing skills they're acquiring in these crucial years is something everyone agrees on—*it's major.*

The first of these are skills related to executive functioning, or the "command central" of the brain. Executive functions are made up of a collection of skills Ellen Galinsky, president and co-founder of Families and Work Institute, labels as the "seven essential life skills" all kids need for future success. In her book *Mind in the Making*, Ellen talks about skills such as:

1. learning to be focused and have self-control,
2. learning to take on life's challenges,
3. being able to communicate well with others,
4. having empathy and ability to take someone else's perspective,
5. the ability to think critically and
6. make connections to the world around you, and
7. being motivated to continue to learn.[2]

So yes . . . pretty much everything! You can see why the "command central" metaphor fits.

According to Harvard University's Center on the Developing Child, "Children aren't born with these skills—they are born with the potential to develop them." And while executive functioning continues to develop well into the early elementary school years and adolescence, during the preschool years many areas of executive functioning experience rapid growth.[3] For example, a child's working memory, which is the ability to acquire, store, and recall information, powerfully switches on around the age of three. Impulse control—a concept that is sometimes touted as a key predictor to future success—is a skill that is generally learned in the preschool years as well. Really, since all executive functions are acquired and not innate, the preschool years are the ideal time to begin supporting and nurturing their development.

Other cognitive skills taking center stage in the preschool years include understanding the use of "symbols" as objects that represent something else (like a drawing of their family being a *representation* of their family or using a penny to represent a missing player token in a game), developing problem-solving skills (such as figuring out that two children, each with the color of balloon they don't want, can trade them so that each gets what they want), beginning to use logical thinking (such as being able to organize toys by color, shape, or other characteristic), and understanding the concept of cause and effect (such as recognizing that furiously pumping the water pump at the playground water station will ultimately result in the makeshift stick dam being washed away).

. . . .

A TYPICAL MORNING

From the moment preschoolers wake up in the morning, they are learning and developing by taking everything in—the tone of the morning, the smells of what's cooking, the mood of everyone around them. On a Saturday, they hop out of bed early and run into our room, jumping on our bed singing "good morning!" (meanwhile, we have to pry them awake on the weekdays). We urge them to go potty (asking about ten times), and then they hop down the stairs and sit at the kitchen table (still hopping or at the very least bopping). They look at their breakfast of oatmeal and blueberries, which we may or may not have arranged into a smiley face (always a crowd pleaser!). They eat a few bites while counting how many blueberries they have, making a game out of it, and then launching into questions about the coming day as we hurry them along. Bouncing out of their chairs, they run to brush their teeth (singing a song) and get dressed (yep, singing another song). And all before 7:30 a.m.!

The morning routine is an example of an everyday way preschoolers practice *cognitive* development (knowing the routine, understanding what utensil to use, counting blueberries, asking questions, and comprehending what is expected of them), *social-emotional* development (understanding the tone of the room, the mood of the caregiver, saying good morning), and *physical* development (the hopping down the stairs, bopping, sitting, eating, getting dressed, going potty).

. . . .

Physical Development

The preschool years are when our kids' sense of big and small movement, coordination, and agility are growing by leaps and bounds. With every new feat they attempt—from big movements like climbing up the slide, jumping from higher and higher perches, kicking and throwing a ball, riding a bike with two wheels (gross motor skills), to small movements like building with blocks and small Legos, zipping up a jacket (fine motor skills)—their balance and coordination neurons are becoming more and more robust.

As active preschoolers, many kids feel driven to test their bodies and see what they're capable of, and research shows that it's in our best interest as their parents and caregivers to give them the chance to do this, safely, of course. These are also the years when kids may find themselves frustrated with certain fine motor or gross motor tasks that don't come as easily to them as they might for their peers (such as grasping a pencil or catching a ball). Sometimes this is simply a variance in developmental pace, and sometimes it's indicative of an area where a child might need some extra support. A pediatrician will keep his or her eyes on this and let you know when and if these differences warrant more attention.

As is the case in most aspects of growth and development, play is everything. Between zero and five years old, the brain is more pliant than it will be at any other point in life. Providing opportunities for young children to deliberately repeat, test, and practice their gross motor and fine motor movements through play can yield a big payoff.

Social-Emotional Development

When we consider all the tremendous connections our preschoolers are making as they try to understand their huge emotions and begin to make sense of the world around them, it's no wonder this period can get off to a, shall we say, rocky start. In her book *Your Three-Year-Old: Friend or Enemy*, author Louise Bates Ames writes about the generally calm, pleasant nature of the three-year-old in contrast with the tempestuous nature of a three-and-a-half-year-old: "inward, insecure, anxious, and above all determined and self-willed.[4] The three-year-old child seems emotionally insecure from the word go." Six months' difference! It still amazes me.

Erik Erikson, a psychoanalyst known for his psychosocial development theory (and who worked with Fred Rogers), helps us look at the role of preschoolers and their social and emotional development.[5] Erikson's theory has eight distinct stages, and successful completion of each stage results in a healthier personality. The preschool child has already gone through the first two and is now entering Stage Three, called the "play age." During this stage, she is asserting herself, initiating play, and asking questions of her world as she grows and develops. Our job during this stage is to foster this level of growth as we nurture their sense of themselves. During Stage Three, preschoolers work hard to navigate relationships with other children and develop the skills to express their own feelings, understand and respond to others' feelings, and share, as well as discover their own sense of self within groups of other children and appropriately relate to others in group settings. No pressure or anything!

These are also the years when children are putting a lot of time and energy into learning emotional regulation, which refers to understanding how to respond to things that happen in their world in ways that are emotionally appropriate. This age group is intense! It's no mistake that both Erikson and Piaget celebrate the world of play for preschoolers as a great source of learning during this age.

Another typical social-emotional area of growth centers around a preschooler's desire to, often for the first time in their lives, begin to see themselves as independent individuals. As a result, they often start looking for opportunities to assert and demonstrate their independence.

Lastly, it's during the preschool years that children are developing a vocabulary for their emotions, a concept known as emotional literacy. Learning how to identify, label, and talk about the big (and small) emotions they're feeling is a big piece of what's happening in a preschooler's world.

Communication Skills

When we talk about language acquisition for preschoolers, we're talking about huge growth spurts in all aspects of language and communication development, which means in both the giving and receiving of information. Though it may not always seem like it, especially when repeatedly asking our little ones to do something like put their boots on or stop banging on the table with their crayons, preschoolers are developing all kinds of skills related to listening. These include everything from simply hearing what's happening around them (what other people are saying, audio books, a show on the TV) and recognizing what the spoken or sung words mean, but also being able to understand and follow multistep spoken directions.

HOW PRESCHOOLERS LEARN

Preschoolers are naturally curious little people who want to learn about all of the "whys" in the world. As born scientists, preschoolers are always pushing the limits to learn through trial and error. Whether they are running in the park, playing with blocks, painting a masterpiece, or role-playing with their imaginary friends, they are actually making hypotheses, gathering evidence, and finding results. They are also great observers—learning about the "whys" of human behavior by watching everyone around them to figure out motivations, desires, preferences, how to act, and how they fit into the world.

Kindergarten Readiness Skills

Timelines are different for every child and, especially in cases where a child might be developing in some sort of neurologically atypical way, the milestones may be either accelerated or delayed. But generally speaking, kindergarten readiness skills are the milestones schools expect typically developing preschoolers to reach by the time they enter kindergarten, which in most school districts happens when a child is between the ages of five and six.

There is no one set of concrete guidelines for exactly which skills—social, emotional, and cognitive—a child should be comfortable with before beginning his or her first year of full-time school. Ask a half-dozen teachers and you just might get a half-dozen different answers, and requirements also vary by state. But for the most part, these little learners should be able to:

- listen and pay attention
- verbally communicate their needs and wants;
- be patient, take turns, and share;
- grasp a pencil;
- write their name;
- exhibit reading readiness skills like letter recognition and story comprehension;
- show an interest in learning new things;
- be able to follow simple directions;
- identify a variety of numbers, colors, and shapes; and
- perform gross motor movements like running, skipping, and jumping

What your children learn at the preschool and kindergarten age sets the foundation for later learning, both in school and in life.

DIFFERENT LEARNING STYLES, DIFFERENT KIDS

Development is a fluid process and different types of kids learn in different ways. There are, of course, many different ways of learning and experiencing the world, as is evidenced by the most recent statistics showing that one in five school-aged children are in some way neurologically atypical. My writing partner, Debbie, focuses on these unique learners in her book *Differently Wired*.[6] As Debbie experienced firsthand in raising her intellectually gifted son Asher, who at the age of eight was diagnosed with ADHD (attention deficit/hyperactivity disorder) and Asperger's syndrome (now known simply as autism spectrum disorder), there are many variations on the ways preschoolers move through the developmental stages, depending on their sensory issues, the way they process information, or if they have social, emotional, and other developmental delays.

The preschool years can be especially tricky for parents raising atypical kids because it can be hard to ascertain what's "typical" behavior and what might be an indicator that something else is going on that deserves a closer look. Debbie's advice for all parents, but especially those who are wondering if their child is in some way neurodiverse, is to discover what type of learner you have on hand, become curious about their areas of strengths and weaknesses, and commit to becoming fluent in how they see and experience the world. Doing so will help parents navigate the journey in a way that best supports their child, no matter what their unique wiring is.

Doing the work and laying the groundwork in these preschool years will set the stage for our school-aged children and beyond. We want to teach our preschoolers and give them strategies that they will take with them as they grow into competent, independent, happy, kind, and powerful kids, setting their sights on changing our world for the better.

CLUE TAKEAWAYS

▷ The time between the ages of two and five is the most critical.

▷ Preschoolers are learning about who they are and what is most important from *you*—parents hold the keys to a pre-schooler's world.

▷ Everything from brain development to socio-motor skills to language acquisition is growing at the fastest rate during these critical years.

▷ Maximize the preschool years as best you can through the Clues in the next chapters.

Play,
Pause,
Repeat

CLUE #1: PLAY

Playing Opens the Door to a Preschooler's World

Fresh out of college in 1990, I got my start in Nickelodeon's research department as an analyst. I remember that first day, riding up the steep elevators, singing the song "Let the River Run" from the movie *Working Girl* in my head. I truly had stars in my eyes, a skip in my step, and my sights set on conquering the world. One of my favorite parts of the job was going to focus group sessions and sitting behind a one-way glass mirror with a group of network executives and show creators to watch a moderator talk with preschoolers about new show ideas Nickelodeon was considering. During one such session, I noticed that the group of five-year-olds was being uncharacteristically lackluster and noncommunicative, and the moderator was struggling to get them talking, let alone get any insights out of them.

I watched the moderator ask each preschooler to rate the show they'd just screened on a scale of 1 to 10, a challenging task for any preschooler who's just mastered the art of counting. How were they supposed to rate their preference using numbers, where 10 was the best and 1 was the worst? As she went around the circle, calling each preschooler by name, not one gave her a response. Finally, one little boy held out his hand and on his fingers showed five as he said, "Five." Then, one by one, the others followed suit, holding out their fingers and saying "Five."

Out of the corner of my eye, I saw the show creator slowly put his head down and begin quietly banging it on the table, clearly upset. His show wasn't doing well in the market testing and was under scrutiny.

He turned to me, a green research coordinator who was known for her preschool expertise, and asked pleadingly, "A five? How could they give it a five? Why? *Why* did they give it a five?" Which is exactly the question the moderator was asking the kids. But none of them would give her an answer, and now it appeared they were having a standoff, with some even making a beeline for the door. Exasperated, as you can imagine you would be with a room full of preschoolers who are done with you, the moderator stepped out for a moment and poked her head into our room, asking us if we had any other questions.

I had a question. I wanted to know if I could introduce myself to the kids as a "special guest" and ask them a few questions about the show. Happy for the reprieve, the moderator agreed, and I headed to the other side of the one-way glass.

After introducing myself, I began to play with the kids using the various toys we'd set up around the room. And for ten minutes, that's all we did—*play*. We played with blocks, we laughed, and we talked. One preschooler brought me a cup of pretend tea, which I drank. Another, dressed head-to-toe in a Princess Jasmine outfit, started working through my hair with a pretend brush. After we had bonded through play, I decided to ask them about the Nickelodeon show they'd just watched and find out their reasons for giving it a score of five. Their eyes wide, they all turned to me when I posed the questions, but still said nothing. I noticed my little Princess Jasmine friend was now running around the room with her arms outstretched on her pretend flying carpet, so I called to her by her pretend name. "*Princess Jasmine,* why did *you* give the show a five?"

Then something magical happened. Princess Jasmine slowly turned around and sized me up. She gave me a huge grin and flew the magic carpet over to me, animated and ready to talk. She sat down, scooched really close to me, and announced vehemently, "Because I'm five!" She held up her five fingers to prove it. The rest of my new preschool friends joined in—they had *all* given the show a five because they were five years old. Preschool reasoning at its finest. But I wanted to know more. So, we played more. In fact, we played out the entire show that Nickelodeon was there to test. And through play, I discovered that not only did the children understand the whole storyline—they liked the characters enough to act out the twenty-two-minute show for me, sing the songs, and even stop to retell their favorite jokes.

When I said good-bye to the preschoolers and went back to the room on the other side of the one-way glass, I was immediately enveloped in a warm hug by the creator of the show. Play had saved the day *and* the creator's dream of making his show.

LEARNING THROUGH PLAY

That experience in the focus group reinforced the power of play, and it's why I work hard to capture that sense of play in all my shows. As Fred Rogers famously said, "Play *is* childhood."

Whether they are figuring out how their family dynamic works, acting out their preschool fantasies, sounding out a new word, or handling a sharing showdown on a playdate, a preschooler's *play* is intrinsically tied to every aspect of their learning process. In fact, a preschooler's entire life revolves around play—that's why tapping into this power of play is so critical. By knowing how to use play in a way that preschoolers will respond to, parents, caregivers, and teachers will be in the best possible position to support their kids' cognitive and social-emotional development.

THE DEFINITION OF PLAY

Not surprisingly, Merriam-Webster dictionary defines play as: ". . . to take part in a game" with game defined as "an activity engaged in for diversion or amusement." Perhaps because of definitions like this and the way the word *play* is used in our everyday vernacular, the concept of play has a long history of not being taken seriously. For me personally, I don't know how many times I was told as a kid, "Stop playing and learn something!"

Of course, we now know that free play—child led, without any adult guidance—fosters much more learning than anyone once believed. When our kids freely play for even half an hour per day, they will become smarter, more independent, and more adept at solving problems. In fact, there is research-based evidence that dramatic play promotes desire, motivation, and mastery.[1] That's because when kids have control over their own learning, they tend to seek out knowledge through exploration, hypothesis testing, and discovery. And when dramatic play is done in a safe, anxiety- and risk-free environment, children feel free and willing to test the limits of their knowledge and abilities.[2] As a result, they learn to have confidence in their ability to solve a problem.

When Piaget defined play as "the work of the child," he proved that play was not just for amusement, but had real merit in the developing brain of healthy preschoolers. When given the time and space to play creatively and imaginatively, preschoolers are actually practicing key skills. They are engaging in self-directed learning in a way that allows them to make up their own rules about the world and change them whenever they want to.

Learning through play fosters:
- cognitive learning: letters, numbers, patterns, shapes, etc.;
- social-emotional learning: working through their feelings;
- conflict-resolution strategies;
- role playing and perspective taking;
- playing out decisions without the risk of failure;
- bonding with loved ones.

DIFFERENT TYPES OF PLAY

There are many different types of play, each with a different but positive effect on our preschooler's brain development. Here's a breakdown:

Type of Play	What It Is	What It Looks Like
Dramatic Play	Acting out scenarios based on what preschoolers see in real life and in the media, their hopes and dreams, and/or what they're worried about.	Playing house, restaurant, school, going to the store, superheroes or fairies, and more.
Physical Play	This is the play we see in backyards and playgrounds everywhere; preschoolers getting valuable exercise and practicing key gross motor skills.	Running, jumping, climbing, playing physical games like tag and hide and seek.
Expressive Play	Often referred to as "art" play, kids tell stories and share thoughts, which allows preschoolers opportunities to express their feelings.	Playing with finger paints, watercolors, clay, water, sand, musical instruments, and more.
Manipulative Play	This play is about figuring out how things work and the beginning of scientific discovery, beginning in infancy when the child begins to understand what they do has an effect on their environment.	Throwing a toy on the floor just to have Mom pick it up and give it back to them . . . *over and over again*, playing with puzzles, using arts and crafts items.
Intellectual Play	Interactive gaming that broadens and deepens a preschooler's cognitive development.	Drawing and telling a story that leads to writing and acting out their stories, letter identification, tracing in shaving cream, playing with letter blocks, playing letter bingo, and writing words.

JUMPING INTO THEIR WORLD OF PLAY

Dramatic play provides preschoolers the most educational benefit and parents the most valuable insight, so I'll be focusing on this type of play in this chapter. Preschoolers' play is immersive, all consuming, and purposeful. Like our own little Meryl Streeps, preschoolers completely lose themselves in their characters as they try on different types of play scenarios. Sometimes they insist on dressing like their favorite character (capes, hats, flight suits, tutus, and tiaras), other times they might eat like their character (I knew one preschooler who would only eat oats during her "horse stage") or only respond when they are addressed as their character, as was the case with my friend, Princess Jasmine. So, I say, why beat it when you can join in? Play can be the portal to enter a preschooler's world and get them expressing their points of view. And to do this, we need to get down on the floor, on their level, and play.

Immersing preschoolers in the world of play is the reason why the live-action characters of Steve and Joe are shown living inside a book on *Blue's Clues* as real people in an animated world. It's why Blue is a *blue* puppy—completely fantastical. It's why Steve and Joe literally jump to *skidoo*—magically travel—into felt boards, pictures, and chalk worlds. In this way, we are literally modeling how to enter the fantastical world of preschool play when the TV is off and cheerful objects are all around and available for play. Because preschoolers are so much more communicative and open when playing, there's no limit to what we can learn about them when we embrace this notion.

I remember one weekend with my daughters. Hope was seven and Ella was four, when they were busy playing in our family room. Dressed head to toe in pretend ball gowns, plastic shoes, and lots and lots of "jeweled" necklaces, they were singing at the top of their lungs.

"*A moment like THISSSSS . . . !*" Hope belted Kelly Clarkson, as Ella danced around her. Then suddenly their play pivoted. Here's how the scene unfolded:

Hope: Let's play house! I'm the mommy.
Ella: Great! I will be the daddy. I want to be the daddy.
Hope: You *can't* be the daddy!

Ella looked at Hope, puzzled.

Ella: Why?
Hope: Because you are a girl.
Ella: So?!
Hope: So girls are mommies and *boys* are daddies.

Ella, my budding philosopher, wasn't having it.

Ella: Playing pretend is for being people you *love*. Not for being
  people who you *are*.
Hope: Oh, yeah. Like a princess? Or a fairy?
Ella: Or a daddy. I want to be daddy. I love Daddy.
Hope: Yes, sure, of course. Okay, you can be a daddy, or a frog,
  or a mermaid!

The negotiation ended as they learned, together, that playing pretend means they can be whoever they want and, in Ella's mind, whoever you "love." As they happily continued their play, Ella kicked off the high-heeled shoes, literally stepped into my husband Greg's big slippers, and said, "Ready!" Hope surveyed Ella's outfit, finding another problem.

Hope: Daddy doesn't wear a dress or necklaces.

Ella looked down and considered her dress-up outfit, trying to devise a plan.

Ella: *This* one does.

This scene highlights an interesting developmental difference between Hope and Ella, and shows how play bridged the gap so they could both continue their own learning journey from their unique vantage points. At seven, Hope's mind was beginning to form rules and understand gender norms and roles. Ella, still her four-year-old fantastical self, begged to differ. But Hope was willing to go with it. Their play was engaging her flexible thinking capabilities and continuing to expand her mindset.

Hope shrugged and continued to play, sitting at the coffee table pretending to type feverishly on a make-believe computer. Just as I do when I'm working, Hope stopped typing for a second, looked up, cocked her head to one side, and then began furiously typing again.

> **Hope:** Okay. So, I'm the mommy. I'm writing. Then I have a meeting. It's about a new show. In New York City.

Ella barreled in, running around and making beeping sounds.

> **Ella:** I'm the daaaaaddy! Beep! Beep!
> **Hope:** Daddy, what are you doing?
> **Ella:** Picking up my girls. From school. Beep! Ugh. Traffic.

Then suddenly, Hope stopped and got up, no longer in imaginary play mode.

> **Hope:** Wait, let's play house the *regular* way.

Ella looked at Hope, unsure of what she meant, as this *was* her reality.

> **Hope:** You know, the *regular* way. Where the mommy stays home and the daddy goes to work.

Hope's understanding of the norms and rules were again pushing against the preschooler view of play. And again, Ella was having none of it. Learning and playing with her highly verbal big sister definitely had a positive impact on her negotiation skills.

Ella: This *is* the regular way! Daddy works. See? I'm on my phone. On my computer.
Hope: Yeah. But not in New York City!
Ella: Yeah. So now *I* go to New York City?
Hope: Yup. You go on the train now. And I'm the mommy. I pick you up from school.

Ella came bouncing by, this time pretending to be on the train:

Ella: Oooooon the trainnnnnnnn . . . Chooo chooo . . .
Hope: Okay, now you come home 'cause the Daddy needs to play with us.
Ella: I'm home!
Hope: I'm Hope now. Let's dance! *A moment like thiiiisssss!*

Hope and Ella took each other's hands and danced around. I walked into the room with some blueberries, and decided to jump into their play by using guided learning and contributing my own feelings about who works, who stays home, and what families look like.

Me: Mommy's home with some snacks!
Hope: Oh good! The daddy's home *and* the mommy's home. Sometimes she works in NYC, but then we play.
Me: I love to play.
Ella: Yay!
Me: Let's sing! "A moment like thiisssss!"

We dance . . .

Hope: When the mommy's home and the daddy's home, we all play, and it's like we're on vacation all the time!
Ella: Hurray!

And . . . *scene.*

So, what did I learn through that afternoon of play? I learned that my girls were debating the real versus the fantasy of being "anything you want," including being a daddy if you're a girl. They were also trying to understand the way their family dynamic worked as compared to what they've seen modeled for them in their friends' families. Hope and Ella's daddy was home, picking them up, taking them to everything, and working from home, while their mommy worked in the city. And their real dream? Playing like they were on vacation *all the time,* with everyone free and available to play. (Isn't that everyone's dream?)

PLAY MAKES PRESCHOOLERS SMARTER

In the early years of life, children spend most of their waking time exploring their world, their caregivers, and the objects around them. It is a time of rapid brain growth, and brain development theories suggest that the structure of these early experiences actually shapes a child's functional neuronal circuits. Both play and exploration help build a solid foundation of skills needed for such brain development. In fact, as a linchpin for intellectual development, play helps preschoolers learn how to understand the perspectives of others, invent strategies for play by themselves as well as with others, and solve problems.

We can see the results of play right away. When preschoolers play, they are cooperative and communicative. They take initiative and creative risks, and engage in hands-on learning that promotes intellectual change. And in the long term, play makes preschoolers smarter by supporting their growth, self-direction, and sense of self-worth.

PLAY IS PRESCHOOL "SPEAK"

In addition to promoting brain growth and intellectual development, I consider play to be a preschooler's first language. Back in 1990, when I was sitting in that focus group with a room full of five-year-olds, the children were much more willing to express their feelings, thoughts, and opinions when I allowed them to play. Through their play, they talked and showed me what they understood about the show, what they liked, and how much of the story they retained. In that situation, play became the preschool equivalent of Google Translate, bridging the gap between our two distinct perspectives and languages.

When an adult joins a preschooler's play, they are essentially saying, "I understand you." We're allowing preschoolers to be completely comfortable in being who they are. And what could be more powerful than that?

PLAY PROMOTES ONE OF THE MOST IMPORTANT ASPECTS OF LEARNING: INTRINSIC MOTIVATION

Ask any child development expert about whether we want to foster intrinsic or extrinsic motivation in our children, and they will overwhelmingly tell you YES. Intrinsic motivation—motivation that is driven by internal rewards such as satisfaction, pride, or the boost of having successfully tackled and met a challenge—is what we're going for. As Iain Lancaster wrote on the website TeachThought, of the importance of intrinsic motivation, "Only students who are intrinsically motivated to be engaged in school will end up truly challenged, enriched, energized, and ultimately fulfilled by their experience. Yes, it's an ideal, but it's worth keeping in mind."[3]

Enter play as an ideal vehicle for encouraging preschoolers to be actively engaged and intrinsically motivated. Through play we observe their zest, their spark, and their passion, as well as their focused attention. In play, preschoolers are employing all their senses and practicing all levels of education—from using language to communicate with others and developing critical and flexible thinking to solving problems and working on fine motor skills through activities like drawing and gross motor skills in riding trikes and running. But the most important aspect of play—one that cannot be underestimated—is that a child's sense of autonomy, initiative, and industry is rooted in intrinsic motivation and active engagement.

Put yourself in the mind of a preschooler for a moment. What would it do to you if, as a four-year-old, you were paid money every time you threw a ball into the basket? Or imagine you received a new toy *every time* you sat on the potty? Or a new doll every time you got on stage to perform in your school play? While reward systems like this might work in the short term and may help motivate a child, in the long term, they do the exact opposite. It steals the level of pride a child feels when they figure something out. It replaces the happiness they feel over what they accomplished and puts a monetary value on it. This has a negative impact on their sense of self.

It has been well documented, including in Dan Pink's fantastic book *Drive: The Surprising Truth About What Motivates Us*, that finding joy in the work you do versus working for money is what leads to a happy, healthy, and fulfilled adult life.[4] So how do we teach fulfillment? How do we teach happiness or spark or passion? *We teach it through activities that support intrinsic motivation.* Finding something that sparks your preschooler so much so that they are intrinsically motivated to do it.

PARENTING PRODUCTION NOTES
Turn Your Child's Sparks into Play

Here are some ideas to get you started when thinking about how to take your child's sparks and passions and turn them into engaging play:

If your child is SPARKED by . . .	Activities
Space	Create a baking soda rocket ship, interact with a constellation app, visit a science museum, engage in astronaut dramatic role-playing.
Building	Draw a building and then attempt to build it with blocks.

If your child is SPARKED by . . .	Activities
Cars	Create a soap box derby car, make cars out of vegetables, pretend be a car.
Superheroes	Make a cape to wear around the house, write your own comic book, film your story.
Movement	Sign your child up for preschool-aged running groups, gymnastics, swim lessons, and more.
Nurturing activities	Invest in some house-based props like dolls, stuffed animals, and blankets, get them involved in playfully helping around the house.
Storytelling	Get some drama-based props including costumes; read a book to your child and encourage them to act it out.
Arts and Crafts	Simple sewing, making masks, recycled sculptures . . . the sky's the limit.

FORMS OF PLAY

Play itself comes in three different forms: spontaneous play, guided play, and adult-directed play. Each of these forms has its own merit:

Spontaneous Play

This is the type of play preschoolers do naturally, mostly in the form of pretend play. For example, your preschooler might pick a saltshaker up off the table, turn it into a character, and make it talk (sound familiar?). She might then have a little wedding ceremony with Mr. Salt and Mrs. Pepper and then add to the family a sweet little baby named Paprika. Another example of spontaneous play would be when a preschooler picks up a new prop or object and begins to play or picks up a paintbrush to paint, a crayon to draw, and so on. In spontaneous play, preschoolers are on their own to explore, create, and imagine.

Guided Play

To up the ante, we can introduce guided play, which is defined as a nudge from someone with more knowledge providing information to elevate the learning. For instance, in guided play a parent or teacher might show a preschooler she can use tools beyond a paintbrush to paint, like a sponge or a roller or even a potato. On *Creative Galaxy*, Chef Zesty shows Arty how to use vegetables to make dye for coloring eggs!

When doing a puzzle, guided play might look like showing a preschooler the strategy of building the edges of the puzzle first. When solving a conflict in play, the guide will give preschoolers insights to solve their own problems. These small guided pieces of information or strategies help get preschoolers to practice and discover what they can do on their own. On *Daniel Tiger's Neighborhood*, our musical strategies help to empower preschoolers to solve their own conflicts in play. For example, when preschoolers are having a problem playing together, we sing "Find a Way to Play Together."

Adult Guided and Directed Play

We can get more educational benefit out of dramatic play when we guide or direct the play. Used in classrooms, an adult-directed play technique has a parent, teacher, caregiver, or even an older sibling model something new. Adding in a new prop or asking questions to direct the play can take the learning to a deeper level. In adult-directed play, an adult initiates play by providing a new prop, craft, or theme for preschoolers to play and explore. For instance, adult-directed play could be reading *The Three Little Pigs* to our preschooler, discussing it, assigning pretend play "roles" (e.g., "You be the pig and I'll be the wolf!"), and then letting your preschooler act it out. In another example of adult-directed play, we set out certain items, like clay or paint or even some new props like a magnifying glass and take a nature walk. Preschoolers didn't choose the play, but when offered the idea, they typically latch on and soar.

Just like the best preschool classroom, play is at the center of the curriculum of any good show or app. We want preschool media to enhance and extend the learning for preschoolers, even when they're not watching or playing. We want to choose for them media that sparks them, ignites their thinking, and invites them to play in a creative way after the show is over. When choosing shows and apps, look for ones that feature play at the heart and preschoolers as the leaders of the play.

In my shows, we employ both adult-guided play, showing how to play a game or break down a new skill, as well as adult-directed play, where we start with a theme and walk preschoolers through that theme by scaffolding the information and key skills. We also demonstrate *spontaneous play*, such as when we show Daniel Tiger and his friends playing at home or in the play corner at school. Other preschool shows frequently tap into these different types as well, such as Disney Junior's *Doc McStuffins*, which frequently shows six-year-old Dottie engaging in *spontaneous play* with her dolls and toys before shifting into adult-guided play as she is faced with a problem (a broken toy or doll) in need of fixing.

. . . .

PLAY IN APPS

When it comes to apps and virtual games, we're looking for the same type of experiences to extend the learning through play. Interacting with a favorite character through an app offers real-time interactivity. For younger preschoolers, those two to three years old, opt for the free play apps that allow your preschoolers to play out a story and be the leader in that play. These free-play, or "sandbox"-type, apps are those where preschoolers are encouraged to free play and use trial and error in a way similar to dramatic and sensory play.

Examples of such apps include Busy Shapes, an exploring-to-learn app for the youngest preschoolers; Toca Band, also exploratory yet based in music and instruments; and Explore Daniel Tiger's Neighborhood, which is a "virtual dollhouse" that lets preschoolers explore Daniel's world and lead the play. These apps and others like them let preschoolers be in charge as to *how* and *what* to play and do. For older preschoolers (four to five years old), look for apps that explore and ignite their curiosity and spark them to play as their learning goes deeper on their terms, such as PBS Games, Daniel Tiger apps, The Monster at the End of This Book app, and Toca apps.

PLAY EVERY DAY

So, how do we bring more play into our everyday lives with our preschoolers? Don't worry—it's not about playing with our kids around the clock. But it is about regularly dedicating time for our preschoolers to learn from spontaneous play, coupled with keeping an eye out for opportunities to guide and sometimes even direct their play. We can do this by setting aside some "free time" for play, choosing media and apps that reinforce and model this type of play, and using the play our kids are already engaged in as a tool for communication, comprehension, and mastery.

We know that play helps preschoolers fully comprehend a concept by interacting within it so, as parents and caregivers, we can be on the lookout for ways in which they may be engaging in play to make sense of big feelings they might be trying to sort out. For instance, maybe they are desperate to get a puppy, and so their play evolves into constantly "being" the puppy. By being an involved co-player, we support them in being immersed in the play. We may even let them eat out of a bowl like a puppy instead of a plate. When we can participate in their dramatic play on this level and show respect for their play language and script, they will open up and express their feelings, worries, and points of view. Interestingly, this same approach works even as they move into the tween and teen years, when we enter into their teen-isms (watching *Gilmore Girls* together or going indoor rock climbing), they can put their guard down and give us deeper insight into what's happening in their world.

By being involved co-players and verbally or physically checking in with our preschoolers, by making eye contact or nodding, we can also extend the learning of their play and/or offer clues to guide them. For instance, if a beloved pet fish has just died, a preschooler might be stuck in fish play for a while as he figures out his emotions. Noticing this, we can use some play therapy techniques, such as putting out paper and crayons and suggesting they draw a picture of their beloved fish, setting out a preschool book about losing a pet like *The Tenth Good Thing About Barney*, or even role-playing the scenario to better understand their interpretation of events.

Similarly, if we see our child engaged in a lot of sad play, or even angry play, we might have an easier time discovering the underlying reason if we make the effort to join in. Play is a safe way to express feelings. It's much better for them to be acting out negative emotions in dramatic play than at another child. Through role-playing or actively listening, we can understand what's at the root of the play and then offer solutions. The other upshot of this type of interactive, involved co-playing is that it provides yet another opportunity to give preschoolers clues and coping strategies that they will model and use, independently from us.

PARENTING PRODUCTION NOTES
Be An Involved Co-Player Every Day

- Pay attention to those activities your child is highly engaged in, and set aside dedicated time every day to join them in this play.
- Create rituals with your child around this play (for instance, listening to a book on tape while playing Legos or enjoying a snack of apples and raisins while coloring).

> • Commit to really "going there" with your child by fully immersing yourself into their pretend play. (You'll get so many great insights about the way they think and feel when you do!)

We Are the Greek Chorus

Vivian Paley, a renowned expert on preschoolers and play, spent her career in preschool classrooms and has written thirteen books, most notably, *Mollie Is Three.* In it, Paley equates adult engagement in a preschooler's play to a Greek chorus, writing, "We observe from outside the drama and comment in the manner of a Greek chorus, sometimes repeating something a child or character has said. We make connections that help reveal the player's intentions."[5] The connections are questions about their play, similar to the way we might ask questions while reading a storybook aloud such as, "Why is the superhero running around so fast?" "Where is he going?" "I wonder what is going to happen next in the story?" "Can we make room for a friend in the spaceship to the moon?"

This type of play is regularly modeled on *Daniel Tiger's Neighborhood* as we offer repeated strategies to help Daniel deal with play-corner squabbles. We call them strategies "with handles" because they are easy to grasp and hold on to for both parents and preschoolers. One of our most popular episodes has been our "sharing" episode, in which Daniel goes to the park to play "cars" with his friends. In the story, everyone was to bring their own toy car so they could play together by racing them, but Daniel's preschool friend Prince Wednesday (Backstory: he's the later-in-life son of King Friday and Queen Sarah Saturday!) forgets to bring a car and is visibly upset. Modeling empathy, Daniel is upset too and wants to help. After the two talk about the situation, Prince Wednesday asks to take a turn with Daniel's car. At first, Daniel isn't so sure. After all, this is *his* new toy and he wants to play with it.

Then we bring guided interaction into play, and have Dad help him by singing the strategy song with him about sharing: "You can take a turn and then I get it back." In the end, in addition to better understanding the concept of sharing, Daniel learns that if he does share, he will always get his toy back, something an adult clearly understands but a preschooler may not be too sure about. This adult-directed strategy helps Daniel resolve the situation, and he ultimately gives Prince Wednesday a turn with his car, reminding himself that he will get it back. This modeling of conflict resolution through adult-directed play is repeated, with different strategies for different feelings and situations, throughout every episode of the series. We always show Daniel first learning the strategy from an adult, then singing it so he fully understands it, and then ultimately, in play using the strategy by himself to solve his own problem.

Similarly, on *Wishenpoof*, Mom, Dad, and even Bianca's "sage" of a bear best friend Bob will give Bianca "words of wisdom," which is food for thought to help her solve her own problems. For instance, in different episodes, Bianca has learned "You can think of how your friend is feeling" or "The best way to know what your friend needs is to ask him." Rather than tell Bianca exactly what she needs to know—*Your friend is sad!* or *Your friend needs to rest, he's not feeling well*—we use adult-directed play so Bianca can model thinking on her own to solve the problem while armed with her "words of wisdom."

PARENTING PRODUCTION NOTES
What Being the Greek Chorus Looks Like

The Situation	What *Not* to Do	Do
Your child falls down.	Rush in.	Assess the situation. If your child isn't hurt, then *Pause, encourage* with your face, eyes, and words, and *watch* her get up and play again.

The Situation	What *Not* to Do	Do
Your child is having trouble sharing a toy.	Reprimand; take the toy from her; make her share.	*Pause, watch,* and use empathetic language ("How do you think your brother is feeling right now?"); give them language for solving the problem ("You can have a turn and then I'll get it back").
Your child is angry and wants something *right now*.	Give in to his wants.	*Pause,* wait for him to calm down, give him encouraging words, help him breathe, and ask him what he thinks he can do to solve the problem.
Your child gets upset when he makes a mistake while painting.	Tell him how to "fix" it.	*Pause, watch,* and guide a conversation around the idea that there are no mistakes in art.

Involved Co-play and Self-Worth

When a parent or older sibling takes the time to play a game with a preschooler—whether it be playing a board game, reading a story, sharing a bike ride, or doing a wacky freeze dance game—we are bonding through play in a way that teaches our kids self-importance and boosts their self-worth. At this age, virtually any shared experience becomes a highlight in our preschooler's experience, and they will want it to be repeated. For instance, snuggling and watching a favorite show together fosters positive, pleasant, sweet sharing moments and leads to inside jokes, talking (about what's going to happen next or how a character is feeling, for example), and bonding one-on-one time.

PLAYING WELL WITH OTHERS

I know many people are turned off by the fact that these days most of us have to make a "date" to "play." Back in my day, as a kid, we used to just run next door to "play," unannounced and with zero fanfare. But I actually see today's playdates as a positive thing. While there is something to be said for the innocence and freedom we had as kids to just play and do our thing, truth be told, the date to play gives kids more structure and additional parental involvement, which ultimately elevates the play. Now that you make a "date" to play, the rules and stakes are higher for what a playdate entails. And I happen to think that's a good thing.

PARENTING PRODUCTION NOTES
Organize Preschool-Empowering Playdates

Since playdates are such a big part of a preschoolers' lives these days, here are a few strategies to ensure playdates are successful, for both the children *and* you!

- Make a Plan: Have a conversation with your preschooler about what she and her friend are going to do on the playdate by making a list of activities both children love and thinking about ways to combine them (don't forget to give your child some ownership over it). The idea that you can "make a plan" and have an activity or theme in mind brings the play to another level.
- Choose an Activity That Sparks: Promoting bonding and teamwork, create a homemade treasure hunt, put out a craft, bake a "no-bake" snack together, or bring out props to promote dramatic play.
- Design Playdates for All Kids: Scheduling playdates is a chance to get your preschooler matched up with kids who are both similar and different from themselves. Setting them up with appropriate

activities will help them be the best they can be while learning how to negotiate the play with others, a good experience for life.

- Tailor Experiences to Personalities: Think about ways to adapt the playdate experiences to the little (or perhaps *big*) personalities involved. For instance:
  - Have a kid who's a leader (a.k.a. a bit bossy)? Have your child be the "director" of a play and assign the roles for the other kids or have them play restaurant and make the bossy kid be the chef.
  - Have an introspective, shy kid? Start with an old-fashioned game of charades to break the ice or put out a craft that puts the kids on the same side of the table to create together.
  - Have a kid with lots of energy? Get outdoors and get physical—play games with rules, bring out the hula hoops, make an obstacle course, or paint outside with splatter paints or finger-paints.

Angela's Clues

With the onset of apps, educational toys, educational classes, and media, the time our preschoolers are spending doing their own thing has become increasingly sparse. The more we understand about how important dramatic play and free play is, the more we can make some time for it and see inside our preschooler's mind as to what they are learning and what sparks them.

When we incorporate play into the lives of our preschoolers, we are giving them a leg up, not to mention ultimate control over learning through trial and error, learning to find their spark, and learning to expand their knowledge of the way the world works. When we are playful in our approach to parenting, we are also creating a lasting bond with our kids so they can grow up independent, strong, and ready to take on the world with their own opinions and values modeled by us.

In media, I use a model for play by engaging and interacting with the preschooler at home and sparking dramatic play for after the show is over. As a media creator and a mom, I also understand the importance of finding the time to promote dramatic, creative, and imaginative play, and some of that time is consistently being eaten away by media. Using media to inspire our preschoolers to turn it off and go "do" is one of its best uses. And as parents, we need to model putting our phones away or turning off media to focus on our family time, too. To a preschooler, even our "just checking email every now and then" while at the park doesn't feel good. When they look over at us after launching themselves super high on a swing only to see us deep in our phones, it feels like a betrayal . . . like catching our significant other canoodling with someone else while out on a date with us. *Ouch.* I remember once when we were on vacation and I went to check my email. Ella, four at the time, looked me square in the eyes and said, "This is not an *email-cation*, this is not a *phone-cation*—this is a *VA-cation!*" Out of the mouths of babes . . .

. . . .

- **Be Involved** by immersing yourself in your preschooler's world of play.
- **Ask Questions** to discover why they love to play the way they do.
- **See the Spark** to find a way to extend their learning through play.

. . . .

YOUR MEDIA "YES" LIST

How does your child's media stack up with regard to its relationship with *play*? Go through the following checklist (and do the same with the checklists at the end of each of the remaining chapters) to refine your personal media "Yes" list and deepen your understanding for how to apply the strengths and tenets of best shows for your child into your parenting notebook.

☑ The show is asking my preschooler to be involved and play.

☑ The play is enriching, new, different, and/or challenging.

☑ My child is motivated to try new things, solve problems, and/or explore something new after engaging with the show.

☑ The play themes in their media are extending into real life in a positive way.

· ·

Clue Takeaways

o Play is the work of the child.

o Play helps preschoolers develop intellect and intrinsic motivation, understand the perspective of others, and problem solve.

o Preschoolers benefit from spontaneous play, guided play, and adult-directed play.

o We can look for opportunities to participate, ask questions, and be part of play to extend our preschooler's learning.

o Co-playing with our preschooler builds his or her self-worth.

CLUE #2: PAUSE

Pausing Helps Preschoolers Find Their Voice

After my now infamous research session, I became known around Nickelodeon as the "research girl" and resident preschool expert. I started coming to meetings to give my point of view on new projects in development. In one meeting, we were listening to pitch after pitch for a "game show for preschoolers" that involved giving preschoolers a "clicker" to answer questions like on *Jeopardy*. I couldn't help but roll my eyes. *Three-year-olds with a clicker?* Suddenly the tables turned, and everyone looked at me. I shrugged and said, "Preschoolers won't play the show—they'll be too absorbed with the clicker." Then they challenged me, and said, "Well, what would *you* do?"

As if I were on my own game show, I feverishly researched and wrote and three weeks later, I presented a *research memo*. That's right, my first show pitch was a research memo. What would I do? I started with what I know—research—so I had outlined the idea of an intentional "Pause" as the secret sauce of what a game show could be for preschoolers. Pausing so preschoolers *at home* can interact with the show would make them feel as if they were part of the show. A preschool version of a game show! Viewers would be the contestants, and the games would be based on all the skills they need to learn before starting kindergarten, like colors, numbers, matching, patterning, and preliteracy skills. I had seen this work in a research session—kids were talking back to the TV, but the content wasn't sticky enough to sustain a whole series. I wanted to perfect the interactive approach with a preschool-appropriate game concept and a good storyline that would make it a hit show on television.

To be honest, in that very first pitch meeting, everyone nodded in agreement, but no one truly understood what I was talking about. After all, it was 1993 and *Barney & Friends* had just taken preschool television by storm. Also, while the idea of "interactive" media was being tossed around, the available technology wasn't able to support it yet. To put things into perspective: Sony's PlayStation wouldn't debut until 1995. Even AOL didn't appear on the scene until 1995, and the interactive toy phenomenon of Tickle Me Elmo didn't come out until Christmas of 1996. Having a toy Tamagotchi pet was revolutionary in 1997, and the first iMac debuted in 1998.

When *Blue's Clues* premiered in September 1996 and we introduced this idea of the four-beat Pause—Steve, our host, asks the viewer a question and then Pauses—we ended up changing the landscape of preschool TV forever. The Pause was a way to do interactivity for preschoolers—a simple, low-tech approach with a "game show" spin for the entire twenty-two minutes of an episode. Breaking the fourth wall and talking to the camera had been done before, of course, but not in the way we approached it on *Blue's Clues*. Steve would wonder where a clue was, ask the viewer, "Have you seen a clue?" and then very closely lean into the camera. His eyes were wide with interest and curiosity, as if the home viewer wasn't only his cool best friend but also had all the answers. And if you were the home viewer sitting in your living room watching *Blue's Clues*, you couldn't help but feel Steve's intent gaze and get the sense he was talking directly to you. Then after asking his initial question, Steve would lean in even closer and wait. And wait. And wait. (And wait.)

He would wait for our now infamous four-beat Pause, which is *a long time* by television standards. Scratch that. It's a long time by *anyone's* standards! But Steve was waiting for us at home to answer. And when we would answer and point and say, "There! There's the clue!" he would smile, acknowledge us with a genuinely impressed expression, and turn in the direction we were telling him to. This was the *Blue's*

Clues way of storytelling—pausing to listen—that brought the home viewers into each episode. It was powerful.

For *Blue's Clues*, the "Pause" made kids feel like they were an active part of the story. This wasn't a "play" they were watching. The kids watching our show actually felt like they were *inside* Blue and Steve's world playing along *with* them. In fact, many preschoolers believed that if they didn't help Steve and answer the questions, the show wouldn't go on. And the preschoolers loved that power. So, they continued to talk to Steve—and he listened. The kids "helped" Steve all while learning and practicing kindergarten readiness skills in the form of interactive games. The first preschool game show!

From the very beginning, the preschool home viewer has been at the center of my thinking as I create shows—he or she is a key character in every story, and in everything I do. And my signature "Pause" has had to be carefully timed and reflect a keen understanding of who preschoolers are, where they are in their level of development, and their need to play in a world that's part reality and part fantasy. With the Pause, my characters are respectfully listening to our preschool home viewer. I'm giving them time to think. I'm giving them a sense of power. And it works.

WHY THE PAUSE?

As preschoolers' brains are developing, they need more processing time than adults do. When asked a question, they need time to think about what the question means, process an answer to the question, form the words needed to communicate their answer, and then verbalize it. When we fill the silence and follow up with a second question, we are forcing them to start the process all over again from the beginning.

University of Florida educator Dr. Mary Budd Rowe called this "wait time" in the classroom.[1] She found that when teachers purposefully employed wait time, students gave higher-quality answers, and their self-confidence increased because they were able to spend time recalling the information and articulating a good answer. In essence, wait time or pausing sets us up for positive interactions with our preschoolers.

According to the Center on the Developing Child at Harvard University, interactions actually *shape* the architecture of the brain. They wrote, "When an infant or young child babbles, gestures, or cries, and an adult responds appropriately with eye contact, words, or a hug, neural connections are built and strengthened in the child's brain that support the development of communication and social skills. Much like a lively game of tennis, volleyball, or Ping-Pong, this back-and-forth is both fun and capacity-building."[2]

But is it possible for that same "ping-pong" back-and-forth dynamic to apply to the relationship between preschoolers and their media? Can "virtual" interactivity result in young viewers understanding and applying what they pick up from their educational shows or apps? *Yes.*

Research from Dr. Sandra Calvert of Georgetown University tells us that until around three years of age, depending on task complexity, children learn better from a live demonstration than from an equivalent televised demonstration, a problem that researchers have since labeled the "video deficit." However, the entrance of "interactive media" with programs like *Blue's Clues* and now interactive educational apps, has challenged this notion, and updated research continues to shed light on how the Pause has changed everything.

In one study in which Dr. Calvert and her team looked at the differences between the way young children respond to passively watching videos versus playing a computer game, they found that adding pausing and interactivity helps kids to learn and transfer what they know to real-life situations. Another found that preschoolers who *interacted* with key parts of a program via a computer understood the content better than those who simply observed the program with an adult, suggesting that it is the interactivity with content that leads to greater learning.[3]

I am a fierce believer in the "power of the Pause," as the use of the Pause has a real and profound impact on the learning of our young viewers. A summative study of *Blue's Clues* by media researcher

Dr. Jennings Bryant found it was indeed working. In fact, he found that kids who watched *Blue's Clues* scored better on standardized tests than kids who didn't watch *Blue's Clues*.[4] I was thrilled—like "over the moon" thrilled—to discover our curriculum and interactive model helped to elevate preschoolers' learning. This was further proof that educational media can teach and that how we approach the learning, through the use of the Pause, makes all the difference.

THE PAUSING PHILOSOPHY

By employing the Pause in our preschool programs, we are supporting cognitive development because preschoolers, like any other man, woman, or child, *love to feel heard*. Preschoolers are empowered by the fact that their favorite characters Pause and wait long enough for them to absorb information, formulate a response, and actually state their point of view. The Pause does wonders from a child development perspective.

Whether in kids' media or in real life, this idea of being interactive and taking the role of an active listener is what I like to call the *pausing philosophy*, a philosophy that addresses a preschooler's feelings of being powerless, models empathy, and supports them in learning to understand their feelings and the feelings of others. By listening to and caring about what preschoolers have to say, parents and teachers reinforce the idea that (a) our children have value, (b) our kids' feelings are important, and (c) our kids' voices deserve to be heard. And just like anything else, its success depends on *how* we Pause and interact and with what *content* when utilizing this tool in our everyday lives.

THE MAGIC IN THE PAUSE

The truth is, there is magic in the Pause. In fact, this super simple technique actually makes our job as parents easier. That's right, I said it, *easier*. Because when we take the time to enact the four-beat Pause, we:

o don't need to have all the answers,

o don't have to be perfect,

o don't jump to conclusions,

o don't answer the question we think our kids are asking,

o answer only the questions they *are* asking, and

o give our preschooler time to gather their thoughts and verbalize them.

Yes, a four-beat Pause may feel like forever, but, in real life it can be a godsend. When I was pregnant with Ella, two-year-old Hope was rubbing my belly when she looked up at me and asked, "I know you are going to be the baby's *mommy*, but who is going to be the baby's *daddy*?"

I would like to say I Paused instinctively, the expert use of a correctly timed Pause, but the truth was she caught me completely off-guard and I had no idea what to say. During my Pause, Hope scrunched up her face and ran over to Greg to protectively give him a hug and said, "Is it my daddy? Is my daddy the baby's daddy?"

I Paused and then nodded, waiting for her mind to be blown.

She continued, "So, I have to share?"

Again, I Paused, sure that her head was about to blow off her body. And before I could even nod, she shrugged, as preschoolers often do, and said, "Okay. I can do that. I love OUR NEW BABY!!!"

I just love preschool enthusiasm!

If I hadn't Paused, I may have jumped in before she was ready to hear the information. But with the Pause, she led the conversation and the information was better received.

. . . .

PRACTICING THE FOUR-BEAT PAUSE

Implementing a "Pause" in real life the same way we do in our shows might seem unrealistic at first. And I understand why. After all—four beats is a *long time* to wait for a response, especially in a world where we're used to multitasking and rushing around trying to fit everything in. And it's not something we experience in most (if any) of our day-to-day real-world interactions. Think about it. Have you ever seen someone talk with a child and ask, "How's school? Good? Great!" So often, we as adults don't leave any room for kids to think about what was asked, formulate a response, and actually provide an answer. As a preschooler, my niece used to think this was a ritual of sorts. For Morgan, "Good!" always came after "How's school?" Just like for most of us, "Fine" always comes right after, "How are you?"

But once we become conscious of this, we can begin building the four-beat Pause into our day-to-day interactions with our kids. The payoff—higher self-esteem and the time to think and absorb what is being asked of them so they can find the right words to give us insight into what they're thinking—is priceless. A little practice goes a long way:

1. Ask a question to your preschooler, making eye contact and PAUSING (it works with your spouse too, and even to yourself in a mirror).
2. Wait for an answer, slowly counting to four, Mississippi style (in your head, of course!)
3. Respond.

PHEW! It's a long time, right? Well, that's the power.

. . . .

Pausing for Our Kids to Talk

Have you ever caught up over coffee with a friend who couldn't help but interject her feedback, opinion, or advice about whatever you were sharing before you even finished getting the story out?

Me: We were in NYC until Hope started kindergarten and then—
Friend: Really? How could you have babies in the city? It's so loud and crowded. I love the suburbs!

Me: Well, we loved walking everywhere and going to the museums—

Friend: I would hate it! I mean, you have no space, and it's dirty . . . isn't the city so dirty?

Me: We loved the city with the babies . . . it was easy—

Friend: No way. I couldn't even imagine it.

Doesn't feel so great, right? Yet we often do the same exact thing with the young children in our lives. We may have the best intentions of trying to help our child formulate his or her thoughts or let them know we understand what they're trying to say, but the truth is, nothing stops a conversation with our kids quicker then jumping in with our point of view before we are asked. But when we Pause, we're telling them that we're open to hearing anything else they have to say.

Adele Faber taught us *how to listen* in her groundbreaking book *How to Talk So Kids Will Listen & Listen So Kids Will Talk*, because *we want our kids to talk*. We want our preschoolers to find their voice. We want them to have and express opinions. Practicing active listening not only boosts their self-worth and helps them gain confidence in the notion that what they have to say matters, it also plays an important role in setting up a powerful foundation for tweens and teenagers.

Pausing to Reflect

This act of pausing, repeating back what we hear in a positive way, and letting go of any "agenda" is known as *reflecting*, and by actively choosing to do this, we are encouraging our preschoolers to not just recall information but to be aware of what they learned, what was interesting, how they feel about it, and what they can do to build on the experience. With reflection, we are setting the stage for mastery of deeper thought.

Case in point. My four-year-old niece, Reese, came home from school devastated one day, telling her mom, my sister-in-law, Alicia, that no one had liked the picture she made. As she burst into tears, Alicia hugged her while simultaneously noticing her own anger at the other child who'd made her daughter feel bad. But rather than speak to that emotion, she kept those thoughts to herself, Paused, and then repeated back, "It seems like you're sad about your picture."

Reese was instantly engaged. "I really like my picture. It's a dog. See?" She shoved the picture in Alicia's face.

Alicia nodded, and noticing that the dog was purple, once again reflecting back her daughter's sentiment. "You sound so proud of your *purple* dog!" She then shared a thought to give some insight into the problem. "It's creative!"

Reese perked up, feeling a bit better at being validated. "I am creative, see? Even her tongue is purple!" She giggled and continued to tell a whole story about her favorite purple dog and how much her brother would love it and how she wished purple dogs were real. Alicia agreed—purple dogs would be cool.

In the end, Reese not only felt heard, but she got to work on learning how to label and cope with her feelings by talking to someone, namely her mom. And this is a strategy that will be incredibly useful to her as the problems she'll face get increasingly complicated as she gets older.

Pausing to Find Solutions

In the story of Reese and her purple dog, Alicia's pausing followed by reflection gave her daughter the opportunity to more deeply understand what she was feeling. Another powerful benefit of active listening through Pausing is that it helps us find solutions together. When we listen and Pause in response to our child's upset, we model compassion and empathy, which are great precursors to solving whatever problem is happening for the child. On *Daniel Tiger's Neighborhood*, we always try to go the extra step. Even when Daniel learns to apologize, our strategy is, "I'm sorry, *how can I help*?"

Perhaps what I love most about Pausing is that it is active "listening with heart," as parenting expert Julie Ross has called it. Julie sees Pausing as a power capable of drawing our kids into us in a "magnetic and creative space." In doing so, we're encouraging independence in our children while still helping to collaborate with them on the big decisions life brings. And isn't that exactly the dynamic we want to foster in the long term?

Pausing to Solve Problems

Taking the time to Pause when confronted with a conflict enables us to remember to use it as a learning moment. The results of being calm enough to be positive and non-judgmental will allow our preschoolers to grow and learn from each situation.

The scenario	Old response (shuts down conversation)	New response (keeps conversation going)	Possible response from child after Pause
Your child is upset that she lost her library book.	"How many times are you going to lose your book? I tell you all the time, put your book on your desk so you always know where it is."	"I can tell that you're upset" + Pause	"I am! I'm looking and looking . . . I'll look by my bed."
Your child doesn't want to do his homework.	"If you don't do your homework you'll never get into college."	"It seems like you might be stuck. What could help?" + Pause	"Maybe a snack and then I'll do some more?"
"My sister is so mean . . . she's the worst!"	"Tell her to come over here! It makes me so mad when you both fight!"	"Hmmm" + Pause	"Sometimes I hate her, but I love her too."
"I don't want to go to bed! I'm not tired. I'm never going to bed!"	"That's it! I'm picking you up and putting you in your bed myself."	"You have so much to do tomorrow—I'm not sure how you'll do it all if you don't get a good night's sleep" + Pause	"Well, maybe . . ." (Stays up longer, but in his bed, and eventually goes to sleep.)

The scenario	Old response (shuts down conversation)	New response (keeps conversation going)	Possible response from child after Pause
"Everyone is invited to the party but me."	"That's not true. Not everyone. You're exaggerating—again."	"You sound disappointed" + Pause	"I am."
"Why are you sooooo mean????"	"Really? I'm mean? You are being ungrateful."	"I know this is important to you. But it's my job to keep you safe" + Pause	Grumbles.

Pausing to Understand

One of the greatest benefits of the Pause in the way we communicate with our little ones is that it gives them a chance to process new, confusing, or potentially difficult information and fully understand it. When we Pause, we are also giving us, as parents, a chance to process the situation and formulate thoughtful responses that respect our child's emotional well-being.

Pausing for a purpose can be seen in one of our most challenging episodes of *Daniel Tiger's Neighborhood* to date. In the episode, Daniel Tiger, our three-year-old protagonist, has to deal with the death of his beloved fish. After Daniel observes the fish isn't moving, he calls to Dad Tiger, who comes over to investigate. With Daniel, he pokes the fish gently, showing that he's not moving. Daniel doesn't understand, so Dad explains: "It looks like Blue fish has died." Daniel looks at Dad quizzically. Dad Tiger *Pauses*, waiting for Daniel to respond.

He finally asks, "What does that mean?" Dad responds, "It means that Blue fish is not breathing or moving anymore." Daniel again takes some time to process this new information, while Dad Pauses. Daniel, not completely understanding, says, "Well, I'll play with Blue fish later."

Dad bends down, looks Daniel in the eye and says, "Blue fish died, which means he can't play with you." Daniel frowns, his eyes watering with tears and says, "I'm so sad." Dad embraces Daniel. For the rest of the episode, we deal with Daniel's feelings about the subject. Mom and Dad Tiger model active listening, pausing, and helping him cope by offering some solutions, including drawing a picture of Blue fish to help him feel better.

The use of the Pause gave Daniel a chance to absorb Dad's information and create meaning from it, while also giving Dad a chance to collect his thoughts and consider the best way to share this sad news with his son. What resulted was a respectful, connected conversation. And when we as parents and caregivers can follow Dad's lead in the way we communicate with our own children, we can reap the same benefits.

Pausing While Playing to Learn

Pausing can be an extremely effective tool while playing with our children—one capable of turning any kind of dramatic play into genuine and meaningful learning experiences. The key is to jump into the play, Pause to let our child lead, ask relevant questions, be in the moment. Do this and you're primed to empower, challenge, and build their self-worth, all while making them laugh!

For instance, say you call your daughter to get her shoes on so the two of you can run to the grocery store, and she surprises you by coming down the stairs dressed as Supergirl, complete with cape and bright red tights. Instead of being annoyed or embarrassed or inflexible because your expectations haven't been met, try jumping into the play. Suddenly you've gone from dad and daughter picking up eggs and milk to superheroes saving the day from hunger. You stay in the moment and ask, "All right, Supergirl, ready to save the day?"

"Ready!" she says as she jumps to her best superhero stance.

As you get her into the car, you say, "Okay, let's soar to the grocery store. Supergirl, what do superheroes eat?"

"Food!" she declares.

You listen, Pause, and then probe for more creativity. "What kind of food would make you stronger, Supergirl?"

She thinks and you Pause, all the while getting her into the car to go. "Lots of veggies for strong muscles!" she shouts.

You continue to actively listen, adding some more flavor to the conversation. "Green veggies are the healthiest for superheroes. Which are the green veggies?"

Play your cards right, and she may spend the rest of shopping trip labeling all the green veggies she knows as you fly around in the grocery cart, quickly, because that's what superheroes do.

Simply put, asking questions and pausing is in and of itself a game. Much like we've shown through *Blue's Clues* or *Super Why!*, asking questions of kids promotes learning and a strong bond. Whether on screen or in real life, playing an interactive game in the grocery store has all of the same effects.

Pausing to Promote Mastery

The research shows that kids learn more when they are interacting and learning for themselves, but the same is also true when we as parents and caregivers are interacting and using the "pausing philosophy" with our preschoolers in our everyday lives as a way to encourage our child's self-discovery, self-knowledge, and eventual mastery.

Julie Ross wrote about the idea of letting kids learn from themselves in her fantastic book, *Practical Parenting for the 21st Century*. In her book, she presents the well-known story of a boy finding a butterfly cocoon. Fascinated, he examines it and notices that, in fact, a butterfly was struggling to come out. He watches and waits as the butterfly desperately pushes and pulls to try to get his wings outside of the cocoon. The process takes such a long time and the boy gets increasingly sad and wants to help. So instead of watching the butterfly continue to struggle, he very carefully opens up the cocoon wider and wider until the butterfly is able to break free. The butterfly flies right out of the cocoon high over the boy's head and then comes crashing down and dies. The heartbreaking moral of the story, of course, is that the butterfly needed the struggle to ensure her wings were strong enough to fly. Without the lengthy struggle, the butterfly didn't develop the tools it needed fly on its own.[5]

In her book *The Gift of Failure*, author Jessica Lahey has pointed out how we, as parents, are too often making the same mistake the boy made with the fledgling butterfly. She describes loving, well-meaning, yet helicopter-like parenting practiced by so many moms and dads and calls us out on it. As she reminds us, when parents constantly rush in to help our children—when they fall down but are fine; when we bring them their forgotten gym clothes; when we swoop in and fix a friendship fiasco—they will never learn how to help themselves. By barreling ahead without leaving breathing room for Pauses, observations, reflections, and yes, mistakes, we're taking away opportunities for personal growth and mastery.[6]

Perfect example—my girlfriend and fellow writer, Becky, recently sent me a video of her fifteen-month-old daughter, Meadow, at a small trampoline park. Mind you, this sweet little girl had just mastered the art of *walking*, so even I caught myself holding my breath as I watched the video of her attempting to jump on the trampoline. Yet as I watched, I realized she had quite possibly the best coping strategy I'd ever seen in a child that age. First, she Paused and observed how the "big" kids jumped. After a minute, it becomes clear by the way her face lit up that she made the decision to jump, too. She then "hopped" her way over to the trampoline, as if to prove to herself that she had the chops to do it. When she got to the trampoline, she was immediately flung backward. But her mom knew she wasn't hurt, so instead of swooping in, she continued to watch, testing the level of resilience (both hers and her daughter's). Meadow Paused, got herself up, and tried it again, and this time she was successful! The pride and happiness on her face beamed through the video. A perfect example of how pausing *on both sides*—Becky and Meadow—had great effect.

Pausing for Self-Worth

The next time you Pause and really take that moment to *listen* to what your preschooler has to say, watch what he or she does. In my experience, preschoolers tend to lean right back into you, stand up taller, hold their head up high, and speak in a measured, excited voice. By giving them this pausing time, we are giving them a voice. We're letting them know that their opinion matters. When we validate what they have to say without judgment and simply ask for more information, we're letting them think things through. We are boosting their self-worth.

My mother has an uncanny way with preschoolers. She's very in-tune, very in-the-moment, and loves her one-on-one time with them. Once, when my daughter Ella was little, she looked at my mother and said, "You would look pretty with blue hair."

I thought maybe my mother would balk at her statement or brush it off. Instead, she looked right at her, smiled, Paused, and eventually said, "Then my hair would match your eyes!"

Ella laughed and said, "I know. You would match me!"

Knowing that this made Ella proud, my mother said, "I would like that!" My mother took out some crayons and paper and they went on to draw my mom with blue hair. Ella felt proud, heard, and like her ideas had merit.

Truth be told, the reason that *Blue's Clues* became interactive in the first place was to let preschoolers know that their voice mattered, just the way Mister Rogers made me feel when he looked at me through the television screen and said in his legendary gentle tone, "I like you just the way you are."

HOW TO PAUSE EFFECTIVELY

The Pause is the tool, but it's how we *use* the tool that makes all the difference. We need to be conscious of our body language when we Pause and what we say when we interact. Being intentional with the Pause results in positive outcomes for both our kids and ourselves.

For example, what we choose to say and how we say it after we Pause is important. In fact, sometimes we can Pause and say nothing at all. We use body language like leaning in to our preschoolers and looking into their eyes. This is definitely a sign of interest and our preschoolers feel it. To them it says, "You're important." When we do want to make a strong point, getting on our preschooler's level and looking into their eyes is a powerful tool.

Your child says: "My friend made fun of my picture."
    You say: "That makes you feel . . ."
    Pause and listen for response.
    You say: "What can we do?"

Your child says: "I can't do it."
    You say: "You sound frustrated . . ."
    Pause and listen for response.
    You say: "How can I help?"

Your child says: "I'm so sad."
    You say: "That makes me sad . . ."
    Pause and listen for response.
    You say: "Can you tell me more?"

WHEN THINGS GO OFF-SCRIPT

If yours is like most families, there's a good possibility you and your child have "trigger" words that arise during conflict, or words that conjure up feelings of upset, annoyance, or worry. For instance, when your child pouts that she's *bored*, are you instantly put-off and angry? It could be that it conjures up a feeling of disrespect, as if you haven't done enough for your child! How could they be bored?! Before you react, take a Pause and think, What is your child really saying? Perhaps if we dig deeper, we can find out they're feeling left out because they weren't invited to a friend's party or perhaps they are being shut out by their sister. They are still learning to maneuver through their emotions and don't have as strong a handle on them as we do.

When we take the time to Pause and listen, we are giving ourselves the chance to *calm down* and reflect on underlying issues our kids may be facing. My friend's trigger was when her son would stomp his feet and say "I don't wanna!" Any time her preschooler was adamant like this, she pictured him as an adult, acting like a big baby when he doesn't get his way. Taking a Pause, she was able to put her emotional fears and annoyances on the back burner and deal with what was going on right then for her son. The truth is, parenting is day-by-day and behavior issues that bubble up at the age of four can be emotionally dealt with so that they don't erupt when they are twenty-four!

Pausing to Bond as a Family

Sometimes it takes a conscious effort on our part to create true family bonding interactions between us and kids, but these almost always provide rich opportunities to introduce and play with the power of the Pause. Here are some ideas:

o Family meals, whether shared daily or weekly, are an ideal time to practice the Pausing Philosophy and active listening.

o Interactive games you can play as a family help promote pausing through turn taking in a fun, silly way. My favorite games that can be adapted for preschool play? Apples to Apples, Cranium, Guess Who, *Super Why!* Board Game, Heads Up for Kids (app), charades, I Spy, tag, and freeze dance.

o Family movie nights can offer fantastic opportunities for thoughtful conversation, intentional listening, and lots of pausing both during the movie (hit the "Pause" button on your remote, first!) and afterward as you reflect on the characters, storyline, and message of the film. The same goes for good television programs.

o Interactive meal prep can be a great time for thoughtful conversations full of Pauses—working together to bake up a batch of yummy banana bread, personalizing homemade pizzas with your favorite toppings, or prepping the ingredients for a make-your-own taco night.

○ Reading together is an ideal time for practicing the Pause. In fact, studies have shown that preschoolers' learning soared when parents and caregivers actively and interactively read the story by stopping to ask the preschoolers questions or have them predict what would happen next.[7] This might include simple questions about the pictures such as, "Where is the ball?" to more thoughtful questions like "What do you think is going to happen next?" or taking time to study the faces of the characters and asking, "How do you think this character is feeling?" One of my favorites is, "How would you write the ending to this story?"

○ Take a walk or go for a drive. Two words: captive audience. Combine intentional listening with the pausing philosophy, and you've got all the ingredients for amazing conversations. My friend Maddie has said that her mom always missed a tricky highway exit in her hometown because as a child, Maddie *never* stopped talking from the backseat of the car!

Angela's Clues

If you remember one thing from this chapter, remember that interactivity, vis-à-vis the Pause, is a technique, a tool, and a philosophy that will make parenting easier. Pausing and waiting for a response and then being nonjudgmental, positive, and interested in what your preschooler has to say will boost a preschooler's self-worth and give them time to tell you what they know, which gives them a "voice"—a voice they will need to change the world.

When we Pause and don't rush in, we are helping our kids learn how to be resilient and independent, fostering grit, and teaching them to handle conflict. In this way, we won't only see our preschooler's smart insights, but we'll have a powerful strategy to handle their meltdowns and the push and pull of a preschooler's strong will. Modeling the Pause and delayed gratification is also a powerful example for our preschoolers to emulate.

When we use the power of the Pause effectively and consistently throughout the preschool years, we set the foundation for a respectful, empathetic, and caring relationship dynamic.

. . . .

- **Be Involved** and set aside time to Pause *life* and bond as a family.
- **Ask Questions** and be aware of how long you Pause while awaiting a response.
- **See the Spark** and actively listen to what your preschooler has to say.

. . . .

YOUR MEDIA "YES" LIST
- ☑ The characters Pause to ask viewers direct questions.
- ☑ The characters give a four-beat Pause.
- ☑ The interactive moments in the app or show are used to promote learning.
- ☑ The interactivity is integral to the plot and propels the story forward.

. . . .

Clue Takeaways

- ○ Preschoolers need time to think about what a question means, process an answer, form the words, and verbalize it.
- ○ Intentionally pausing helps our preschoolers find their voice.

- Pausing gives preschoolers an opportunity to foster independent thinking, grit, and resilience, and promotes learning, understanding, and mastery.
- The ability to delay gratification has numerous benefits later in life.
- Pausing during challenges and conflicts allows for more thoughtful, calmer responses.

CLUE #3: REPEAT

Repetition Leads to Learning and Mastery

It was 1995. We'd been busily producing the first season of *Blue's Clues* for the past twelve months and our premiere date was fast approaching. One afternoon, co-creator Traci Paige Johnson and I found ourselves meeting in a conference room at 1515 Broadway discussing the rollout plan for *Blue's Clues* with the programming and marketing executives.

We knew the programming team wanted to get the show out as soon as possible, and those of us on the show's staff were writing, researching, and animating like our lives depended upon it, which in our case meant we were being diligent and *slow*. In fact, at this rate, by our premiere date we would have completed only seven out of twenty episodes. *Seven*. If we aired one episode per day, as was the norm for Nickelodeon and other kids' networks at the time, we would go through all our shows in *one* week!

We also knew the marketing group was trying to figure out how to let the world know just how different our show was from the other preschool shows on the air. They knew we had a strong curriculum. They knew we had a different look with a live-action character living in an animated world. And, of course, they knew we were truly interactive in an unprecedented way. But how could they present these breakthrough aspects of our show without any context? It was 1996— no one would understand what "interactivity" meant. Thinking about this marketing conundrum, I had gone back to my roots. *Research*.

As if I were playing my own personal game of *Blue's Clues*, I had looked around for clues to help me step back and get clarity on what made the most sense for sharing our important show with the world. My first clue was that I knew without a doubt that preschoolers want to hear the same bedtime story over and over again. The second clue was that when we tested the first episode of *Blue's Clues*, the kids in our research groups wanted to watch the same episode over and over again. That's right . . . *the same episode*. And the third clue was that those kids who *did* watch the same episode repeatedly were on their feet—screaming, laughing, and perfecting playing our curriculum-based games and finding the clues—after the fifth repetition. They interacted the most, were louder and more confident, and, most important, answered more questions correctly.

I had found my answer.

So . . . in that conference room, packed with about fifteen of the smartest executives at Nickelodeon seated around a huge boardroom table, this once meek twenty-six-year-old girl from New Jersey piped up. "What if we aired the same episode every day for a week?"

Suddenly everyone at the table turned and looked at me, mouths agape. But I kept on talking. And really fast. "For preschoolers, repetition is the key to learning. *And*, if we air the same episode every day for a week, kids will be able to watch our seven episodes over a *seven*-week period versus just *one* week!" Then I looked at the marketing team. "And . . . parents would clearly know our show was different from all the other shows because by Friday the preschoolers would definitely be screaming at the TV, 'A clue! A clue!'" And then I smiled, you know, for good measure.

Knowing I'd need some big guns to back up my theory, I had enlisted the support of Dr. Dan Anderson and Dr. Alice Wilder, who shared relevant research on how preschoolers learn through repetition. This sealed the deal.

Nickelodeon agreed to try out what, by all accounts, was a crazy programming schedule. I distinctly remember the head of programming saying, "Well, let's try it. If it doesn't work, we'll pull it. And we'll all probably be fired." We all chuckled nervously. I knew she was joking, but *still*.

When *Blue's Clues* first premiered in September 1996, we had the highest ratings of any premiere at the time. Nickelodeon received phone call after phone call from parents. Some were confused by the programming schedule, and some were wondering why their kids were screaming at the TV. But most were calls of parent pride—the game play on *Blue's Clues* showcased just how involved, invested, motivated, and interested their preschoolers were to learn. Nickelodeon was thrilled at the results and more committed than ever to continue the programming strategy that put us on the map.

Before premiering our second season, journalist Lawrie Mifflin wrote an article for *The New York Times* called "The Joy of Repetition, Repetition, Repetition." She wrote,

> *A muddled mother telephoned Nickelodeon to complain. Her three-year-old daughter absolutely loved the new show called* Blue's Clues, *she said, but there must be some mistake: the same episode had been shown every day that week. It is no mistake. In fact, it tells parents that this show's creators deeply understand the world of people under the age of five, people who love to watch the same videos over and over again. Making children feel reassured this way is not a gimmick—it's a recognized concept of early-childhood learning. Another is that preschool children love active, not passive, ways to learn, and* Blue's Clues *gives them that, too.*[1]

So, as it turns out, repetition *is* the key to learning. And it was also the key to our new kind of preschool show. (And no one got fired.)

. . . .

PRACTICING REPETITION
WHILE MAINTAINING SANITY

My niece, Morgan, used to want to read the same book—*Owen* by Kevin Henkes, the story of a little boy mouse who was reluctant to give up his lovey (a blanket)—over and over and over again. It was sweet for a while, as Morgan would read it and cuddle up to her mom, holding her own lovey (a "baby"). But by the forty-ninth reading, my sister-in-law felt like she was going a little crazy. So, she changed it up a bit. She began adding little surprises and making up her own lines. This made Morgan laugh and it made Dawn feel a better about reading it for the fiftieth-plus time.

. . . .

WHY REPETITION?

Parents may wonder why important concepts on educational preschool shows are often repeated multiple times within a single episode, sometimes to the point where they're convinced their child is hitting the Rewind button on the remote. There's a reason for that.

Not only are preschoolers soaking in information and experiences, but it's these early experiences that affect the brain structure. A child's brain develops in an iterative, interactive process from birth through adulthood, but in the preschool years, a child's brain is especially pliant. According to the Center for the Developing Child at Harvard University, in the first few years of life, seven hundred new neural connections are formed *every second*. The more frequently information is repeated, the better the brain recognizes it, the thicker the associated neural pathways become, and more powerfully a concept or learning is reinforced and retained.[2]

This insight about the development of neural pathways is a foundational piece of what we know about early education. It's also what excited me about weaving repetition into my shows as an intrinsic part of the curriculum. I knew that the more we exposed our young preschoolers to words, concepts, experiences, and activities, the more robust their brain development would be. By utilizing repetition in our programs, we are providing preschoolers with the opportunity to:

o fully comprehend concepts,
o practice skills,
o build mastery,

- o boost their confidence, and
- o increase their love of learning.

REPEAT AD NAUSEAM, DELIBERATELY

How long did it take you to learn how to drive? Ride a bike? These aren't skills we learned overnight. We had to keep practicing and practicing and practicing. The same goes for our children. And the great thing is, they seem to be hardwired to inherently understand the importance of repetition, for they tend to naturally want to repeat things over and over (and over) again—the same book, the same songs, the same games, the same play. But it's not exactly this repetition that makes something stick. It's *deliberate* repetition.

Deliberate repetition may be the most important differentiating factor when it comes to success. People at the top of their game are so sparked, so passionate, that they focus and repeat, refining their work as they go, until they master it.

Author Malcolm Gladwell, who coined the idea of the ten-thousand-hour rule, stated that success is correlated with repetition and that "natural ability requires a huge investment of time in order to be made manifest." Gladwell shed light on this concept through the work of researcher K. Anders Ericsson and his colleagues, who interviewed a group of violinists at the Academy of Music in Berlin. After interviewing the students about their practice habits during childhood through the age of twenty, they found a direct correlation between the number of hours they practiced (i.e., repetition) and their abilities. In fact, the best players were those who'd logged more than ten thousand hours of practice (twenty hours per week for ten years!). Gladwell correlates success to practice. But author Cal Newport argues that it is not just practice that makes the difference—it's *deliberate* practice, where you expand your abilities day after day. Newport says, "Successful people are *experts* at practicing. If you're not expanding yourself in such a fashion, you'll never be ridiculously successful."[3]

My co-writer Debbie has been living out this focus-and-repeat strategy since moving to the Netherlands in 2013. I give her so much credit for picking up and moving from the United States to a new country, but of course, she was worried about immersing herself and she's never been naturally good with foreign languages (her admission!). However, determined to learn Dutch, she is counting on the idea that by committing to her weekly Dutch lessons, doing homework daily, and consistently engaging with baristas and other locals in her fledgling new language, she's eventually going to become fluent. She's highly motivated, and though she has plenty of setbacks (acquiring a new language is a very "two steps forward one step back" kind of thing), through mindful repetition, continually putting herself in situations where she can practice her phrases in context, and regularly putting in the time to build up her vocabulary and strengthen her verb conjugation, she'll eventually get there.

As Debbie is experiencing, the more you do something, the better you will be at it. There's an art to the way repetition is undertaken. It's not mindless "drill and skill" we're after. It's repetition in a way that also reinforces the love of learning. For our preschoolers to reach their full potential, the most useful ways to reinforce repetition is through scaffolding, routine, and positive reinforcements.

THE SECRET OF SCAFFOLDING

Deliberate repetition, called scaffolding, is the *key* ingredient we use in all of our programs to garner mastery. When most people think of scaffolding, they picture the temporary structures erected alongside buildings during construction. Typically built out of metal poles and wooden planks, these makeshift structures offer tangible support to workers as they go about doing their job of building or cleaning or repairing. When they've completed the job, they remove the scaffolding, and continue on to what's next.

In the context of education, scaffolding plays a similar role. Coined in the 1950s by cognitive psychologist Jerome Bruner, *instructional scaffolding* is the support given to children in order for them to achieve more than they would by themselves. The most effective scaffolding uses a trusted guide and hands-on activities that are repeated in deliberate layers of increased difficulty.[4]

I use this educational concept of scaffolding as a foundation for everything I create. It always begins with our main character—he or she is the "guide" who theoretically holds hands with the preschool viewers as they experience our stories, conflicts, and curriculum. Then, we thoughtfully scaffold each game we play in an episode by presenting increasing levels of difficulty throughout. It's this very approach of scaffolded games that has differentiated our shows from the rest. Just as construction scaffolds grow along with the needs of the workers so they can safely go higher and higher, we are supporting our child's learning and growth. Like training wheels, but smarter.

USING SCAFFOLDING AS A TOOL FOR LEARNING

Step 1: Be an Involved Guide

Before a construction team builds up their scaffold, they must first create a sturdy foundation. In education, this foundation comes in the form of a positive, trusted, and involved guide who can support the depth and growth of a child's learning. In our preschoolers' lives, parents, teachers, caregivers, and carefully chosen media guides and peers play this critical role. As an involved guide, our role is to spark an interest in our preschoolers, keep the learning on target, ask guiding questions, and repeat all of the above until they've mastered the task or behavior. Not to be mistaken with "helicopter parenting" that is overly hovering, an involved guide takes cues from the preschooler and repeats questions and strategies while modeling to support the learning with the end goal being our child not needing the scaffold anymore.

Fred Rogers on *Mister Rogers' Neighborhood* was the first to use creative production and editing techniques to convey this idea of his being an involved guide who was virtually "hand-holding" the preschooler. If you watch closely, you'll notice that Mister Rogers would be shown in an exterior shot opening the door to his house and in the next shot, filmed as an interior shot of his "house," he would walk through the open door. He then continued to show the transition of where he was going—to his closet, to the living room, to the kitchen—as if the preschooler at home were walking with him.

When Fred Rogers introduced this virtual hand-holding, for the first time ever a program considered the cognitive development of their young viewers in the way it was edited. Unlike adults, preschoolers can't make the same sort of cognitive leaps that many television shows expect their audience to make. For instance, consider a show that cuts from a shot showing a family walking out their front door to a shot showing that same family playing on the beach. As adults, we recognize the transition that needed to take place to get to the beach—walking, biking, or driving to their sandy destination. But preschoolers can't make this cognitive leap, which means they get confused. And when they get confused, they stop paying attention. And yes, you guessed it—when they stop paying attention, they stop learning. I make sure this idea of "hand-holding" is used in all of my shows, but it's also analogous to the way in which we, as parents, need to hand-hold our kids as their trusted guides so they feel safe and secure in order to learn.

Step 2: Slowly Increase the Levels of Difficulty

Lev Vygotsky, a Soviet psychologist and theorist in the early 1900s, added to the child development work of Piaget's stages by emphasizing the importance of social interactions. Like Piaget, he believed that children learn best through hands-on experiences, but he also believed children could learn new tasks on a deeper level and get to another stage with the right kind of intervention. Specifically, Vygotsky believed a child's "zone of proximal development"—essentially what a child can do herself—can be elevated with scaffolded intervention by a knowledgeable guide.

For example, imagine a preschooler is playing on the swings at the playground. She is able to swing by herself but is unaware of the fact that pumping her legs just so will increase her momentum and allow her to swing even higher. But when someone else shows her how it's done, coaches her, and encourages her to repeat it until she's mastered it, she can literally take her swinging to a new level. As a parent or caregiver, you're not swinging for her, you're not tearing her down for not knowing how to swing higher—you are modeling a tool for her to use and learn for herself.

Parenting Production Notes
Be an Involved Guide Using Scaffolding

Using Scaffolding for Learning About Building

Spark Interest	Keep Learning on Target	Ask a Guiding Question	Mastery
Place a set of building blocks out. Play with blocks alongside your preschooler.	Model building a simple house out of blocks alongside your preschooler.	As your preschooler starts to build a house, offer affirmations and encouragement, and then scaffold by asking what certain blocks could be, adding to the house, making it bigger, more detailed, more expansive.	Preschooler plays with blocks on his own, experimenting with trial and error and creating his own masterpieces.

Using Scaffolding for Learning About Writing

Spark Interest	Keep Learning on Target	Ask a Guiding Question	Mastery
Set a piece of lined paper and a pencil out for your preschooler. Write your name and the child's name.	Model making a grocery list with simple words preschoolers can copy.	Provide affirmations and encouragement for preschoolers to copy and add to the grocery list, and give your preschooler letter-by-letter guides to write down words for items.	Preschooler can use the grocery list in context, potentially even copying the list in its entirety, making her feel proud.

A CASE STUDY: *BLUE'S CLUES* AND *SUPER WHY!*

Repetition and Scaffolding to Promote Problem Solving

As I've described before, for *Blue's Clues*, we repeat three levels of the same game, and incorporate a factor of increasing level of difficulty for each game. And using Steve (or later, Joe) and Blue as our involved guides, we "hand-hold" our preschoolers as they play the games. Because the rules are always the same for the three layers, our viewers know how to play and can focus on the next level of challenge.

We incorporate scaffolding into our games in several different ways. First, we always begin with the easiest level of a game and gradually work up to the hardest level of that game. Second, over the course of a half-hour episode, there are three distinct games played, which we likewise scaffold, starting with the easiest and ending with the most difficult, which is to remember what the clues were and think about how the clues relate to each other and add up to answer the question of the day.

Dr. Dan Anderson conducted a study to test the effects of the repeat viewing of *Blue's Clues*. He found that when preschoolers watched repeated viewings of the same episode, they showed higher levels of comprehension, especially in their use of problem-solving strategies. The show also improved children's flexible thinking, which includes solving educational riddles, creative thinking, nonverbal skills, and verbal skills. Interestingly, Dan and his colleagues found we were actually changing the way preschoolers watched TV in general.[5] Because of the sticky repetition, preschoolers were bringing what they knew to other shows, interacting with their content, and therefore, we can assume, learning more from other shows as well.

For our literacy-focused show *Super Why!*, we know that the skills involved in learning to read build upon each other. For example, preschoolers first need to know how to label and identify letters, next they need to know how those letters have a sound, and then that when the letters come together they form words, and lastly, that those words form sentences, which have meaning. By changing a word in a sentence, a new meaning is created.

Because we understand all of these layers of preliteracy learning, in *Super Why!* we used scaffolded game play in a slightly different way than in *Blue's Clues*. First, in every episode we always started with an Alpha Pig letter identification game. Then we would alternate between having either a Wonder Red word decoding game or a Princess Presto spelling game. Each episode ended with a *Super Why!* game of reading comprehension. Depending on how much time was available based on the story and script, each game was also repeated two or three times. Across the entire series, the level of repetition for each skill was extremely high. By using a variety of examples, we were able to reinforce the mastery of these skills as transferable concepts that preschoolers could (and did) use as they read outside of the show.

I SPY, PUZZLES, AND LAUNDRY

Once we understand the concept of scaffolding as a way to build up the support our children need, the next steps involve slowly *increasing* the levels of difficulty to deepen what they know and what they're able to do and then purposefully *remove* the supports as they become more proficient. We can apply scaffolding to our lives through games, media, and everyday situations and activities. For example, think about the simple game of I Spy. When you first start playing, start by spying something easy, but over time you can choose increasingly difficult objects that are harder to spot and use clues to help your preschooler figure it out. When that becomes too easy, up the ante by having preschoolers take over and be the ones spying something and challenging them to come up with clues so you can guess and find.

Puzzles present another perfect scaffolding opportunity. By beginning with simple puzzles with only a few, large pieces and over time graduating to puzzles with more, smaller pieces, you're naturally increasing the challenge while simultaneously offering them a chance to practice or repeat the same type of spatial relationship problem-solving skill. Even the most mundane activities like sorting or folding laundry can provide all kinds of opportunities for scaffolded learning if you're willing to get a little creative (and realize that scaffolding household chores means they may take you a little longer). Clean laundry can first be turned into big sorting game, for example sorting by type of clothing and by color, and the next level could be matching, such as pairs of socks. Over time, you can introduce folding and putting things away in their proper place.

SCAFFOLDING IS A GUIDING HAND

Scaffolding is about providing a guiding hand in how our kids learn so they will develop not only with a strong sense of who they are, but with the ability to solve their own problems. We:

○ give our preschoolers guiding words, not answers;
○ recognize what our kids are playing and provide a guiding hand to up the ante on their play so their learning deepens;
○ look for opportunities to add challenge and learning when we engage in the same activities with our children;
○ add increasing levels of difficulty to games that we play with our preschooler.

REPETITION, A.K.A.
THE WARM AND FUZZY ROUTINE

One of the reasons repetition is so successful as a strategy with young children is that it is grounded in the *familiar*. The familiar ensures that kids feel safe and secure. And—no surprise here—when kids feel safe and secure, they are primed to learn. I've taken this aspect of child development to heart by creating "routines" for all of my shows, which means they follow a specific format so kids know what to expect. And that's critical for our young audience, because once preschoolers know what to expect and, even more important, what is expected of them, they can relax and just play our games, interact, and learn.

We honor this understanding of preschool development in our shows by creating formal features that open every series, and every episode within a series, in the same familiar place. Our show opens with the camera slowly panning, as if a preschooler is walking up a pathway to a house, replicating a familiar activity. Then, our main character greets the home viewer: "Hi out there, it's me, Steve!" (or ". . . Daniel Tiger!" or ". . . Arty!"). The character then invites the viewer in to get the adventure started.

This repetition is deliberate and purposeful. We want kids to come to the media, ready to play, so we ground them in a familiar setting and create a format for repetition. Here's a summation of an episode of *Blue's Clues*:

o   We open a book called *Blue's Clues*.
o   We dive inside the book and walk up the pathway to the Blue's Clues house.
o   Blue has a problem and shows she wants to play Blue's Clues to figure out a solution by "paw printing" the screen.
o   We sing the *Blue's Clues* song.
o   We find three clues.
o   We play three games, each with three layers of game play.
o   We *skidoo* through something and go somewhere even more preschool fantastical (inside a chalkboard, inside a picture frame, inside a game board!).
o   We have "mail time" at some point in every show, and it's so exciting that we sing about it.
o   We end by sitting in the Thinking Chair and figuring out Blue's Clues.

○ We celebrate and sing.
○ We say good-bye and sing our closing song.
○ We end in the living room, open the door to the house, and the camera pans out.
○ We close the book.

Take the time to view a variety of preschool programming and you'll find most employ this technique of simple, familiar routines to help viewers easily connect with the show, the characters, and the learning.

At home, we can take clues from our preschooler's favorite shows and create routines that are simple, short, and easy to follow. Since familiar, repetitive routines help preschoolers know what is expected of them, their use tends to help them become more compliant, understanding, and helpful. Just as they love the repetitive format of our shows, preschoolers take pleasure in these little routines at home, and for the same reason: *they love the feeling of control.* Ask any preschool teacher how they get an entire classroom cooperating, and they will invariably respond it is their adherence to a consistent and repetitive routine. That's because when preschoolers understand the rules of the day, they feel more in control and safe. And when we can help them feel safe and secure, we've just eliminated one of the biggest triggers for meltdowns.

Lest you think you've got to create a ten-step routine à la *Blue's Clues* involving games and several musical interludes, fear not. In real life, even the simplest of routines can be extremely effective. For example, the simple morning routine: we get dressed, eat breakfast, brush teeth, shoes on, and off to school! And the evening routine: we eat dinner, put pajamas on, brush teeth, read a story, and off to sleep! Want to up the ante? Sing your routine! Songs help preschoolers do anything. (More on that later.)

Another simple routine could be a weekly routine centered around dinners. Taco Tuesdays and Meatball Mondays and sundaes on Sunday will be a hit! Again, these simple routines make it easier all around, for us and for them.

CLUE #3: REPEAT

My friend Becky found solace in creating a new repeated element to her bath time routine. Ever since her twenty-month-old daughter was born, she has loved her bath, but as joyful as bath time is, getting *out* of the bath was inevitably a nightmare. Meadow would cry, thrash, and refuse to get out—even stomping, splashing, and flattening herself in the tub. Sometimes the crying lasts through pajama time. Fun times. After asking herself what was going on (too cold? scruffy towel? wet hair?), Becky realized the problem was the *transition*. By adding a new repeated routine, she could give her daughter a new sense of control over the situation. So she invented the "Bye-bye bath time" song (sung to the tune of the old folk song "Goodnight Ladies"), whereby she lets her daughter sit in the tub until it drains entirely (natural consequence) while they sing "Bye-bye water, bye-bye soap, bye-bye bath time, thanks for getting me clean." Then Becky pulls out the towel and sings "Hello towel, it's time to get dry." By this point, Meadow is happy to be lifted out of the tub to be dried off. Becky spends an extra two minutes doing the bath time song routine, but the rest of the night is infinitely easier. A new repeated routine with respect for her daughter's feelings (loves the bath!), plus a natural consequence (no more water in the tub), plus a repeated song routine (bye-bye bath, hello towel) equals parenting win.

CONSISTENCY: A FANCY WORD FOR REPETITION

We hear a lot about the importance of being consistent in our parenting, and it makes sense because, at the end of the day, being consistent is all about following through on our routines and sticking to our overall parenting point of view. Easier said than done, I know, but repetition in the form of consistency has a major payoff for parents. Because when we're consistent, repetitious, and yes, perhaps as a result "boring," our preschoolers will be less resistant and grow up grounded in who they are and where they belong. They'll know how Dad would feel in this specific situation; they'll know how Mom would react. That means if we create a rule, as in "No soda," we need to follow through, no exceptions. This no-exceptions rule can be tough to get behind, but ultimately it ends up being both easier on us *and* our kids when we don't give in. Because once preschoolers know there is a hard-and-fast rule, a line that can't be crossed, they relax into it. The routines we set up—the aspects of our parenting philosophy we are consistent with—helped when they were toddlers and build a foundation that will come in handy as our kids get older.

PARENTING PRODUCTION NOTES
Tap into the Power of Routine

To maximize the benefits of routine as a repetition tool in your daily life, remember to:

- create simple routines that can be repeated,
- share the schedule,
- create a simple consistent, repeated mealtime (e.g., Taco Tuesday),
- talk through a plan (another form of routine) before going to appointments, and
- be consistent.

THE ROLE OF POSITIVE REINFORCEMENT

Because preschoolers are essentially active "sieves"—regularly sifting through information to make sense of their world—they utilize repetition by *doing*. Every time they find something they love and repeat it, they're looking to us for feedback. By giving positive feedback in the form of reinforcement—such as smiling, nodding, or asking a related question—we are setting the foundation for motivated learning, a.k.a. resilience, self-confidence, and, ultimately, mastery.

During play, preschoolers are increasing the level of complexity and scaffolding naturally, through imaginary play and storytelling.

And when we allow time for play and are involved in their play, we are also providing positive reinforcement. For example, when my sister's daughter Bella was a preschooler and her son Aidan was just a newborn, she was noticing repetitive play. Bella was playing that s*he* was the baby, with wanting to be swaddled, rocked, and given a pacifier. Jenn sat with her for a bit and played as she guided her to see what was going on. As they played together, Jenn rocked her as the baby. Suddenly, Bella changed up her play. Feeling in control again, she was back to being the big sister, and the *new* baby was crying and crying and crying. Jenn, seeing what was going on, scaffolded the play to show her all of the things she can do, talked about why babies cry, and explained how Bella can help. Loving that she was part of her mom's team, she happily complied. We all know it isn't always sunshine and rainbows, so for those times when she didn't want to help, and the crying was too loud, Bella put on a pair of headphones.

If we see our preschoolers getting stuck in their play by acting out the same exact story script over and over, that's our cue that they're struggling to make sense of something in their world such as, using the above example, dealing with a new baby sibling who cries a lot. This is where we as parents, caregivers, and teachers can step in, offer positive reinforcement, and scaffold. Because we're involved and know what they are playing, we smile and offer ways to add to the play. Perhaps the new baby is hungry, or sleepy, or needs his big sister to read him a story? And off they'll go in a new direction to solve the problem they are struggling to comprehend.

The use of positive reinforcement can also build up a preschooler's self-confidence by encouraging her to be persistent as she tries things that may initially feel challenging or push her outside her comfort zone. When Daniel wanted to learn how to ride a bicycle, we showed him trying over two episodes as he dug deep with resilience. Dad Tiger affirmed his interest, added encouragement, and sang a musical strategy: "Grr, grr, grr out loud, keep on trying and you'll feel proud." Daniel sings the strategy to himself and then continues to use it over and over again as it gets hard to pedal and steer the bicycle. In the end, he even teaches his friends the strategy as he continues to master riding a bike.

We can use positive reinforcement to build self-confidence in the same way with our preschoolers. Consider a preschooler who's nervous about going down the big slide by herself. Through an adult's thoughtful positive reinforcement repeated over time—*I noticed you're showing a lot of courage by climbing up the ladder with me and sliding down while sitting on my lap. I can see that you're becoming less nervous about how high we are*—the child will slowly build up her self-confidence and eventually (and on her own timeline) become comfortable enough to tackle the high slide all by herself.

A quick reminder: positive reinforcement isn't the same thing as "praise" without purpose. In fact, Carol Dweck, an author and prominent researcher in the field of motivation known for her work surrounding mindset, found that repeatedly telling a preschooler they are great at doing something can actually inhibit growth and result in an eventual hit in self-confidence when a child is suddenly faced with a task or activity they aren't already "great" at. *Focus on reinforcing the effort rather than the result.*[6]

. . . .

DRILL AND SKILL: THE ANTI-MASTERY

When we talk about preschoolers' level of interactive learning, what comes to mind are flashcards and "drill and skill" worksheets. Sure, they are interactive in that preschoolers are filling them out. Sure, they are steeped in repetition, which is why they are called "*drill* and skill." So, what's the missing ingredient? The fact that kids are not learning experientially and with spark, purpose, and motivation. Drill and skill will work, in the short term, to learn a particular *skill*. What it won't do is motivate kids to *love to learn* as well as learn within different contexts, which is the key to promoting mastery of the concept.

. . . .

Angela's Clues

One of the things I love most about preschoolers is how passionate they are about everything they do. This passion is easy to recognize because it will cause them to jump into an activity they love with gusto and repeat, repeat, repeat. It also gives us as parents, caregivers, and teachers a powerful tool to help them learn. The key is harnessing their natural inclination for repetition in a thoughtful, scaffolded, purposeful way by repeating positive words, actions, and strategies they'll want to emulate. We know that when given something they can do, they will jump in, feel proud, and do it. Using that excitement and pride, we, as the involved guide, gently add another level, "plussing up" the learning. Attempting this next level, we then "plus it up" once more and continue until our preschoolers max out. Similar to a game of Jenga, you never know how high your preschoolers will get unless they try—with you as the gentle guide at their side, creating a strong and safe foundation for their learning.

. . . .

- **Be Involved** by finding opportunities to be an "involved guide."
- **Ask Questions** and offer positive reinforcement as a way to encourage mastery and growth.
- **See the Spark** and scaffold concepts with increasing levels of difficulty.

. . . .

YOUR MEDIA "YES" LIST

☑ The show promotes purposeful repetition and scaffolding.

☑ The skills in the show are taught in a way that promotes mastery.

☑ The vocabulary is defined and used repetitively across different scenarios.

. . . .

Clue Takeaways

- Repetition thickens neural pathways and allows learning to be reinforced and retained.
- Repetition is the key to full comprehension, practicing skills, building mastery, boosting confidence, and increasing a preschooler's love of learning.
- Scaffolding uses a trusted guide and hands-on activities that are repeated in layers of increased difficulty.
- Creating simple and predictable routines for everyday aspects of home life helps preschoolers know what is expected of them and results in their becoming more compliant, understanding, and helpful.

Think,
Resolve,
Respect

CLUE #4: THINK

Unlocking the Genius Within

When I create a new show, I'm always trying to put the right amount of each "ingredient" into the smoothie, and when doing so, my team and I research the script drafts in real preschool classrooms. Some say that research is one of the key ingredients to creating shows that are so loved by preschoolers. At the beginning, before I had a team, I'd personally come into the classroom, sit down on the floor with the group of preschoolers, and launch a conversation to get to know them. A conversation, incidentally, that would invariably end up focusing on *snacks*—either they'd just *had* a snack, or they were *going* to have a snack, or there was some conversation on what the snack was going to be *tomorrow*. We would talk for almost ten minutes about snacks— sliced grapes and cheese was always a favorite, with graham crackers and milk a close second. Carrots and hummus was much debated.

When I went to research our first ever episode of *Blue's Clues*, I brought in the games to test. I showed them a "picture book" that Traci Paige Johnson, co-creator, had illustrated based on the games I had written. Traci had even made cutouts of the characters and manipulatives so we could move them around and play the games like we would on TV. So, for example, our "chick" in the "chick" game could be moved around and "talk" directly to the preschoolers we were playing with, giving them instant access to join the story and play. The kids loved it. And teachers in those classrooms would often ask us to leave Traci's cutouts behind so they could use them in their lessons.

The research went well enough that we knew we'd figured out the games for our premier episode, but we still didn't have a handle on the overall theme of the story that would have preschoolers emotionally invested, interested, and engaged for twenty-two minutes. I wanted them to be learning *how* to think, not *what* to think, so the overall story and "uber" clue game was critical to our success. We were stumped.

On our way back to the office, Traci and I talked about what we wanted for a snack. Apparently, all this talk of snacks had made us hungry. And then it hit me. SNACKS! The theme of our first episode . . . the overall narrative arc . . . should be about *snacks*.

And that's why the first episode of *Blue's Clues* was based on the question, "What does Blue want for snack?" Now, you may not think this is a big question or something our preschoolers even need to learn about. And you'd be right. Because *what* Blue wants to have for a snack isn't actually what's important here. What is important is *how* we solve that problem, and we do that through what are called *higher-order thinking skills*, a type of learning that includes critical, logical, reflective, metacognitive, and creative thinking. It requires heightened brain functioning and cognitive processing. In creating a story and games where preschoolers are challenged to figure out what Blue wants for her snack, we could specifically focus on teaching those higher-order thinking skills through accessing their motivation, interests, and emotions and using the storyline to build in conflict, empowerment, and play in a powerful way.

LEARNING HOW TO THINK: HIGHER-ORDER THINKING SKILLS

So why are higher-order thinking skills so important to nurture in preschoolers? Because they're the skills used to understand information, make decisions based on that information, and create new ideas that are founded in the knowledge. Luckily, preschoolers come prepackaged with fledgling thinking skills, and as natural players and explorers, they use these skills any time they try to make sense of new experiences, take things apart, build with blocks, create crafts, solve problems, make decisions, and ask questions.

For example, in preschool when we ask students to share or repeat facts and figures they may know, we're building their skills related to the first level of thinking: *remembering and recalling information.* When we want preschoolers to apply those concepts, we are moving up the ladder of thinking skills to a higher level: *absorbing the information and fully understanding it.* Even higher still, we want our preschoolers to understand and think about new ideas and create new solutions and new ways to think about solving problems. At this highest level, we want them to *use the new information.* Scaffolding higher and higher levels of thinking is at the foundation of teaching our preschoolers how to be higher-order thinkers.

HIGHER-ORDER THINKERS ARE GENIUSES

Michael Michalko, a creativity expert and author of *Thinkertoys*, recognized that it was not "smarts" or a high IQ that separates geniuses from others—it's their ability to think out of the box.[1] Theorists studied notebooks, conversations, and ideas in the arts, science, and industry, and found that it was looking at problems in creative ways that made the difference. More specifically, it was making thoughts *visible*, creating ideas out of *interesting relationships*, and putting *different things together.* Sounds a lot like what a preschooler does naturally in play, doesn't it? When we let our preschoolers play, we're not only fostering their higher-order thinking skills as they create, ask questions, and exhibit their relentless curiosity—we're unlocking the genius within.

Higher-order thinkers see possibilities as opposed to obstacles. They develop unique ideas to solve problems, they brainstorm, they work cooperatively, they research, and they see more than one way to achieve a goal. On top of that, higher-order thinkers are more positive in general because they see multiple ways to look at the world and get out of a situation when stuck. Ultimately, higher-order thinkers are smarter, happier, and do better in life in the long run. Plainly put, *higher-order thinkers are our future.*

Higher-order thinking skills, such as critical thinking skills, are at the forefront of education because, in this age of technology and innovation, we need them now more than ever. Yet unfortunately, the way much of today's high school and college curricula are structured is resulting in many graduates entering the workforce with a deficit of skills such as grit, curiosity, attention to detail, and those very same critical thinking skills. While we don't know if the facts and information we're teaching our preschoolers will be relevant in the future, we do know that understanding *how* to gather information and apply it, will be. If parents and educators could do just one thing to set preschoolers up for success, it would be *teach them how to think.*

Though many of today's students aren't necessarily developing these higher-order thinking skills as a result of a school culture focused on testing and drill and skill, this isn't a new concept. In fact, in 1956 educational psychologist Benjamin Bloom and his colleagues published a framework for categorizing educational goals for success. Dubbed Bloom's Taxonomy, it outlines the levels of learning from lowest order to higher order. They are, in hierarchal order: Remember, Understand, Apply, Analyze, Evaluate, and Create. The chart below shows how to offer preschoolers ways to play and practice these important skills.

Preschool Higher-Order Thinking Skills	
1st Level: Remember→	Preschoolers can repeat facts from memory (memorizing a few Spanish words, counting from 1 to 10, labeling colors, shapes).
2nd Level: Understand→	Preschoolers can explain what they know in detail (after watching a show or reading a book, they can tell you what happened in the story).

Preschool Higher-Order Thinking Skills	
3rd Level: Apply→	Preschoolers start to master ideas and use them in their lives (notice shapes, numbers, letters all around them).
4th Level: (Higher-Order) Analyze or Analytical Thinking→	Preschoolers think about information in a new way (seeing a picture of a dog, noticing it's the same type of dog that they have, understanding other people have similar dogs).
5th Level: (Higher-Order) Evaluate or Critical Thinking→	Preschoolers start to be critical thinkers by looking at information and solving problems (making associations between distinct pieces of information to come to a conclusion, deductive reasoning, express opinion, defend, criticize).
6th Level: (Higher-Order) Create or Creative Thinking→	Preschoolers create something new based on what they know (creating a new story, a new way to play, using art to work through a problem).

While teaching preschoolers *how* to think isn't measurable in the way school smarts might be, it's important to recognize that what kids are tested on—remembering and recalling information—is at the lowest order of skills. But when we focus on helping our children learn *how* to think, we're giving them a head start on learning how to form a creative, analytical opinion, and therefore understand the information on a deeper level. Simply put: lecturing and "telling kids what they need to do" is *out*, and active learning is *in*.

When *Science* magazine published an article entitled "Lectures Are Not Just Boring, They're Ineffective, Too," the headline couldn't have been more spot on. The piece references a study of undergraduates that found students in traditional lecture classes were one and a half times more likely to fail than students in classes "that use more stimulating, so-called active methods." What's devastating is that in recent years, most preschools and kindergarten classrooms across America have taken a step backward due to the Common Core state standards, to a point where much of the day's school work focuses on sitting and being taught in a straightforward lecture style.[2] The best preschool classrooms have a focus on active learning by using play as the center of their approach, and we as parents can re-create the same fun, conducive-to-learning environment at home by simply asking questions of our preschoolers, giving them hands-on "interactive" activities to further learning, guiding them, and PAUSING to hear what they are thinking.

. . . .

BLUE'S CLUES 101: A CASE STUDY OF LEARNING *HOW* TO THINK

As a pre-verbal preschooler, our lovable animated character Blue represents just how smart preschoolers are even before they can talk. Because what we know is that preschoolers have *a lot* to say and they often know so much more than they can verbalize. Since our preschoolers at home are bonded with Blue, they want to nurture her, care for her, and, as is in alignment with a preschooler's nature, help her.

Now we add some simple *conflict*. It may not seem like a true conflict, or a conflict with big stakes, but when Steve, our playful *adult*, doesn't know what Blue wants, it's frustrating and upsetting. Think about it. What happens any time an adult doesn't know what a preschooler wants? Conflict. Meltdown. All hell breaks loose. So, when Steve doesn't know what Blue, our animated puppy of a preschooler, wants, we have a problem.

Add a bit of *empowerment*. Now, Steve, the adult, looks to the preschoolers at home and asks for their help. An adult asking a preschooler for help is a pretty big deal. Suddenly preschoolers stand up taller and are full of pride, taking what is being asked of them quite seriously.

And *how* do they help? In the best way they know how—through *play*. Our preschool viewers are asked to play a game—*Blue's Clues*—to figure out what Blue wants. And that is something our audience can totally do. After all, they are *experts* at play.

So, triggered by a question like "What does Blue want for snack?," motivated by a love of snacks and their innate desire to help, emotionally invested due to their love of Blue the puppy, empowered by being needed by an adult character, and armed with the power of play to solve the problem, we have set the stage for our preschool audience. We are now ready to showcase, model, and practice *critical thinking skills*, a.k.a. the process of learning *how* to think, not *what* to think, through the game of Blue's Clues. Which is really the whole point of the episode. (And you thought the question about what Blue wanted for a snack was simple!)

So how does solving the problem the Blue's Clues way teach critical thinking skills? First, Blue stamps "paw prints" on objects that will allow Steve and the home viewer to think through what she wants. But since we're looking to practice critical thinking, Blue doesn't just paw print the *answer* to the question of what she wants for a snack. Instead, over the course of an episode, she paw prints three "clues" in a very specific order, one that's been thoughtfully mapped out by our formative research team led by Dr. Alice Wilder, so the viewers can spend twenty-two minutes figuring out the answer out for themselves.

The first clue Blue marks is open-ended, allowing for the widest possible range of answers for them to consider. For example, Blue's first clue is a *cow*, and Steve asks the viewers, "What does Blue want for a snack?" while drawing a cow in his Handy Dandy Notebook. Steve models thinking, in a preschool-relatable way, about how this clue relates to the question, "Does Blue want a *cow* for snack?" He quickly rejects this idea and we move on.

Later in the episode, Blue marks her next clue—a *straw*. Steve thinks through this, modeling how these two clues could relate to each other. "A cow and a straw? What could Blue want with a cow and a straw?" Tricky.

Our third clue is the clincher: a *cup*. And now that we have all three clues, Steve is ready to sit in the Thinking Chair, a prop that helped to support the idea of critical thinking concretely and visually. Sitting in the red chair, Steve looks at the three visual clues and, with the magic of animation, we can see the drawings on display over his head as he begins putting the three clues together to answer Blue's dilemma.

So, what does Blue want for snack with a cow, a straw, and a cup? As he models solving the problem, Steve plays with the clues in different ways until they make sense. By animating the clues above his head, we visually show his thinking process, while Steve uses "thinking" dialogue. The successful thought process that finally results in the answer to Blue's Clues is: "A cow makes the sound moo, a cow makes milk, and milk could be poured in a cup with a straw! *Milk!* Blue wants *milk* with her snack of graham crackers!"

So, now you know every last detail of how we use the game of Blue's Clues to model and foster critical thinking skills, because our clue game is the epitome of what learning *how to think* looks like. The preschoolers, at home, are asked to interactively solve a problem, step by step. At a higher-order level of thinking, preschoolers need to *remember* the question, then *relate* that question to what all three clues have in common, and then *apply* it to Blue's question of the day. And of course, because they're preschoolers, when we've successfully figured out Blue's Clues, we sing!

PROMOTING ACTIVE LEARNING AT HOME

Just as is true with active listening or interactive media, active learning is a two-way street. In fact, and this probably goes without saying, preschoolers themselves are the key ingredient in the learning. What we as parents and caregivers want to do is work directly *with* our child, incorporating their ideas and interests while considering what they're capable of developmentally, to "teach" them in a way that is custom-made just for them. And then we can tweak the environment to make it as conducive to active learning as possible.

PARENTING PRODUCTION NOTES

Promote Active Learning and Foster Critical Thinking Skills at Home

Just as I described in the *Blue's Clues* example earlier in this chapter, we can foster critical thinking skills in a number of different ways, including:

- Interesting Materials or Information: Offer preschoolers tangible objects they can touch, feel, and explore, along with information and experiences that excite them (snacks!), as well as put them in situations where they can learn something new.
- Interactivity: Provide a rich atmosphere and time to reflect, think, ask questions, answer questions, and/or interact with the new object or information so they can form their own opinions about it.
- Intrinsic Motivation: Tap into their sense of intrinsic motivation and their desire to learn and find out the information for themselves through play, an emotional bond to a person or character who needs help, an intriguing problem, and/or an idea that sparks or excites a preschooler.

While there are undoubtedly so many things you're already inherently doing at home to promote your preschooler's development of higher-order thinking skills (and in many cases, you may not even realize that's what you're doing), here are a few ideas for taking your efforts to the next level:

Play!

Since we know that play is the work of the child and it's something our preschoolers are actively engaged in throughout much of their day, the opportunities to tap into this play to promote active learning are truly endless.

Type of Play	How to Do It	Activity Idea
Build!	Provide building materials (blocks, Legos, cups, props) so your preschooler can explore and experience at his own level.	Build a "set" from building materials for special friends such as dolls, stuffed animals, or Lego figures to have adventures in.
Dress Up!	Offer pretend play material and the chance to try out different identities (dress-up clothes, simple props to play restaurant, school, architect, etc.) to help spark them.	Join in with the dress-up and suggest a silly or dramatic scene for you and your child to act out. Could be a scene from a book, a favorite movie or one that you make up! Put on a performance for the rest of the family!
Create!	Set out art materials (clay, paint, glue, paper, crayons), and/or nature materials (rocks, leaves, pinecones, craft items) to spur interesting inventions, collaborations, and new ideas.	Encourage kids to explore, and collect interesting objects in nature or set out objects that are different and interesting (old socks and buttons) and encourage preschoolers to play with them together. What kind of story can they create with the socks and buttons? What kind of action figure can they make from clay?
Go on Journeys!	Take your preschooler on a ton of various outings, from the usual grocery store runs and the fascinating hands-on children's museum to a road trip or an outing to a nearby aquarium.	Designate a low-key, close to home weekly "field trip" for you and your child to have an adventure together, explore something new, or just experience a regular routine in a new way (i.e., instead of the grocery store, head to the local farmers' market).
Read!	Have different and interesting books with rich photographs accessible for your child to flip through and be read to from.	The next time you go the library to stock up on books, select at least one book that's just about exposing your child to new, interesting concepts (nature, the ocean, art, birds, space exploration, and so on).

CLUE #4: THINK

Answer Preschoolers' Questions

Answering preschoolers' questions is one of the best ways to promote higher-order learning skills. Of course, it's *how* you answer the questions that makes all the difference. For example, say your child is nervous and scared about starting a new preschool. Rather than downplaying her emotions or trying to talk up what you know is going to be great about the school, you could use it as an opportunity to support her development of critical thinking skills and higher-order learning by:

o Providing an encouraging (not dismissive) response: "I'm sorry you're feeling scared. Why do you think that is?"
o Encouraging brainstorming, open to any and all ideas (not judgmental): "Maybe it's because you've never been to preschool before? I wonder if it's because it's something new."
o Encouraging diving deeper into the questions: "What do you think preschool will be like? Do you want to draw a picture? Would you like to talk to your sister about what preschool was like for her?"
o Evaluating the deeper look of ideas and answers: "Okay, tomorrow, let's dig deeper and figure out the answer to this. Maybe we can go visit the preschool and meet your teacher? Then we can talk more about how you feel."

Ask Questions of Your Preschooler

How you *ask* questions of your preschooler is just as important as how you *answer* them, and it can also affect the level of thinking they need to do in order to give you an answer. Generally speaking, probing and asking deeper, more thoughtful questions will always promote higher-order thinking. An easy way to do this, and in situations you surely find yourself in every day, is to get curious with your preschooler when doing things such as reading a story, watching a show, baking, doing a craft, or even just looking at photographs or out the bedroom window. For instance, say you're watching the world go by on the street outside your house:

○ Ask a *labeling* question: "What do you see?" *A yellow car!*

○ Ask a *comprehension* question: "How are these two different?" *One's yellow and one's blue!*

○ Ask a *contextual* question: "Have you ever been in a yellow car?"

○ Ask a *probing* question: "How do you think a yellow car is different from the other cars?"

○ Ask an *opinion* question: "What kind of car do you like best? Why?"

○ Ask an *out-of-the-box* question: "If you could make any kind of fantastical car, what would it look like? Can you draw it?"

Before you know it, in the span of just a few minutes of loving bonding time while taking in the view from a bedroom window, you've nurtured your child's fledgling skills surrounding remembering, understanding, applying, analyzing, evaluating, and creating. How awesome is that?

Have Conversations . . . About Anything!

In addition to asking and answering questions of your preschoolers, I encourage you to simply commit to regularly starting up new conversations with your preschooler, about any topic, and be sure to leave time for Pauses as they reflect on their thoughts and feelings. Conversations about what they're learning at school, what they're interested in, and what could be upsetting them are the perfect entree for encouraging higher-order thinking.

Respectfully Debate

Of course, today's preschools don't have a debate team, but that doesn't mean we can't help our little ones learn debate skills as a way to encourage their formulation of reason and logical and critical thinking skills. So, when having a discussion (or possibly an argument) about something, ask preschoolers to start debating. For example, if they want to go apple picking, ask them to give you a few reasons why they should go (critical thinking), what they could do with all the apples (analytical thinking), or to think of a fantastical contraption they could make that would help them get the apples all the way at the top of the tree (creative thinking—one preschooler answered this last prompt with "How about a ladder-saurous . . . a really tall big dinosaur ladder!"). Or if they don't want to go to bed, ask them to give you three reasons why (critical thinking) they believe they should be able to stay up and then ask them, if they could create something fantastical to help them to stay up later, what would it be? (Ella, age four: "What if I was an Owl Me? Half owl, half me"!)

Another approach for nurturing debate and advocating your point of view is the game Apples to Apples Junior. Not only does this game focus on preschool play with expressive vocabulary, but part of the game is debating and getting the "judge" to pick your answer as the best. The debates my kids have had over this game are the best part—debating why mud pies are scrumptious? Hysterical.

Create—Using Interesting Materials

Put out some craft materials or paper and crayons and have your preschooler create. To elevate, put different materials together and/or challenge your preschooler to make different things with the same object. Here are some suggestions for marrying crafts with fostering higher-order thinking skills:

o Grab an apple and encourage your preschooler to come up with as many different things as possible to do or make with it (apple pie, apples and peanut butter, painting using apple prints, apple toss).
o Find or make cutout shapes (circles, ovals, triangles, rectangles, squares, etc.) and see how many different things your preschooler can create using just those shapes.
o Draw a favorite book, movie, or TV show character in a silly environment (Blue under the sea? Blue going grocery shopping?).
o Make something new out of recycled objects.
o Bake or cook a new recipe together!

PROMOTING A GROWTH MINDSET

When we focus on activities and conversations to support sparking our preschooler and igniting their love of learning, we are also promoting a "growth mindset." Researcher Carol Dweck's work shows that it is "process" and not "ability" that is the key to success.

But when we focus on a growth mindset, or mastery through activity, we're not only fostering how to think—we are postulating that intelligence is malleable. In other words, we're reinforcing in our kids the idea that working hard will pay off. Mindset especially comes into play as concepts and tasks become more difficult. For example, if preschoolers have always been told that they're "smart," they may internalize a belief that intelligence is fixed and, unfortunately, come to the conclusion that they are "not smart *enough*" when they butt up against work or tasks that challenge them, especially as they move on to elementary school. When a child has a "fixed mindset" or believes their intelligence is fixed, they see themselves as incapable of becoming smarter or learning new skills. Since we know from the research that hard work, resilience, practice, and grit are what make the difference in a child's long-term intellectual development, it's critical that we commend, or for lack of a better word, praise *effort* rather than ability.

And as children get older, mindset becomes an increasingly bigger factor in the way they approach what they're learning at school. As Carol Dweck wrote in *Scientific American* in 2015 about a study featuring junior high students and math, ". . . as the work became more difficult, the students with a growth mindset showed greater persistence. As a result, their math grades overtook those of the other students by the end of the first semester—and the gap between the two groups continued to widen during the two years we followed them. The focus on learning strategies, effort, and persistence paid off." When a child is able to embrace and truly own a growth mindset before they begin elementary school, they will enjoy many long-term benefits as they go through their academic (and life) path.[3]

Teaching our preschoolers how to think versus what to think carries with them long after their preschool years and all the way through to adulthood. As with all of our clues, these ideas form a philosophy of learning that has its foundation in preschool, but lasts a lifetime.

Angela's Clues

In this age of innovation and technological invention, it's important that we encourage our preschoolers' capacity to think analytically, creatively, and critically as they thoughtfully move through their world. Teaching children how to think is an integral part of my core mission, both as a media creator *and* as a mom.

We all want our children to be kind, healthy, and smart, but the goal of academic achievement is often measured by metrics like standardized test scores and grades. If we start to evaluate achievement based on higher-order thinking skills, we would put more emphasis on building knowledge through experiences, boosting comprehension, applying information to the real world, analyzing that information, evaluating and critically thinking about the information, and then using our knowledge and information to create. What's really important is that our children develop the ability to know how to approach and solve their own problems, big and small.

I strive for my kids to learn how make their own good choices, not just memorize facts or be robotic in their answers. To me, the smartest kids are the ones who can survey a situation, have a point of view, express that point of view, and attempt to take steps to improve the situation. And, we hope, one day to change the world. My research assistant for this book, Maddie, remembers having to memorize to prepare for her "map quizzes" in elementary school. Her parents knew that memorizing the information did not translate to retaining or mastering the information, so they took that content and upped the ante. Together they chose a country from that section of the world, and Maddie would research the culture, traditional dress, history, and they would even cook dinner a dinner based on that country during the week! Maddie says that it not only made the content more interesting and comprehensible, but that it sparked and inspired her life path as she went on to concentrate in international studies in college, study abroad, and is now living in the Netherlands. What an amazing way to take studying maps to the next level—holy higher-order thinking skills!

. . . .

- **Be Involved** to answer and explore all your preschooler's questions in a meaningful, thoughtful way.
- **Ask Questions** and encourage your preschooler to support their points of view with reasons and logic.
- **See the Spark** by exposing them to new information and cognitive stimuli.

. . . .

YOUR MEDIA "YES" LIST

☑ The storytelling in the show offers examples of thought-provoking ideas.

☑ The lessons from the show can be applied in real-life situations.

☑ My child uses examples from the show as a launching point to think more deeply about things.

. . . .

Clue Takeaways

○ Higher-order thinking skills are used to understand information, make decisions based on that information, and create new ideas that are founded in the knowledge.

○ Preschool play fosters higher-order thinking skills as kids create, ask questions, and exhibit their relentless curiosity. (And it also unlocks the genius within.)

○ Praising efforts and process rather than results will promote a child's development of a growth mindset.

CLUE #5: RESOLVE

Conflict Develops Grit, Coping Skills, and Strategies

Holed up in a conference room at Nickelodeon for six weeks, Traci and I were having a blast realizing our dream of creating a show for preschoolers—we were batting ideas around together while she was sketching different poses of an adorable kitten and I scripted a handful of preschool-appropriate games. We had named Traci's adorable kitten Blue, and we were convinced she would be a preschooler's best friend and the star of our show. That's right . . . Blue was a blue kitten first! We put together a presentation of the materials we'd been developing and headed off to a meeting with Nickelodeon's preschool department, Nick Jr., where we showed them the beginning of the script and our kitten main character. But no sooner had we launched into our pitch then we were told that another show in development at the network already had a cat character in it. So, um, we needed to change the cat.

What? Change? We Cannot Change Our Kitten Main Character! Well, it was either that or drop the show.

Conflict.

That's it. Traci and I were done. We had no show. Our career in children's television was over before it had even really begun. Heads down, we took a Pause. After a brief quiet, the two of us began talking about other things. I remember one of us trying to diffuse the tension by making a joke, which resulted in a bit of laughter. And, I won't lie . . . we may have shed a few tears. How were we going to resolve our conflict?

Then Traci flipped open her notebook, grabbed a pen off the table, and began to draw. When she set down the pen a minute later, we all looked over to see what she had doodled. It was something she'd drawn since she was a kid. A puppy. Our blue puppy. In the midst of this conflict, we had taken a Pause, and creatively resolved it. Blue was born. We were back. We had a show. And an adorable blue puppy to boot.

The truth is, conflict is part of life for everyone. No one gets a free pass. Not you, not me, and not our preschoolers. And because conflict is interwoven into the human experience, it's also at the heart of any interesting and motivating story. *Harry Potter*? Conflict. *Star Wars*? Conflict. Any epic adventure or heartfelt drama or hilarious comedy that grabs us and immediately brings us in? Conflict.

The same goes for media created for preschoolers. But instead of being filled with charged battles over control of the galaxy or young wizards fighting against evil, in preschool terms, conflict looks like this:

Oh no! Why is the big bad wolf so big and scary?
Whoa! Green Puppy just knocked down Blue's blocks!
So sad! We can't have our scooter parade in the rain!
Ahh! The giant is having a huge meltdown!
Help! Jackson's puppy is missing!
Prince Wednesday has my car. It's mine!

This is the preschool version of drama. Conflict. Big problems. Huge emotions. Watch any preschool TV show, and you'll notice there's at least one preschool-appropriate dramatic element in every episode. That's because drama and conflict don't just make good stories—they are the stuff that life is made of. As parents, we often swoop in to save the day the second we notice our child feeling uncomfortable or struggling with a difficult social or emotional problem. Yet the research shows that learning how to deal with challenges and conflicts as a child, as well as have active strategies and clues to deal with them, isn't just an important part of the human experience—it's critical to developing into happy, thriving adults.

In every one of our series, we have an overall approach to solving our conflict at the core of our curriculum. In the end, since we're teaching kids *how* to think and not *what* to think, the journey itself is of the utmost importance. One of the many ways we repeat our approach to learning how to solve problems is by modeling what preschoolers can do in their everyday lives. We want them to see what our characters are doing, aspire to be like them, and model their approaches to different situations. We believe that all children are different and learn differently, and therefore we have different series, different characters, different stories, and different approaches to problem solving in hopes that one of them speaks to each child. For instance:

- "When you have a problem, you look in a book!" Solving conflicts by using research in books.
- "Let's play Blue's Clues to figure it out." Solving conflicts through play.
- "Take a deep breath and count to four." Solving conflicts through emotional regulation.
- "Think, think, think!" Promoting the idea of pausing to gather thoughts before solving conflicts.
- "Think about how someone else is feeling." Using empathy to solve conflicts.
- "We can solve this, with art!" Using art to solve conflicts.

Our approach to solving problems and conflict varies, but they all have key ingredients in common that engage and actively include the home viewer so they can model and learn, especially when experiencing the strategies in different ways.

THE IMPORTANCE OF EMOTIONAL INTELLIGENCE IN SOLVING CONFLICTS

Understanding and labeling emotions is our preschoolers' first step toward boosting their emotional intelligence which, according to

Psychology Today, is the "ability to identify and manage your own emotions and the emotions of others." It's also most definitely something we want to foster in our children, considering that research has shown that "young people with high Emotional Intelligence earn higher grades, stay in school, and make healthier choices."[1]

Fred Rogers, a huge advocate for teaching preschoolers how to express feelings and label feelings, once said, "What is mentionable is manageable." Fred believed, and so do I, that we need to teach our preschoolers that *all* feelings are okay, and when we talk about them, we can find solutions to conflicts. Fred reinforced this thoughtful message in every episode of *Mister Rogers' Neighborhood*, and it made quite an impact on his young viewers. In fact, researchers who studied the television show found that preschoolers who regularly watched *Mister Rogers' Neighborhood* had an increased use of positive reinforcement and an increased understanding of their feelings, and as a result, were calmer and happier.

Continuing Fred's legacy, we tackle emotional intelligence on *Daniel Tiger's Neighborhood*, and knowing that media can influence these effective outcomes for our preschool viewers, we were curious to know if our show would have long-lasting effects. Were the strategies we were teaching "sticky" enough to change behavior? Eric Ramussen and his colleagues at the University of Texas found that children who watched *Daniel Tiger's Neighborhood* over a two-week period exhibited higher levels of empathy, self-efficacy (confidence in oneself in social situations), and the ability to recognize emotions than those who watched a nature show. And when parents were actively involved and asked questions about the content, the results were even greater.[2]

PARENTING PRODUCTION NOTES
Help Your Child Connect with His or Her Emotional Experiences
Experiencing big emotions happens on two levels—in our brains and in our bodies. Helping kids learn how to recognize not only the role their

thoughts play in the way they feel but also how their bodies respond physically to strong emotions is a powerful part of their developing emotional literacy. Understanding the physical manifestation of emotions, such as how different emotions literally feel (hot head, energy surge, "engine running hot," etc.) can be especially beneficial for kids who struggle with emotional regulation.

Here are some suggestions for activities to help your preschooler label and identify their feelings, as well as begin to have body awareness and control to manage emotions.

- **Game: Name That Feeling!** Play a charade game where your preschooler names the feeling you're acting out. For a media twist, consider the illustrations in the books you're co-reading or Pause the TV while watching a program together and analyze the expressions on the characters' faces. Encourage them to use a variety of emotional words.

- **Game: Freeze Dance.** In this oldie but goodie, when you start the music, your preschooler dances, and when you stop it, he freezes. The freeze dance game helps with body awareness and learning how to control one's body, one of the first steps in understanding feelings and actions.

- **Craft: Draw your body.** Get a large sheet of butcher paper and trace your preschooler's body, and then encourage her to color in the outline to create a life-sized picture of herself to promote body awareness.

- **Craft: Create an "All About Me" Book.** Ask your child to make their "expression faces"—mad, happy, sad, confused, frustrated, excited, worried, etc.—and snap photos of each one. Then print out the pictures, ask your child to label them, and compile them to create a personalized "All About Me" book. To extend the learning, you can also have him draw a picture of a situation that results in each emotion and place it on the opposite page.

- **Create a Language: Find the Feeling:** When your child is responding with a big emotion (positive or negative), ask her to point to where she feels that emotion most in her body. Together you'll begin developing a language for understanding and working through emotional reactions and conflicts in the future. I.e., "I'm wondering if you're feeling like your engine's running too hot?"
- **Develop a Coping Routine: Red zone/green zone.** Work with your preschooler to create a simple routine he or she can do when feeling big, uncomfortable feelings that are threatening to bubble over. Be conflict-resolution detectives and try out different coping strategies—deep breaths, counting to ten, clenching fists and releasing, and so on—to see which ones help your preschooler's body go from the "red zone" back to the "green zone."
- **Media: Use media as a teaching tool.** Look for shows like *Daniel Tiger's Neighborhood*, apps, and books that deal with emotions. Use the media to further reinforce the emotional learning.

CASE STUDY: *DANIEL TIGER'S NEIGHBORHOOD* SMUSHED CAKE CONFLICT

The main storyline of the very first episode of *Daniel Tiger's Neighborhood* is that it's Daniel's birthday (birthdays are intrinsically motivating for preschoolers). Daniel was beyond excited and couldn't wait for his birthday party, especially for his *birthday cake* (more motivation). He goes with Mom to the bakery to pick up his cake, and while there, the home viewer helps Daniel decorate it so it's extra special—a tiger cake with frosting stripes that looks just like him (upping the ante of investment in the cake). Empowered to help, Daniel tells Mom he wants to carry the cake home all by himself. After an especially bouncy Trolley ride (you can see where this is going), they arrive at his house, where he runs in the front door jostling the cake even more. Once inside, Daniel wants to show Dad Tiger his cake. Excitedly, he opens up the cake box only to discover that his beloved cake is . . . *smushed.* Smushed! *Big problem.*

So how do we handle this problem? Well, we start by showing Daniel do what most preschoolers would do. His eyes well up with tears and he throws himself into Dad Tiger's lap for comfort. This creates even *more drama*—the home viewers love Daniel so much they become even more emotionally invested to help him with his problem.

Then Dad Tiger empathizes with Daniel about the problem and acknowledges Daniel's feelings. Daniel softens with the affirmation and visibly relaxes even more into Dad's lap. Dad Tiger then takes Daniel through our musical strategy of the episode by singing, "When something seems bad, turn it around and find something good." (This is actually the second time viewers have heard this strategy in the eleven-minute episode. The first time was when Mom sang it to him in the bakery after he messed up while decorating his cake.) After his dad reminds him of the strategy, Daniel sings it back to him, reinforcing the idea that he is comprehending it. Then, taking the thinking one step further, Dad Tiger talks through the problem-solving strategy with him.

> **Dad Tiger:** "Tell me something that you like about birthday cakes?"
> **Daniel Tiger:** "That they're not smushed?"
> **Dad Tiger:** "What's something else that you like about *all* birthday cakes?"
> **Daniel Tiger:** "That they taste yummy?"

Then it dawns on Daniel . . . a solution to his conflict.

> **Daniel:** "Maybe the cake still tastes good even though it's smushed?"

Dad reinforces that Daniel has come to a good conclusion by taking out a spoon (yep . . . he happens to have one handy) and offering Daniel a taste. And what do you know? It *does* taste good! Hurray!

Now, as with everything we try to teach in our shows, the end goal is mastery. We want preschoolers to be able to "own" this conflict-resolution strategy and apply it in their real lives for themselves. So, before we even finalized this episode for air, we conducted formative research with real preschoolers. The director of research for *Daniel Tiger's Neighborhood*, Rachel Kalban, MA, read the story aloud to the preschoolers, assessed and observed their questions and interactions, and asked a series of comprehension questions after she was finished reading. One of her questions was the *mastery* question for the purposes of this episode. She asked the children: "What would *you* do if *you* were disappointed?" One by one each of the preschoolers replied, "Taste it!" "Yup, taste it." "It tastes yummy!"

Whoops. Now, this was a *conflict* for *us*!

What we *wanted* the preschoolers to do was revert to our musical strategy for dealing with disappointment and say, "Turn it around and find something good!" We would have even been happy with just "find something good." Unfortunately, no matter how yummy a cake is, "Taste it" is not a strategy for disappointment. We went back to our research on repetition, scaffolding, and mastery, talked the situation over with Rachel, and devised a plan. I wrote a revised version of the script incorporating some new ideas based on our findings, including making sure it was chock full of purposeful repetition for mastery, added in a one-minute strategy song as well as a second eleven-minute story reinforcing the same strategy. By the end of a twenty-two-minute episode, preschoolers had the opportunity to model and interact with four specific examples of the strategy in two distinct stories and hear two different strategy songs that each had from three to four additional uses of the strategy. That's ten to twelve times, generalizing across multiple storylines and scenarios. This time, when we tested the script, *all* of the kids sang the strategy back to us. And, most important, when Rachel asked the big question—"What would *you* do if *you* were disappointed?"—they all blurted out, "Turn it around and find something good!" Conflict resolved. And we had a show.

SIBLING CONFLICTS

Anytime my friend Claire's kids have a sibling conflict, she asks them to sit down and not get up until they can verbalize how the *other* one is feeling. For example, once Claire asked her four-year-old son Sam how his sister was feeling. He answered that Lilly was sad because she wanted to play with Sam's bubbles. Claire asked Lilly if that was correct, and she nodded yes. Then Claire turned to Lilly and asked her what Sam was feeling. Not even two years old, Lilly tried her hardest and said, "Blah blah blah SAM blah blah blah SAM!" Claire turned to Sam and said, "Is that right?" to which Sam replied, "Yes."

Sibling conflicts can be especially heart-wrenching because, let's face it—we've all dreamed of our kids being each other's best friends. But when guiding our children through such conflicts, our job is to promote empathy from the very beginning so they can learn how to understand and respect each other's differences and points of view. If we do this right, our kids, just like Claire's, just might be considering each other's feelings even before they can talk. Proactively promoting empathy not only helps children learn how to solve conflicts in the future but it also allows for current conflicts to become teachable moments. Through this practice, ideally, our kids will learn how to argue respectfully and successfully, both in and outside the family.

SOLVING CONFLICTS AT HOME

Whatever the root of the drama in your preschooler's world, the ultimate goal with any conflict is to get them *invested in their own outcomes* in the same way they are invested in their own drama.

While a dramatic story written for preschoolers and a drama of their own making may be completely different in content and context, they have one important similarity—*investment*. In both situations, we are working toward developing a preschooler's ability to understand that what they do impacts everyone around them. And in order for them to fully be open to that learning, they need to be invested and feel that what they do and how they do it will affect the outcome. Of course, preschoolers are already invested in their own drama. They want that cookie. They need that iPad. They have to have what they want and they have to have it *now*. Our goal is to get that same level of passion, spirit, and drive into *solving* the drama, too.

What we learn from watching our kids watch media is that when they are emotionally invested in the story, they *have* to know how it will end. Have you ever tried to turn off the TV on your preschooler before a show was over? I have. And I witnessed a major meltdown! That's because they are invested. They care. They are so motivated that they will jump to their feet and do what they can to figure out a solution. We want to harness that unabashed preschool drive and investment and steer it in the direction of solving their *own* problems with similar zest.

Breaking it down, here are the steps we use in our TV storytelling that we can also use with our preschoolers in real life to help them *be invested* in solving their problems.

Step 1: Pause

The benefits of taking a moment to Pause when solving conflicts can't be overstated. Think about it: many of the best mindfulness strategies begin with taking a *deep breath* and pausing to *collect your thoughts*. In the quiet of the Pause, many of the best ideas come to be. When we Pause in real life, sometimes we're *giving our preschoolers time* to have their meltdown (yes, even in the middle of the grocery store) and time to for us to breathe and think. Though it's not always easy to remember when we're facing a DEFCON 1–level crisis, it's important that our preschoolers realize that they need to first calm down before anyone can successfully resolve any conflict. The Pause allows us to take a moment to *figure out our best coping strategies*. As parents, we can identify some coping strategies and offer them to our preschoolers. The best coping strategies need to start with a moment to calm down. After that, we can affirm our preschooler's emotions and reassure them that a solution can be found.

Step 2: Empower

After we take the time to Pause, we want to empower our preschoolers. We empower them by being *positive and affirming, empathetic,* and *understanding.* We don't belittle or shame. Just because they are preschoolers doesn't mean their problems are small (to them). The way in which they deal with their preschool problems will directly correlate to how effectively they deal with bigger problems when they become middle schoolers, then teenagers, and then successful adults. Empower by:

o Affirming: nodding to show you understand.
o Giving a hug to show them you're on their side.
o Staying calm to show this problem can be solved.
o Leaning in to show we're actively listening.

Step 3: Interact

We interact with our preschoolers to help them come up with their own best tools for coping and resolving conflicts. To do that, we *ask questions* that guide them to solving conflicts in their own way. We are there to help brainstorm ideas, nudge them toward new ways to think about something, and offer thoughtful *questions* to help them come to grips with their overwhelming feelings, such as:

o "How did this make you feel?" (*Feeling* question)
o "That sounds terrible. Sounds like you really want that." (*Affirming* question)
o "What do you think we should do? What are other ideas you have?" (*Brainstorming* question)
o "What would make you feel better? How can we solve this problem?" (*Solution-oriented* question)

PAUSE, EMPOWER, INTERACT: A CASE STUDY

Here's an example of what the above approach looks like in action in a scenario you've likely experienced from time to time:

The situation: Your child is having a crisis, and as a result, is feeling BIG emotions such as anger or frustration, or perhaps is in full-fledged meltdown mode. You . . .

Pause	Give them some time to feel their emotion—anger, frustration, etc. Use this time for them to learn how to calm themselves down. Offer strategies for this.	Play with clay, dance the mad out, jump, run, breathe, take a break.
Empower	Provide affirmation, understanding, and respect for their feelings.	"It seems like this is hard for you." "You sound upset." "I see that you really wanted that."
Interact	Ask feelings questions, brainstorm solutions, offer coping strategies, actively listen, and respectfully communicate.	"How are you feeling?" "What could make you feel better?" "What are some things we could do?" "We can't do that, but we can . . ."

And . . . *repeat*.

If your preschooler gets upset again, you can begin all over, but give her more space and time to Pause before you interact. Overall, think of this as a solid investment with payoffs for everybody involved. Because every time we reinforce these strategies with our preschoolers, it will require less and less time as they begin to master the concepts and start having control over *themselves*, their *world*, and find their own *solutions*. With that said, I understand that each preschooler is unique, and so the way each strategy works may look different depending on the child's wiring and social-emotional maturity. For example, preschoolers who struggle with emotional regulation, have difficulty reading social cues, and/or aren't naturally empathetic may need extra support in developing these conflict-resolution skills.

INTRINSIC MOTIVATION AND CONFLICT RESOLUTION

Just as we want our preschoolers to *want* to learn, we also want our preschoolers to *want* to solve their conflicts—on their own. Luckily, intrinsic motivation is found in steady supply in the language of the preschooler: *play*. Therefore, the more a preschooler *wants* to do an activity, including resolving his own conflicts, the more sparked he will naturally be.

When we approach conflict in a positive way—as a learning tool for our preschoolers— we can then detach ourselves from needing to fix it or being overly worried or even annoyed by it. (Who knows . . . you might even embrace it!) The more we give our preschoolers time to come to terms with their own emotions and the space and help to solve their own conflicts, the more they will do it. For example, when we believe our preschoolers will do well and offer clues to empower, challenge, and build their self-worth, we'll see the positive results— fewer tantrums and more problem solving. We need to find ways for our kids to achieve, give third, fourth, and fifth chances, and catch them doing things "right," not wrong, to keep that mojo going as their self-worth grows right along with their ability to deal with problems.

A teacher friend of mind recalled the year she had a preschool-aged student who found a new way to be challenging in the classroom: trying to control and manipulate the kids around him. Billy was a strong and dynamic personality—smart, big ideas, creative and, yes, a "handful." He'd also entered the class with a new swagger—a new baby sister. With less control over his home life, he began taking a strong leadership role in the classroom, which quickly transformed into a dictatorship. He bossed kids around in the dramatic play area, insisting only he could decide who could be who, and tormented kids in the block area, excluding anyone he didn't want to play, with an evil cackle. It got to the point where kids would ask him if they were "allowed" to make a picture at the art table. While my friend could have easily reprimanded Billy or continuously let the kids know Billy wasn't in charge, instead she took an empathetic, positive approach with the cooperation of his parents. In a class meeting, and while Billy had a comfortable and secure seat by the teacher, students were encouraged to talk about their experiences with Billy and how they felt when he excluded or bossed them around. Then they talked about how *Billy* might feel so kids could see him as a person with feelings. Lastly, they turned it around and talked about what the kids liked about Billy and why he's fun to play with. By the end of the meeting, the class agreed they were going to help Billy be a better friend and classmate. As a result, Billy softened and turned from a bully back into a sweet preschooler. It took a few weeks, but eventually the classroom went back to normal. Billy was still an engaged, passionate, and challenging kid . . . but he wasn't the boss anymore.

PARENTING PRODUCTION NOTES
Play Games to Help Our Children Practice Conflict-Resolution Strategies
Here are some ideas for practicing conflict-resolution skills in distinct and meaningful ways through play, media, and hands-on experiences:

- Storytelling: Have your preschooler tell you a story and draw the pictures. Ask questions about the story, probing for the conflict, and brainstorm lots of different ideas of how to solve the problem. Then have your preschooler illustrate the solutions.
- Play: Act out a story with your preschooler through dramatic play and role-playing with dolls, stuffed animals, or action figures. Focus on stories with lots of conflict and high emotion, and be sure to exaggerate facial expressions. To take it a step further, you can film your play and play it back together.

- Bond: Play the game "What you would you do if . . ." and bring up preschool-relatable problems that will help them to think about and brainstorm different solutions. For instance: "What would you do if . . . you forgot your lunch?" (conflict resolution); "What would you do if your puppy was lost?" (worry, problem-solving strategies); "What would you do if you couldn't go out and play?" (disappointment); "How would you help Mommy if she was sad?" (empathy).

NURTURING HEALTHY CONFLICT RESPONSES IN OUR PRESCHOOLERS

As parents, we can look for these clues to see how our preschoolers are dealing with conflict. Notice if they are in the "unhealthy" column and use activities to move them into the "Healthy Responses to Conflict" column.

Unhealthy Responses to Conflict	Suggested Activities	Healthy Responses to Conflict
Unable to identify their emotions	Play "Feelings Charade" and practice naming the feeling.	Can name emotions and understand them
Angry, hurtful, and resentful reactions	Take a Pause and help redirect the reaction to reflect what is truly going on.	Calm, nondefensive, respectful reactions
Withdrawal of love, shaming, isolation, and fear of abandonment	Give a hug; redirect shame away from the preschooler; affirm their feelings and give them some one-on-one time.	A readiness to forgive; many chances to do right

Unhealthy Responses to Conflict	Suggested Activities	Healthy Responses to Conflict
An inability to compromise	Play board games to practice compromise through taking turns, following the rules, winning, losing, and debating.	The ability to seek compromise
The fear and avoidance of conflict	Try to ease fears and gently guide toward a resolution when a child makes a mistake or is afraid of "getting in trouble."	A positive view of conflict and a means to resolve

Conflict is an unavoidable fact of life, and most of us experience it on a daily basis. But when conflict turns into stress every day as we are trying to get everyone out the door in the morning and continues to getting everyone fed, in the bath, and off to bed at night, we need to alter our coping strategies. Understanding and noticing our own stresses as well as those that trigger our preschoolers will help us to change course and tackle these problems head on. Plus, our preschoolers also see and sometimes experience conflict as stress in their everyday lives at school, with peers, and even with trips to the doctor's office. Other preschoolers may experience high stress surrounding transitions and changes to routine, especially children who are differently wired.

It's important that we use our same conflict-resolution clues to help turn stressful situations into learning experiences by giving ourselves and our preschoolers a way to cope. Just as learning how to think is more important than getting the right answer, how we cope and handle these situations is more important than coming up with the perfect solution. In that way, *helping our preschoolers master conflict-resolution strategies* may help rewire their brains to jump into problem-solving mode and utilize a coping routine rather than freak out when under stress. Imagine the benefits of learning these skills as preschoolers when it comes to alleviating long-term stress, and ultimately reducing the chances of developing chronic illness as they age.

. . . .

. . . .

THE POWER OF ONE PERSON

The truth is, most everyone feels vulnerable when faced with resolving a challenging conflict, and this is especially true for our young preschoolers. Being your child's advocate, ready to offer positive coping solutions, will make all the difference in the world when it comes to how they experience conflict. Research has shown us that we need only one person—a teacher, even the crossing guard or the local store clerk—who repeatedly smiles, looks us in the eye, and lets us know that they believe in us. That human connection can make all the difference in the world, especially to a preschooler. For me, that person was my Italian grandmother whom I was named after. Angela Ferrante was a tough Italian woman who'd been through a lot in her life, and therefore she felt no remorse in telling it like it is—the good, the bad and the ugly. So, when she went out of her way to repeatedly tell me how smart it was of me to "look in a book for whatever I wanted to know" and say that I'd "go far in life" and that she "believed in me," it impacted me deeply. I would *feel* her message and hold my head a little bit higher. To this day, one of my favorite necklaces to wear is hers—with a large gold "A" for both of our names.

. . . .

THE I MESSAGE

One of my favorite ways to approach conflict, especially when we as parents or caregivers are the ones feeling the conflict and all the emotions that go along with it, is to express ourselves in bite-sized, preschool-appropriate words. Parenting guru Julie Ross was the one who first taught me about the "I Message." The I Message incorporates *what the issue is* (so it's explicitly clear what exactly is going on), *how it makes you feel* (for motivation), a simple *why* (for clarity and learning purposes), and the *want* (for a clear idea of what to do about it). Not only does this tool give us a simple approach for navigating difficult moments with our preschoolers, but it is an ideal strategy to model for our little ones.[3]

For example, let's say you walk into the living room and there are toys strewn all over the floor. You've already asked your child to put them away several times, so naturally, now you are upset. You're upset that (a) your daughter hasn't listened to you, and (b) that the living room is still such a mess. What do you do?

State the I MESSAGE. You say:

"When you . . . *don't pick up your toys,*

"I feel . . . *upset,*

"because . . . *I've asked you to do it a few times.*

"I would like you to . . . *pick up your toys.*"

Why the I Message Works

I know—the above script sounds so simple and rational, right? Well, that's exactly why it works. I won't beat around the bush: it's kind of magical, because the dialogue is clear, concise, repetitive, emotional, motivating, and action-oriented, all at the same time. When used correctly, preschoolers will clearly understand:

"When you" = What the problem is (your preschooler didn't pick up her toys)

"I feel" = How the behavior affected someone she loves (Dad is upset)

"Because" = Why the other person feels this way (Dad has asked a few times)

"I would like you to" = What action we want her to take (pick up the toys)

CLUE #5: RESOLVE

How many times have you gotten upset with your preschooler but neglected to concretely state what you wanted to happen? Or how many times have you been upset without explicitly saying why you feel that way? Remember: preschoolers are literal and concrete. They need to know a very specific thing that they can do to fix the problem, and they need to be told. If you incorporate this I Message into your parenting notebook and use it in a calm, natural way every time you have a conflict with your preschooler, she will learn to know what to expect and will flourish in the repetition.

PARENTING PRODUCTION NOTES
Using the "I Message"

Using the I Message can take some practice. Use this chart to fill out typical scenarios where you can incorporate the message in a calm, clear manner. Once you've mastered it yourself, teach it to your preschooler and encourage him to start using it to resolve his conflicts, too. I've filled in a few examples for you:

When you . . .	I feel . . .	Because . . .	I would like you to . . .
When you don't use your words	I feel confused	because I don't know what you need.	I would like you to use your words.
When you throw your food on the floor	I feel frustrated	because the food makes a mess and stains the floor.	I would like you to keep your food on your plate or in your mouth.
When you kick me	I feel upset and threatened	because it hurts.	I would you like you to stop kicking me.
When you scream	I feel annoyed	because it startles me and is hard to understand.	I would like you to stop screaming and speak calmly.

When you . . .	I feel . . .	Because . . .	I would like you to . . .
When you won't eat dinner	I feel worried	because I want you to grow.	I would like you to try to eat your food.
When you don't get dressed in the morning	I feel nervous	because I don't want us to be late for school.	I need you to get dressed.
When you run so fast down the street	I feel anxious	because I'm worried you will get hurt.	I would like you to walk and hold my hand.

Angela's Clues

Conflict helps us to learn and grow. How we deal with it and how we resolve it in our everyday lives will make a huge difference in our preschoolers' development of empathy, respect, and positivity. Our preschoolers follow our lead with regard to how we model responding to conflict and how we help them to deal with tough situations. Using clues such as pausing, empowering, and interacting, as well as coping strategies and the I Message, can help us resolve conflict in a positive way. Taking examples from our preschooler's favorite shows, we can help our kids to work through some of their tricky situations, such as having your preschooler remember when this happened to Daniel Tiger or Arthur. Thinking of conflicts as a learning tool changed the way I look at my own daughters' highly charged emotional outbursts. It is always important to me that they have the time and space to think about their problems and actively engage in a solution. And of course, sometimes our kids just wanted to cry and be hugged (don't we all?). Truth be told, these strategies have continued to come into play now that my children are teenagers as they persevere in conflict, try new things, and many times fail, but continue to reach for what they want.

- **Be Involved** by affirming and embracing conflicts.
- **Ask Questions** to help your preschooler foster their social and emotional skills.
- **See the Spark** and build on your child's approach for resolving conflict.

YOUR MEDIA "YES" LIST

☑ The characters model healthy responses to conflicts.

☑ The conflicts aren't too stressful or scary.

☑ The shows spend more time portraying the resolution than the conflict itself.

☑ The conflicts shown are surrounding preschool-relatable situations.

Clue Takeaways

○ Conflict is part of everyday life, even for preschoolers.

○ Conflict offers opportunities to foster resolution strategies that will benefit preschoolers throughout their lives.

○ Developing learning strategies is more important than coming up with the "perfect" resolution.

○ The I Message is a simple, clear tool for dealing with conflict in your family in a way that supports growth.

CLUE #6: RESPECT

Respectfully Communicating
Builds a Preschooler's Self-Worth

When I first sat down to write the pilot for what would eventually become *Blue's Clues*, we called it *Blueprints*, because we wanted to create a show based on the "blueprints" of child development. Research geek that I am, I'd spent years absorbing everything I could get my hands on about how children learn, what contributes to their healthy growth and development, and what was the biggest influencer in developing their self-worth. My goal was to blend my master's degree, my years of working with kids, and my passion for media to formulate the recipe for the show.

A key ingredient at the heart of that very first episode and all that followed was a model for *respectful communication*. Everything I'd learned and experienced confirmed that the quality of *what* we said—from the words we use to the concepts we convey—combined with *how* we said it, was hugely influential when it came to contributing positively to preschoolers' brain development and honoring their unabashed curiosity and desire to learn.

This consideration was at the forefront of my thinking as I wrote the very first episode of *Blue's Clues,* as it was critical that respectful communication be modeled through the show's host. As we were casting for the role of the "host"—a part that was originated by Steve Burns and then went on to be played by Donovan Patton—we looked for someone who could strike that perfect balance of being a young adult with the vibe of an awesome camp counselor coupled with a childlike energy and sense of wonder. Steve talked to the home audience as if he knew that they were cool people who constantly amazed him with their knowledge and unique perspective on the world. And preschoolers responded because they felt heard, respected, and understood.

Respectfully communicating with the audience is a tenet of any well-made preschool show. Making conscious choices about the language we use, the concepts we convey, and the way we speak with preschoolers empowers, instills confidence, and builds self-worth by:

o making them feel smart;
o encouraging them to explore, discover, and make meaning out of their world;
o reinforcing the notion that they have a right to be heard;
o expanding their vocabulary and language reasoning skills;
o boosting their school readiness;
o encouraging their healthy social-emotional growth; and
o letting them know we believe in their ability to comprehend, which further sparks their curiosity.

Does talking with respect truly do each of these things? The answer is a resounding *yes*. So how can we put these important tenets into practice in our day-to-day life?

USE RICH LANGUAGE: THERE'S NO NEED TO DUMB IT DOWN

Binky. Woobie. Ba ba. Milky. I don't know a parent of a preschooler who doesn't use cute or silly nicknames at least some of the time. It's part of the unique language between a parent and their child, which has powerful benefits when it comes to babies and their development in addition to fostering closeness and close familial bonding. The problem is when parents and caregivers subscribe to the myth that talking to preschoolers always requires using super simplified language for them to understand. It's a problem because it's simply not true. In fact, using challenging words defined in a preschool context respects a child's burgeoning brain, helps develop their vocabulary, and gives them a richer way to express their emotions and experiences, and that fosters their social-emotional growth.

When my daughter Hope was two and a half, she would put her hands on her hips and assert, "I would like to jump up and down right now. It's my prerogative!" Anyone who's parented a child through the terrible twos is familiar with her "my way or the highway" mindset, and I had recognized really fast that the word *prerogative* was, frankly, the most appropriate one to describe her will and ability to make certain choices. So, my husband, Greg, and I introduced and defined the word for her in an organic, preschool context: "Jumping outside where it's safe is your prerogative. You can jump if you want to jump." The word was "sticky" to her because it so clearly matched her desires. Hope wanted to do what she wanted to do, and for a two-and-a-half-year-old, jumping up and down was where it was at, and as she learned, it was her prerogative.

The key is to use the same words with your preschooler that you'd use with an adult and define them in context when necessary. You can define the word at the same time as you use it ("It's your prerogative, you can jump if you want to jump!") or, like my friend Audra, who, when realizing a word may not be on her son's radar, Pauses and asks him, "Do you know what I mean when I say _____?" If he doesn't, she shares a preschool-appropriate definition and—voilà— she's added a new word to her son's vocabulary. And since, like all preschoolers, her son is a porous sponge, he invariably finds ways to weave his new word into his everyday vernacular, because doing so makes him feel smart. There are also real, tangible benefits to weaving complicated words into the way we communicate with our child when it comes to their future success in school, as studies show that learning vocabulary in a "high-quality way" and in context (versus using things like flashcards) is a key factor in successfully expanding a child's vocabulary.

According to a 2014 article in *The New York Times* entitled "Quality of Words, Not Quantity, Is Crucial to Language Skills, Study Finds,"

"The quality of the communication between children and their parents and caregivers, the researchers say, is of much greater importance than the number of words a child hears."[1] The bottom line? When we talk, our children are listening. And the more high-quality words we can use in context, the better.

When it comes to introducing complex language, the biggest payoff comes from using a variety of expressive words. We all know preschoolers feel *big* emotions, yet they often have a limited vocabulary to express exactly how they're feeling. In fact, preschoolers' feelings are often slotted into the three primary colors of emotions: happy, sad, or mad. Chances are there are many different words that could more accurately represent what they're actually experiencing—ecstatic, frustrated, or, possibly, disappointed. This is exactly why, on our shows, we don't shy away from bigger concepts with expressive vocabulary broken down so that our preschoolers can understand. On our *Blue's Clues* spinoff *Blue's Room*, Blue would use words like *scrumptious* and *gigantic* in context and kids picked up on it. Daniel Tiger uses words like *disappointment* when his birthday cake gets smushed and *empathy* when feeling love for his mom and wanting to help her.

At home, we can plus-up our language in similar situations. Instead of jumping to help your child and find out if they are "scared" of something, ask them if they're "feeling cautious" or "concerned." Or if something potentially upsetting happens, why not remark that it's a bit "disconcerting"? For example, when my friend's three-year-old son heard the roar of the aerobatic flying team the Blue Angels during a flight show, the look on his face was pure terror. But instead of simply asking him if he was scared, she calmly said, "That was startling, wasn't it? I wasn't expecting that sound to be as loud as it was. I can tell by the look on your face that you're feeling a little concerned. Are you okay?" This way we are plussing-up their vocabulary and more accurately describing the feeling versus generalizing emotions in a way that might lead to their experiencing a situation more intensely than they may have otherwise.

Beyond learning how to accurately label and appropriately respond to different emotional triggers, we as parents can give our children an active strategy to help. On an episode of *Daniel Tiger's Neighborhood*, Daniel Tiger is ready to go to the beach. He has his sand pails and his shovel, he's wearing his bathing suit, and his friend Prince Wednesday is over to come along. But when Daniel and Prince open the door, they realize it's raining. Feeling disappointed and frustrated, Daniel begins to get upset and his feelings come out as truly red-faced and angry, not unlike a meltdown.

Mom Tiger validates his feelings, labels them, and we even created a mini-song (inspired by Mister Rogers' classic) for Daniel to sing to himself to calm him down: "When you feel so mad that you want to roar, take a deep breath and count to four. One, two, three, four . . ." Because, once calm, Daniel can figure out what to do to fix his problem.

He decides to make an "inside beach" by setting up beach chairs, making a pretend ocean, and bringing real sand from outside into his living room. Yikes! Well, Mom Tiger takes one look at this and begins to get angry herself. Daniel says, "Mom, your face looks funny and your cheeks are getting red. Are you mad?" Mom nods and then sings the calming strategy song to *herself* to calm herself down. Once calm, she talks with Daniel by getting on his level and looking at him in the eye.

We've found that this strategy benefits both preschoolers and parents. Preschoolers identify with this strategy and feel powerful because they can label their feelings and actively calm themselves down. And parents in similar situations have picked up on these cues and used them to communicate respectfully with their preschoolers to label and give legitimacy to their emotions. In fact, we have many episodes based on a range of feeling words in the context of four-year-old Daniel Tiger's life situations on the show such as *disappointed, excited, frustrated, scared, worried, lonely, ambivalent, empathetic, trust,* and *love.*

On any given day with a preschooler, there are undoubtedly countless opportunities to incorporate new expressive words into your world. Tired? *Exhausted.* Big? *Enormous.* Yummy? *Scrumptious.* Scared? *Cautious.* Happy? *Ecstatic.* Angry? *Impatient.* Where can you expand your preschooler's expressive vocabulary?

PARENTING PRODUCTION NOTES
Use Challenging Vocabulary and Introduce Rich, Expressive Words

- What kind of language do you use with your preschoolers?
- Is your default to choose simple vocabulary words?
- Notice the times you swap out more complicated words for simpler ones and challenge yourself to stick with the word you originally intended.

Here's a brief list of different feeling expression words. Which of these words can you incorporate into your everyday beyond the usual happy, sad, and mad?

agitated	ecstatic	impatient
animated	elated	jubilant
apprehensive	embarrassed	lonely
concerned	energetic	overwhelmed
delighted	exhilarated	perplexed
disappointed	frustrated	uncertain

PRIORITIZING HONESTY AND GENUINENESS

Preschoolers have many talents, but reading people's intentions is one that seems to be especially fine-tuned. They know when someone's being disingenuous, or when someone is using an overly sweet and slow tone, or when they're being spoken to by someone who doesn't "get" them. Think about it: why do so many people insist on raising their voice up an octave, turning down the speed dial, and pouring on the saccharine when talking with young children? The truth is, infant-directed speech or "Motherese" or "Caregiver Speak" is a language that has been used by parents since the beginning of time to get an inherent response out of *babies*. Infants respond to the slower speech, higher pitch, and very exaggerated pitch contours. But just as your baby grows, the language you use with them has to grow. For anyone over eighteen months of age, baby talk feels disingenuous and disrespectful.

More than any other aspect of our host Steve's connection with his young audience in *Blue's Clues*, I see his honesty and genuineness as the primary reason he so successfully connects with preschoolers. And it's a fact I've taken to heart in every kids' show I've created. Steve in *Blue's Clues* is expressive, happy, and interested. He doesn't patronize. He doesn't dumb down his vocabulary. And he Pauses for kids to answer him. Steve's character was created to model respectful communication with children in a genuine and honest way so they learn in a warm, nurturing environment. Likewise, Bianca, our animated star in *Wishenpoof*, looks to the camera very closely and speaks to the viewer directly. She respects the home viewers by letting them into her world as she makes mistakes and tries to solve problems, one step a time. With Bianca, we're showing another example for how to bring our kids into our thinking so we can model genuine and honest reactions and the viewers can learn how to problem solve along with us. But how can we as parents replicate this authentic communication approach to the benefit of our children?

It can be a tricky balance. As parents, we are consistently forming a boundary around our children to protect them and to keep them safe. Yet as they grow, our boundary needs to get incrementally wider to continue to keep them safe and secure while also fostering their independence and learning. This is the power of respectful language. We know that preschoolers respond best when spoken to on their level—looking them in the eye when we speak, using appropriate language, defining language for them, as well as using slower and more directed speech, repetition, and playful rhetoric. Child development psychologist Roberta Schomburg is a huge proponent of being honest with our children. "Parents sometimes think it might be easier to just slip away without saying good-bye by telling children, 'I'll be right back' or 'I'm just going to get some coffee.' Sometimes we make promises that we have no intention of keeping. 'Yes, yes . . . we'll do that tomorrow.' These kinds of statements mislead children and, in the end, undermine their trust that adults will keep their word," she says.[2]

Being genuine and honest also means acknowledging when we say things we didn't mean to say or when we lose our cool because we're stressed or frustrated. Since it's our kids' jobs to push our buttons—they are hardwired to test the limits with us so they can figure out who they are independent from us—our job becomes showing them how to toe the line, *respectfully*.

The key? We *admit* to being stressed or frustrated or angry. Telling your preschooler, "I'm feeling like *I'm* going to have a tantrum! I feel stressed. How can you help me?" or "I need a minute to clear my head" or even singing Daniel Tiger's mad strategy to *yourself*, and then walking away to calm yourself down, is an excellent way to cut the tension and even enlist your preschooler's help. These strategies are the very ones we want to teach our kids. And what better way to clue our kids in to our honest, genuine feelings than to show them the power of managing our emotions.

Never underestimate the value of our kids knowing that we make mistakes, too. It's powerful for a preschooler to understand that adults are human, that things go wrong for us, that we have problems and worries of our own. By letting our preschoolers see that we don't have all the answers, we show them that we're open to learning from them and reinforce our goal of growing and developing together as a family that respects each other.

There's an added bonus to talking with preschoolers honestly and genuinely: they will grow up knowing how to respectfully communicate *with us*. This leads to *debates* versus *arguments* as they age. Think about it. When we teach our kids to disagree respectfully with us and each other, they learn how to argue, support their argument, and become passionate without disrespectful screaming matches (or teenage tantrums down the road).

PARENTING PRODUCTION NOTES
Be Open and Genuine and Skip the Baby Talk

Here are three ways you can add some more genuine and honest communication into your script with your child.

- Consider specific circumstances where you could be more genuine in your communication tone with your child. Are you still talking about "going pee pee" or asking your little one if she's "hungry wungry?" Try to notice when you use baby talk with your preschoolers and then consciously think about opportunities to make small, positive tweaks.
- In what type of circumstances are you least likely to respectfully communicate with your preschooler? When you're stressed? Tired? Frustrated? We all have our moments—when dinner's on the table but nobody shows up, or when we're stuck in traffic and running late for school drop off, or when our little one regularly wakes us up raring to go at five in the morning when we've only just managed to get to bed four hours earlier. Think about the times when you're typically not at your "best" and consider ways you can more genuinely "show up" in those moments in a way that respects your own experience while also benefitting your child's social emotional communication growth.
- Many parents don't want their child to see them sad or angry or frustrated, but in reality, modeling these very real emotions in a healthy way has tremendous benefits for your child. When we honestly communicate about these more challenging feelings, we're not only supporting ourselves by not holding it in—we're showing our child we respect them enough to share. An added benefit, depending on what has sparked our intense feelings, calmly sharing can diffuse heightened in-the-moment emotions. Think about a time you were upset but didn't calmly communicate how you were feeling with your child. How would sharing

in that moment have benefitted you? Them? How might it have improved the in-the-moment dynamic?

KEEPING COMMUNICATION AGE-APPROPRIATE

Spending a day with a preschooler can be like one very, *very* long game of twenty questions: *How does this work? Why is this round? Where do these go? Why are you doing that? What will happen if I push this button? Why? Why not?* In fact, that is one of the primary goals behind *Super Why!*—to harness the power of the question "Why?" Super Why asks *why* (hence his name) to understand the motives behind the characters of the stories he jumps into. *Why* do we do this? Because when kids' curiosity evokes a "why" question, this is the moment when kids are most ripe for learning. So, what should we as their parents do? Answer their questions! All of them!

Being respectful communicators means answering their countless questions with true, thoughtful answers, even if the answers might seem cognitively beyond their grasp. Say they want to know how a battery powers a toy or why rides at amusement parks have height requirements. These questions can be opportunities to introduce simple engineering or safety concepts. You don't need to be a physicist to talk about cause and effect or the transfer of energy. By responding to their questions with informative, real answers as opposed to brushing them off or giving them an overly simplified response, you're not only respecting their ability to understand, but you're sparking in them a continued curiosity about the way things work and reinforcing the idea that they can discover the answers for themselves. In fact, it is important to respond with what you know or what you think the answer to the question is. Sometimes it's simply the bond that our kids are after versus the actual answer. And when their questions persist, "looking it up together" is a great way to extend the bonding even further.

I keep seeing ads for our ever-present technology—ask Siri this, let Echo or Google answer that. One commercial that recently caught my eye shows a dad and his daughter reading a book together. Sweet, right? Well, of course, the preschooler keeps halting the book reading to ask a question on every page. Instead of answering her, the dad asks Google to answer for him. Why does this bother me? I just keep wondering if the daughter would rather know what her *dad thinks* as opposed to what *Google knows*. Answering our children's *why* questions makes them feel safe and secure, emotionally. It teaches them to have a voice or have an opinion as we share ours. It teaches them to be passionate about a topic when we show we are. It bonds them with us, forming the attachment relationship we want with them as they grow older. When we as adults take the time to answer our children's questions, we give them so much more than information. We give them an emotional response to learning that will go way beyond that one question in the preschool years. It could very well turn into a lifelong love of learning.

Now, while I am a firm believer in answering every question a preschooler asks (yes, even the tricky ones), I also believe in sticking with answers they are *emotionally* ready for and that protect their preschool innocence. If they don't have the emotional maturity to comprehend a concept or situation, respectful communication means responding in a way that supports their emotional well-being while being honest. It can be a precarious line to walk, especially because the line is always moving.

Having adult programs and the news on the TV and online when kids are around are surefire ways to expose them to things we may not want them to see. While some might argue that kids need to learn about the "real world," remember we are talking about children between the ages of two and five. It's critical that preschoolers believe in the world and trust that they're not in danger. Roberta Schomburg says, "Many people associate trust with honesty and wonder how honest we should be with our children. Certainly, honesty is a trait that we want to instill in children. That being said, giving children too much information or information that adds to their worry and anxiety is not very helpful." The safest bet? Avoid background television when preschoolers are around, period.

Of course, we can't protect our children from everything—tragedies happen and our preschoolers will be looking to us for answers. In their attempts to share honestly with their children about difficult circumstances or events they may have been exposed to, many parents over-answer and go into detail, which can result in an increase in fear and anxiety in their children. This isn't to say parents should brush off painful subjects with an "I'll explain it to you when you're older." Think age-appropriate responses. Use honest but general language to explain what happened while reminding them that you and their other caregivers are here to keep them safe. By focusing on a foundation of safety and trust in the framework of respectful communication, we can find the right words to answer their questions by not over-answering and sticking to concepts they can emotionally take in.

This honesty policy doesn't just apply to tragedies—things like physical differences by gender, a parent getting fired, dealing with financial hardships in the family, and asking questions about how babies are made, all have the ability to stop a parent in her tracks. If you're caught off-guard and don't know how to respond, be honest and say so. "I'm not sure how to best answer that. Let me think about it." (Just make sure you do get back to them, as persistence ranks second to curiosity with these relentless information gatherers.)

At two years old, my daughter asked, "What are babies made of?" My husband and I looked at each other with wide eyes and Paused. (I would like to say we Paused instinctively since I believe so much in the correctly timed Pause, but the truth is, we just weren't sure what to say!) During this Pause, Hope looked at us and continued. "Paint? Watercolors? Arts and crafts?" Greg and I smiled. She was two. She needed a two-year-old answer. So we gave her one. "Love."

HANDLING TOUGH CONVERSATIONS
IN A PRESCHOOL-APPROPRIATE WAY

Real life happens, and no matter how much we try to protect our preschoolers from being exposed to things that may be very upsetting or they may not be developmentally ready for, it's important that we address their questions in age-appropriate ways. Here are a few examples:

The situation	Their question	Our potential response
We stumble upon the aftermath of a car accident where someone is injured.	"What happened? Could that happen to us?"	"There are so many cars on the road and every driver is different. Sometimes someone makes a mistake and an accident happens. Accidents can happen to anybody, but I drive very carefully so I can keep us safe. After all—I have very important cargo in this car!"
They find out about a violent, scary event.	"Why would somebody do that? Are we safe?"	"There are some people whose brains aren't healthy, and so they make very bad choices. We are absolutely safe and you are surrounded by people in your life who work hard every day to keep you safe."
Learning about a natural disaster that has impacted many people.	"Could that happen here?"	"That happened very far away from here—that type of thing [tsunami, etc.] doesn't happen where we live." OR "There's no way to know if a natural disaster like that will ever happen here, but we have a plan for how to keep our family safe if it does."

The situation	Their question	Our potential response
Seeing someone living on the street in obvious poverty and in dire straits.	"What happened to them? Why don't they have a home?"	"Sometimes people make bad choices or get stuck in difficult situations and lose their money and sadly they don't have a home to live in any longer. Luckily, there are many places in our city that provide food and clothing and even shelter for people living on the street. If you like, we could find a way to support one of those places."

PARENTING PRODUCTION NOTES
Answer Their Questions in a Way They're Emotionally Ready For

- What subjects is your preschooler naturally curious about?
- How can you encourage her growth in this area by answering her every "Why?" with age-appropriate answers?
- Think about a tricky or challenging situation you may have to talk with your child about (either now or in the future). How can you communicate respectfully about it while protecting his or her emotional well-being?

GETTING ON YOUR CHILD'S LEVEL

In all my shows, I model adults literally getting down on the floor to play with kids and be on their level when talking with them. This isn't just about avoiding being a domineering parent your child has to strain her neck to look at. Making eye contact when you have something to say to a child actually helps ensure your tone is respectful. It's like magic!

I was reminded of the importance of this eye-level perspective one night when I was wrapping up dinner. I called to my girls in the other room and asked them to stop playing and wash up for dinner. I hollered once. Crickets. I hollered twice. Still nothing. This is where my Italian upbringing could get the best of me and I could easily feel disrespected by my girls. So, I took a few deep breaths and walked into the family room where I found them deep in restaurant play, Hope clad in an apron as the chef and Ella, purse in hand, her hungry customer.

I sat down at the little table and got eye-to-eye with both of them. Hope immediately ran up to me. "Another customer! Here's some soup!" Though I had an agenda—getting the girls to the dinner table—I reminded myself that I had entered their world of play and I needed to respect that world. After all—*play is the work of the child*. So, despite the fact that my schedule was being interrupted, I thought, *At this very moment, I'm not on the biggest time crunch. What's another ten minutes?* This isn't always the case, but I've come to realize that ten minutes of playing trumps ten minutes of hollering to get them to do what I want them to do. So, I *played*. I pretended to eat the soup. "Deee-licious! Did you make this, chef?" Hope nodded. Excited for the script change, Ella jumped in pretending to eat, too. "Deee-licious!" Continuing our play, I said, "It's dinner time in Mommy's restaurant. And I could use some help. Chef Hope could help me dish out the pasta and Ella could help me by being a hungry customer!" *Magic.* They were suddenly totally ready to play (i.e., cooperate!) with me. It works every time. Making eye contact not only helps preschoolers notice we're there and see that we care about their thoughts and feelings—it transports us as parents into their world and onto their level, which is how and where the respectful communication occurs.

PARENTING PRODUCTION NOTES
Look Them in the Eye and Jump into Their World
The next time you have something important to say, get down on your child's level.

- Sit on a chair and pull them onto your lap, crouch down, or get down on your knees, and look them right in the eye as you communicate.
- Notice how it changes their responsiveness and your willingness to join their world. Don't worry if your preschooler isn't much for eye contact—this is more about getting down on their level than anything else.
- Compare the outcome with your regular approach. Which one ultimately takes more time? Which one results in happier feelings all around?

SPEAKING TO YOUR KIDS THE WAY *YOU* WANT TO BE SPOKEN TO

In the past century, the parent-child communication dynamic has gone through remarkable shifts. In the 1920s and 1930s, the norm was an authoritative "What I say goes" approach. Kids were seen as "working" for their parents and were expected to obey their parents' every command. After World War Two, the paradigm flipped, and suddenly parents were "working" for their kids, coddling and babying them and making them the center of their world at any cost.

I advocate a *conscious parenting* approach: finding the balance between respecting our role as parents while respecting and embracing our children for who they are. When it comes to communication, conscious parenting isn't about being our child's best friend—it's about talking with them the same way we would talk with an adult we care about. It's about wanting to hear what they have to say and letting them know what they say matters and is interesting to us.

Peggy O'Mara, founder of *Mothering* magazine, famously wrote: "The way we talk to our children becomes their inner voice." As the most influential adults in our preschoolers' lives, the way we speak to them has a profound impact. Research on the long-term outcomes of talking to children in a disrespectful way shows a strong correlation with their developing low self-worth. It also challenges their ability to problem solve because they become afraid to take risks. In the long run, children who are reluctant to take risks frequently develop high stress levels, which directly corresponds with a lowered cognitive and academic ability.

Go to a place teeming with families and you'll hear plenty of disrespectful communication. And it's easy enough to understand—as parents of young children, we are "in charge" of their well-being, and the way we speak to them often reflects our stress over their safety, and our hierarchy:

- "Get *down* from there . . . what are you *thinking*?"
- "What's *wrong* with you?"
- "I said *stop doing that*!"
- "If you pinch your sister again you're going to get in *serious* trouble."
- "Why are you making me call your name five times? Get over here *right now*!"

Yikes. We've all had our moments. We've all been there. But how would you feel if your friend or your partner or your boss talked to you that way? Yes, we're their parents, and yes, we're ultimately in charge. But that doesn't mean we should place more value on our desired outcome at the risk of devaluing their experiences and dismissing their emotional experiences. Couple this with the fact that children love and admire their parents in a godlike way, and these words carry even more weight.

Does that mean we let our preschoolers run rampant while we bite our tongue? Absolutely not. It all comes down to the words we use and the way we say them. And just think—the more respectfully we speak to our children, the more likely they'll be to talk this way with us as they get older (can you say teenage dream?). Here are some respectful alternatives using the above examples (all said calmly and at eye level, of course!).

Disrespectful	Respectful
"Get *down* from there . . . what are you *thinking*?"	"I can see that you really like to climb, but I'm concerned you might hurt yourself."
"What's *wrong* with you?"	"Wow . . . it looks like you've got strong feelings about that. What's going on?"
"I said *stop doing that!*"	"I've asked you several times to stop, and I would like you to listen to my words."
"If you pinch your sister again, you're going to get in *serious* trouble."	"It seems like you're having a hard time not pinching your sister right now. It's time for you to take a break and do something else."
"Why are you making me call your name five times? Get over here *right now!*"	"You're having so much fun that you must not have heard me, but I need you to come over here and stand by me now."

PARENTING PRODUCTION NOTES
Stay Calm and Patient, Even in Challenging Situations

- Think about the most recent challenging situation you experienced with your preschooler and reflect on the way you spoke to him or her.
- Think about the words you used and the volume and inflections in your voice.

> • Did you talk to them the same way you would hope to be spoken to in a challenging situation? How might you rewrite the script for that scenario?

THE POWER OF EMPATHY

My friend Beth used to call her son "Drama," since the nickname so clearly represented how strongly he felt things and the animated way he let everybody know about it. She called him this in a loving, playful way, but she now acknowledges the nickname probably resulted in her not taking her child's strong emotional responses seriously. At the very least, they sent the message that her son was making a bigger deal out of things than he should have, and everybody knew it.

All preschoolers have their buttons and things they feel strongly about. Some get scared of pretty much anything, some refuse to wear socks, some might think it's the end of the world if the pediatrician's office forgot to give them a sticker. I even knew one mom whose daughter would get incredibly upset if they tried to give breadcrumbs to ducks at the park ("Those are OUR breadcrumbs!" she would scream).

In situations like these, specifically when we're seeing them through our rational, well-intentioned, adult perspective, it's easy to be dismissive. After all, we know there are plenty of breadcrumbs to go around. But brushing off our preschooler's emotions through the words and tone we use does them a great disservice.

Instead, practice empathy. And lots of it. Speaking to a preschooler in a calm, empathetic way—whether they're overreacting, being too sensitive, or just plain being unreasonable— is not only respectful . . . it works. Research has shown that the way in which we talk with our preschoolers can dramatically reduce power struggles with them because they feel heard, empathized with, and emotionally safe to experience their range of emotions. This makes them feel not only validated but also valued. Lastly, speaking empathically with our children teaches them how to communicate with other children in an empathetic way, forming the foundation for healthy relationships outside of the home. According to a 2016 article in *Greater Good*, "Various studies show that the more empathy a child displays, the less likely they are to engage in bullying, online and in real life. Empathic children and adolescents are more likely to engage in positive social behaviors, like sharing or helping others. They're also less likely to be antisocial and exhibit uncontrolled aggressive behaviors."[3] Bottom line: it's never too early to nurture our children's empathy. And even though some children may be more naturally empathetic than others, consistently modeling empathy will, over time, result in their developing this critical trait.

Here's what it looks like:

Dismissive	Empathetic
"It's not scary, sweetheart. You're fine!"	"I can tell that you're feeling unsure about this. We don't have to do/watch/read this if you don't want to."
"You have to wear socks in those shoes, otherwise you'll get blisters."	"You really want to go without socks? I'm concerned you'll get blisters if you do."
"You can get a sticker the next time we come, I promise!"	"Oh boy, I know you really wanted that. It can be hard to want something and not get it."
"Why are you so upset? We have plenty of breadcrumbs! Don't you want to feed the poor ducks?"	"You really want us to stop feeding the ducks right now. What's going on?"

PARENTING PRODUCTION NOTES
Honor Your Child's Emotional Responses

• What kinds of things does your preschooler feel strongly about? What does he or she overreact to?

- What kinds of things make him or her cry, get angry or frustrated, or become fearful? How do you typically respond to his or her strong reactions? Write out three examples.
- For each example, play with the language and tone to see if there is room to build more empathy into your responses. (Remember: empathy isn't being over-the-top understanding or giving in to their demands—it's letting your preschooler know you hear him or her and validate his or her experience).

Angela's Clues

At the end of the day, we want our kids to talk with us, be respectful of us and the world around them, grow up to be in healthy and happy relationships, and succeed in the world in whatever they want to do. The simplest way in which we, as parents, caregivers, teachers, and anyone around children can accomplish this is to lead by example. We need to talk to children with empathy and care. We need to get down on their level and be playful. We need to talk to them with open, honest, and smart words. If we're stressed out, we need to admit it. We need to choose media that models respectful communication in all of these ways. Because, when we do all these things, we'll be creating children who will be respectful themselves, and in turn, continue to want to open up to us, express their feelings, talk with us, and talk *respectfully* to us, as they grow up so we can help guide them along the way.

- **Be Involved** by answering your preschooler's questions honestly and respectfully.

CLUE #6: RESPECT

- **Ask Questions** to show you're interested in their thoughts and point of view.
- **See the Spark** and be a respectful listener as they share their big ideas and dreams.

. . . .

YOUR MEDIA "YES" LIST

- ☑ The characters regularly use nice, juicy words.
- ☑ The stories respect my child's level of development.
- ☑ My child feels happy and positive after watching the show.
- ☑ The characters are patient and empathetic toward one another.
- ☑ The characters talk with honesty and respect.

. . . .

Clue Takeaways

- o The words we use and the way we use them have the power to positively contribute to a preschooler's brain development, expanding their vocabulary, reasoning skills, and school readiness
- o Speaking and listening to our preschooler with respect boosts their confidence and their sense of being heard and seen.
- o Being open and honest about our own emotional state of mind respects who our children are.
- o Asking thoughtful questions, and only answering the questions they ask, encourages the growth of your child's emotional literacy.

Help,
Model,
Observe

CLUE #7: HELP

Asking Preschoolers "Will You Help Me?"
Develops Empathy and Confidence

From my time as preschool teacher's assistant, I thought of the kids as I sat down to write my very first episode of *Blue's Clues*. But beyond incorporating the Pause, how else could I approach the story and characters to achieve all of my goals in one story? I remember sitting and staring at the blank page for hours, unsure about how to meet my milestones for such a young audience. But then it hit me, and I once again went back to my roots, something I've continued to do over and over throughout my twenty-plus years creating kids' media. Knowing preschoolers as well as I do gave me an advantage . . . a kind of secret weapon if you will. And that secret weapon is *asking kids to help*. As I began to write, the phrase, "Will you help me?" became a constant theme, a reminder that our preschool audience was not just watching, but ready, willing, and able to help.

That phrase ended up being a part of every single episode of *Blue's Clues*. Here's how it typically plays out and why it works so well. A capable adult (Steve) looks the preschooler viewer in the eye (the camera) somewhat pleadingly (the bond) and tells the viewers, who are much younger than him, that he needs *their help* to solve a problem (source of pride). Now that's a powerful ask! Not only that, but *after* Steve asks for help, he *Pauses* again. This second Pause happens as Steve looks closely at the home viewer, holding eye contact as a way to encourage the home viewer to answer. After those infamous four beats, Steve follows up with an answer. "You will?" Then he *Pauses again* to take in his surprise and excitement that the kids will help him, as if the kids at home are some sort of mystical Jedi Master. And then Steve looks right in the camera again and says, "Oh great!" (affirmation) and smiles. It looks like this:

"Will you help me?"

Pause.

"You will?"

Pause.

"Oh great!"

So simple, right? So simple and yet *so powerful*. The little four-word phrase *"Will you help me?"* became part of the lexicon of preschool television through *Blue's Clues*, and has since grown to be a common feature in many shows aimed at kids. That's because it's an incredibly powerful question to the ears of a preschooler. And likewise, it's an incredibly powerful tool for a parent. But why?

Babies as young as twelve months old can recognize when others are in distress and may try to comfort them. It's true. And between the ages of twelve and twenty-four months, toddlers typically begin showing signs of empathy and concern. Once children reach the preschool years, for the most part they are naturally sympathetic and have a desire to be helpful. "The desire to help is innate," says David Schonfeld, MD, director of Pediatrics at Cincinnati Children's Hospital Medical Center. "At first, children like to help others because it helps them get what they want. Next, they do so because they get praise. Finally, they begin to anticipate the needs of others, and it becomes intrinsically rewarding to do nice things for people in their lives."[1]

So, what is it that preschoolers want so much that fuels their desire to help? The love and adoration of their parents. The truth is, preschoolers love to help almost as much as they love the idea that someone is *asking* them to help in the first place. When they're asked to help, especially by a role model, they usually jump at the chance.

HOW HELPING LEADS TO KINDNESS

Whether you're asking your preschooler to help you set the table or put away the groceries, you're helping them feel *valued and capable* and, even better, you're giving them an active way to practice kindness and a reason to believe in their own self-worth. If *you* believe in them, they will believe in themselves, too. Research has shown that *all* people, young and old, feel better about themselves when they *practice* kindness.

People who are kind and compassionate are more successful and fulfilled in the long term.[2] In fact, practicing kindness, which is defined as "giving to others" (i.e., helping!), has been shown to make us even happier than giving to ourselves. Better still, performing even one small act of kindness each day for ten consecutive days is linked to long-lasting happiness due to the "positive feedback loop" between kindness and happiness.[3] Even the royals are setting a fantastic example. As Kate Middleton said in an interview about the values she and Prince William are committed to instilling in their preschoolers, "My parents taught me about the importance of qualities like kindness, respect, and honesty. I realize how central values like these have been to me throughout my life. That is why William and I want to teach our little children, George and Charlotte, just how important these things are as they grow up. In my view, it is just as important as excelling at maths or sport."[4] I couldn't have said it better myself! The more we help, the more we give. The more we give, the kinder we are. The kinder we are, the happier we are. And the happier we are, the kinder we are. That's the kindness loop!

. . . .

Fred Rogers has famously said, "When I was a boy and I would see scary things in the news, my mother would say to me, 'Look for the helpers. You will always find people who are helping.' To this day, especially in times of 'disaster,' I remember my mother's words and I am always comforted by realizing that there are still so many helpers—so many caring people in this world."

. . . .

KINDNESS IS ACTIVE

Promoting kindness in our preschoolers is one of the more important aspects of growing them to be positive, successful, empathetic people who value their own self-worth. When preschoolers learn to be helpers, we know that it helps to reduce violence and bullying in the long run. What follows are suggestions for how to reinforce kindness in an active way.

See Kindness Everywhere

It's important that preschoolers witness acts of kindness every day, all around them, as the first step in filling their brain with the kindness gene. Even in times of tragedy, we can find comfort in seeing kindness. Our preschoolers should be surrounded by kindness in the same way that we surround them with books we want them to read or media we want them to learn from. On *Super Why!*, we surround preschoolers for twenty-two minutes with literacy with a goal of modeling the idea that books are a resource for life. We start the show in a *library*, we go beyond the *books* to a world *where fairy-tale book characters* live, we showcase superheroes with the power to *read*, we jump inside *books* to solve problems, and, while on the adventure, we play *literacy* games to propel the story forward, find super *letters*, and figure out the *Super Story Answer* to our problem.

With kindness, we want to follow this same example. Imagine a world where your preschooler is surrounded by neighbors smiling and saying hello; everyone opening doors for each other; adults and kids saying "please" and "thank you" to each other, helping each other without asking, giving little smiles and hugs for no reason. By creating a world brimming with good deeds, kind acts, and positive behaviors we are using kindness as an active strategy, a tool, and a sense of morality in the world of our preschoolers.

Give Preschoolers Opportunities to Be Receivers of Kindness

As with showing love, when we are kind to our preschoolers by speaking to them with respect, talking with them at mealtimes, and being concerned and interested in their day, we are modeling kindness and our preschoolers are the recipients. Saying kind words to our preschoolers—such as praising their efforts, noticing when they're trying hard to do something, acknowledging them being nice to their sister, saying thank you when they do something you've asked them to do, and even apologizing when you lose patience—are all ways of showing kindness. Although they are little, we want our children to know that they deserve to receive kindness. The way we want to be treated by our kids when *we're* older is correlated to the way we treat them now.

Modeling Kindness

It's important that we're mindful of modeling kindness both "inside" the home as well as "outside" the home. We model kindness not only in the way we treat our spouses and friends, but waitresses, store clerks, baristas . . . strangers. And because we know that repetition is the key to learning, small acts of kindness that we perform multiple times a day can make as big an impact, if not *bigger*, than the larger acts do. And of course, the same is true for the opposite behavior. Even if we're a kind person at heart, when we act in an unkind way—even little acts that might seem like no big deal (maybe we're distracted, have too much on our plates, or are caught up in an emotional problem)—we're modeling these unkind behaviors. And our preschoolers are watching and listening.

When we are cognizant of modeling kind behaviors, we're not only showing our children *how* to be kind, but we are showing them what it means to be a friend, a neighbor, a spouse, a daughter/son to our own parents, and how to act once we are older. Essentially, the way in which we model treating people around us is the way our kids will grow up treating other people. If we value a strong familial bond, we need to show that bond with our own parents as well. Our kids should catch us in the act of going out of our way to help another person, upholding our commitments, welcoming in neighbors in times of need, and complimenting another person for their accomplishments. We want to take note of the small things we can put into practice multiple times a day, as they are the simplest, easiest ways to showcase kindness and empathy.

LITTLE THINGS HAVE A BIG IMPACT

What we want to do is find ways to promote kindness every day, in small, yet powerful, ways. Such as:

- asking preschoolers to help,
- pointing out kind acts,
- surrounding our kids with kindness,
- treating our kids with kindness,
- modeling kindness.

PARENTING PRODUCTION NOTES
Find Ways to Model Kindness Every Day

Positive	Negative
Holding the door open for other people	Rushing through the door (*models an inconsiderate action*)
Smiling to strangers	Looking down at our phone (*shows that we aren't caring or involved*)
Stopping to help a stranger in need	Rolling eyes, being too busy, ignoring the stranger (*shows that we are not empathetic*)

Positive	Negative
Being cordial and friendly to someone who is doing something for you (waitress, barista, sales clerk)	Being curt, rude, too busy (*models unkind behaviors*)
Speaking to our spouses in a respectful way	Fighting in front of the kids (*showing that aggression is acceptable*)
Speaking to our parents (their grandparents) with respect	Not being involved with our parents, not respecting time with them, not upholding traditions (*models not respecting family, which may in turn, be how our children treat us*)
Being interested and invested in our friends	Being nice to someone and saying something disparaging about them when they leave (*models inauthentic, non-genuine "petty" behavior, two-faced, phony*)

THE BENEFITS OF CATCHING PRESCHOOLERS DOING SOMETHING GOOD

Getting into the habit of catching our preschoolers "doing something good" and affirming them for this action will send the message that we are mindful of these kind acts. Petting the dog, sharing with a sibling, helping without being asked, are all little kind things that can be affirmed. When we look our preschoolers in the eye, smile, and point out these kind behaviors, we're ensuring they are the ones most likely to be repeated.

Preschoolers get such a rush of adrenaline and good feelings when they do something kind that the very act itself actually taps into and builds upon their intrinsic motivation. And by affirming kindness, we can encourage the growth of this social-emotional muscle by providing opportunities for our preschoolers to be in the "giving" role. For instance, arranging a playdate with a younger child will put our preschooler in a nurturing, leader role where we can encourage him to be helpful and kind by showing his younger friend how to do things like throw a ball, pump on the swings, or draw a house. Likewise, using kind and interested phrases with our preschooler like "Show me how you did that" puts them in the driver's seat as proud people who are capable.

Asking our preschoolers *to help* provides rich opportunities for them to feel capable, confident, and smart, but it also enables them to practice being the "giver." And studies show that being an active "giver" of kindness creates many long-term and tangible benefits including boosting one's energy, strengthening one's immune system, lowering heart rate, reducing stress, and enhancing cognitive function. Just imagine the ongoing and long-lasting benefits of fostering a habit of kindness as a three-year-old!

When we ask our preschoolers to help us, they are in essence "practicing" being kind, and we are making an investment in their knowledge bank as they learn what happiness looks and feels like and, more important, what it means to *them*.

PARENTING PRODUCTION NOTES
Use Kindness Strategies with Your Preschooler

Try out some of these strategies for helping your preschooler practice kindness every day. Where can you easily build a little kindness into your everyday world?

Strategy	Examples	Your Plan
Pay It Forward	Do something nice and kind for your preschooler and encourage her to pay it forward by doing something nice for someone else.	
Chores	Ask your preschooler to help you with simple chores around the house.	

Strategy	Examples	Your Plan
Shopping Help	Give your child a mini-grocery list of three items you need while shopping and ask him to point the items out to you when you're at the store. To take it a step further: encourage him to choose an item that can be donated to a shelter or food drive.	
Mealtime	Ask your child to help you set the table. She can start by setting out the napkins or something equally unbreakable. After a meal, ask your child to help clear the table. Give your child the job of being responsible for filling up the water pitcher at dinner.	
Kindness Jar	Catch your preschooler doing something good (as often as possible) and add their act to a kindness jar (Mason jar) so they can see their kindness bounty adding up. Add to the bounty by recounting examples preschoolers see at home and at school with siblings and teachers—and add those to the jar, too! Examples they see on the media are fair game, too! (What Daniel Tiger does counts!)	

GROWING PRESCHOOLERS' EMPATHY MUSCLES

Once our preschoolers have developed the ability to routinely give and receive kindness, the next level is nurturing their sense of empathy. Empathy is our ability to recognize and respond to the needs and suffering of others, and growing their empathy muscles is an important next step (and unfortunately one that a lot of adults have yet to master).

In order to empathize with another person, we need to know how to read the emotion on a person's face, understand his verbal tone, and/or pick up on visual cues of that person's problem. Developmentally, our preschoolers are egocentric by nature, and as a result, they have a hard time thinking about the world beyond their immediate needs and desires. So, in order to nurture this skill, it's important that we as parents and caregivers model empathy and provide opportunities for our preschoolers to practice it in their own way. As cited in *The New York Times*,[5] psychologists Schumann, Zaki, and Dweck found that "when people learned that empathy was a *skill* that could be improved, they engaged in more effort to experience empathy . . ."

To practice this skill, we want to label and reinforce feelings and emotions and regularly use "feelings vocabulary." We can also model using empathy when resolving a conflict, whether in real life or during play, respectfully communicating with our preschooler, and talking things through with our preschooler by watching and listening in an empathetic way. When we start working on developing empathy young, the payoff is huge—raising children who will grow up to be open, kind, and understanding of other people's experiences.

Research suggests that parents can generate sympathetic responses in our kids by calling out when we see someone being victimized, in real life, on TV, or in a book, and talking with our child about how that person must feel.[6] In addition, kids are more likely to feel empathy for individuals who are familiar and/or similar to them.[7] In this way, we can use media, and our preschooler's favorite characters, to call out emotional vocabulary, "feelings faces," and to practice kindness mantras and strategies in play, such as "feelings charades."

In media, when we are conscious of teaching and practicing empathy for preschoolers, we can use the formal features of television to our advantage. We can slow down the scenarios with empathetic content to get our point across; we can use animation to visually overemphasize facial expressions and "feelings faces"; we can use music to underscore what the scene is trying to convey; and we can ask questions to point out the feelings cues. For instance, on *Daniel Tiger's Neighborhood*, Daniel leans in to the camera to include the home viewer in his thinking process as he figures out how to empathize. Mantras Daniel has used that have also been successfully used at home include "Think of others," "Friends help each other, yes they do," "I like you, I like you, I like you . . . just the way you are," and "Thank you for everything you do." As Daniel practices these strategies on himself and with his friends, the home viewer also learns, along with Daniel, emotional awareness and how to be kind and empathetic of others.

In another way, Bianca on *Wishenpoof* deals with executive functioning skills via musical anthems and "words of wisdom" that she uses to navigate situations as she tries to help her friends. We model Bianca learning how to cope with her emotions and feelings as well as recognize what others are feeling. Once she understands and labels the feeling of others, she leans in to the camera and brainstorms with the home viewer about ways to help in any given situation. For instance, in one episode, Bianca witnesses her friend Penelope's feelings get hurt due to mean words. Unsure about how to help her, Bianca leans in toward the home viewer and models the kinds of questions and observations we want preschoolers to consider and parents to use when coaching their preschoolers. Bianca asks us: "How do you think Penelope is feeling? Look at her face . . . she's frowning." She also asks the home viewer for ideas as to what she should do. After a Pause, we introduce our words of wisdom, "Say Something." Bianca understands she needs to "Say Something" in order to help her friend. Bianca waltzes up to Violet, the friend who caused Penelope pain, and lets her know that her words made Penelope feel sad. Bianca also sings a full-blown pop song about the merits of "Saying Something" when you see something that just doesn't feel right. The preschoolers watching at home are encouraged to think along with Bianca, helping them to practice empathy as well.

NURTURING PRESCHOOLERS' INNER COMPASS

To foster in our preschoolers the natural inclination to be empathetic helpers, the first step is to help them tune in to what's happening around them and encourage them to notice how it makes them feel. For example, when they witness someone doing something that is not nice (either on TV or in real life), ask them to explore the way it makes them feel inside. This helps them nurture their inner compass and learn to know they can rely on their body to give them important information. Then remind your preschooler that friends help each other, and work with them to brainstorm ideas about how they could help out in that type of situation. For example, if a friend is being treated poorly by another child, we could let our preschooler know that he can take the friend's hand and leave the situation, or tell a grown-up, or ask the person to "please stop." Opportunities for our children to build these kind, helpful traits happen every day, and can even help our preschoolers feel more empowered and hopeful by knowing they can be a part of the solution rather than simply feeling sad about a situation.

The Yale Center for Emotional Intelligence has created a Feelings RULER that they use to help kids, from preschool through high school, learn to: *R*ecognize emotions in themselves and others, *U*nderstand the causes and consequences of emotions, *L*abel emotions accurately, *E*xpress emotions appropriately, and *R*egulate emotions effectively. For preschoolers, the Feelings RULER is a visual poster that is put up in the classroom so kids can check in during the day and label how they're feeling. They can also "wear" a "feelings face" sticker on themselves so other kids can know how they are feeling and begin to see the value in recognizing others' emotions. The research on this type of empathy-building work with kids shows staggering benefits—from higher academic performance, increased leadership, better relationships at school and at home, and less bullying.

. . . .

TEACHING EMPATHY THROUGH GIFTS

I've focused on teaching my girls empathy at holiday time as they give and receive presents. Whenever they received a gift, I would talk about all the steps the person who gave it to them needed to go through. For instance, when Grandma gives them a gift, she had to first think about what they wanted, then drive to the store, then pick out the gifts, pay for them, and bring them home. Then she would excitedly wrap them up for Hope and Ella, as she couldn't wait to see the smile on their faces. I also verbalized these same steps any time we would go to the store to pick out a gift for someone else. By reinforcing this same message both in a giving and receiving role, the empathy messages went a long way. Today, my girls are the first to come over and hug someone after they get a gift, and they are super excited to pick out and give gifts to Greg and me. They appreciate and understand the effort, and you can see the happiness—and pride—on their faces because of it.

. . . .

PARENTING PRODUCTION NOTES
Practice Empathy in Simple Ways

- Role-play or point it out to your child when a friend is upset.
  - Take a moment to Pause and then talk to his or her friend to check in with them.

- Ask your preschooler to think about how someone else is feeling.
  - Ask how their favorite media character would help in this situation, using questions like: "How do you think he is

feeling?" "What is her face showing? Is she smiling? Is he frowning?" "Do you see any clues of why they might be upset?"

- Use play or drawings to interact with your preschooler by walking them through how they can help their friend.
    - Probe by asking, "What would make *you* feel better?" *Pause.* "Do you think giving Jack a hug will make him feel better, too?"

HELPING MAKES YOU SMARTER

We know from the research that the idea of helping is a great motivator for practicing and developing key cognitive skills, so we use this strategy intentionally in all of our programs. My interactive approach allows me to get kids labeling, talking to the screens, and pointing to answers—encouraging our viewers to help is extraordinarily effective.

The key to its success has been creating strong "helping" storylines for each episode, as well as simple "helping" storylines for games, so kids know exactly what they need to do. Here's an example of a simple "helping" storyline we used on the very first episode of *Blue's Clues*.

Steve *skidoos* into a picture of a farm. Once on the farm, a little chick wearing a hat hops into Steve's hand and says: "Can you help me? Can you help me find my friend?"

Okay. Let's stop there for a second. Finding a friend is a *big deal* in the world of preschoolers. Kids at home will most likely feel this little chick's pain, as many of them may have been in this exact situation themselves before . . . unable to find their friend anywhere! Because of this connection point, the viewers won't only be motivated, they'll likely be tapping into their sense of empathy as well.

The chick continues: "She has a hat on just . . . like . . . mine." Now we've let the kids at home know that in order to help, they have to find a matching hat. The idea of "helping" has provided the perfect impetus for the home viewer to lean in and have an emotional connection to wanting to help, and as the chick hops around looking for its match, the home viewers help the chick by saying "No! No! No! No!" until finally they spot a match. "YES! That one!" Then the chick says: "See? See how we match? Thank you for helping us!" Affirmed and thanked, the kids feel empowered and proud, and get a little self-worth boost to boot. Through this simple storyline and game, we've set the stage for helping, for empathy, and for practicing matching skills.

We took a different approach to using the strategy of helping as a tool for cognitive development on our show *Super Why!* Since the literacy show's main characters are superheroes—Alpha Pig has Alphabet Power, Wonder Red has Word Power, Princess Presto has Spelling Power, Woofster has Dictionary Power, and of course Super Why has the Power to Read—we decided to give the preschoolers at home a superhero power on the show. Their special power? The Power to Help!

By introducing the Power of Help, we've given our home viewers the motivation and understanding, across the whole *Super Why!* series, that their role in every episode, when up against any obstacle, is to help. In our stories, we are propelled forward through obstacles and games that are overcome or completed only by help from the preschool home viewer.

At home, in our everyday lives, we can use interactivity through asking for help from our preschoolers to teach cognitive skills. Asking our preschoolers questions (as well as answering all of their questions) about everything around us will help to boost these skills, from noticing shapes all around us, to pointing out numbers in our world, as well as colors, words, size comparisons, patterns, etc. Each time we ask preschoolers to help us find what we need or make a game out of it, we are helping to boost cognitive skills as well as their self-worth.

PARENTING PRODUCTION NOTES
Play Helping Games to Promote Cognitive Skills

Where?	What?
In the car	• Ask them to point out everything they see that is the color blue. • Ask them to count the red cars (and then ask for a more challenging color: turquoise or aquamarine).
At the supermarket	• Ask them to count all the rectangles they see. • Ask to point out all the green fruits. • Ask them to find as many vegetables as they can that start with the letter P (and other letters).
On a walk	• Pick up different leaves and ask them to label them when you get home. • Find all things that are green. • Bring an art pad and draw what you see. • Point out different animals.
At a restaurant	• Ask your child to close her eyes, take one condiment away from the table, and see if she can remember which one is missing. • Bring five different shapes and see how many objects can they make with the same shapes.

HELPING BOOSTS RESPONSIBILITY

Asking preschoolers for help not only promotes kindness, empathy, and a sense of purpose, it also underscores a sense of responsibility and investment in the family, the community, and the world. When they are at an age where they are figuring out how they fit into the world at large, giving preschoolers the ability to help adults will contribute to their sense of importance, usefulness, and purpose. And as preschoolers grow, we want to give them the clues to be not only independent but also *responsible* human beings. We want to instill in them the value of being someone others can count on: someone who keeps their word, meets their commitments, does things to the best of their ability, and is accountable. Being responsible also means learning how to contribute as a functioning member of the family, community, and society, which is why it is a key to a child's future success.

Finding even small ways for a preschooler to help and spend time with you (which, after all, is a preschooler's ultimate goal), will go a long way in building their self-worth and improving your family dynamic. Expecting our preschoolers to help with chores around the house for the sole reason that doing so is part of being a contributing family member has been proven to be a successful way to foster independence and responsibility. According to research by Marty Rossmann,[8] young adults who started chores at the preschool age were more likely to achieve academic and early career success and be self-sufficient and have good relationships with family and friends as compared with those who didn't have chores or who started them later.

We can set our preschooler up for engaging in preschool-appropriate chores through the use of positive affirmations. That way we can "catch them helping" and start the kindness feedback loop. For chores to be the most effective for preschoolers in terms of achieving our longer-term goals, they should be:

o simple,
o easily repeatable,
o highly visible (done around us so we can give them verbal positive reinforcement),
o easy to do while also being a bit of a challenge to master, and
o important to the family but not punished if not done.

As preschoolers become school age and older, we can continue to broaden their view of responsibility toward being an active member of their neighborhood, their school, their community, and ultimately, the world. Helping neighbors—such as offering to open the door for them, carry in groceries, water their plants when they're on vacation—is a nice first step, as well as being an active, helpful member of the school community (bringing in school supplies as needed for the classroom, taking part in classroom chores, and so on). To expand your child's reach, she can be part of helping the world through participating in things like clothing, toy, and food drives; volunteering at places like a nursing home or an animal shelter; and even raising money for a cause she is passionate about through a lemonade or cookie stand. With each year, we can continue to find creative ways to open up their understanding of the world around them and set the stage for their role in it.

PARENTING PRODUCTION NOTES
Make a Family Chore Chart

To achieve maximum buy-in, brainstorm different chores with your preschooler to find out what he thinks might be helpful, and then make a list and put his name on it. Remember: it's his responsibility to the family to help out around the house. No rewards necessary. To make the chore chart a family affair, you can also have a conversation about what you and your partner do to help out (cook dinner, pay bills, prepare lunch for the next day) and add your names to the list as well. To affirm and impact responsibility, we (including siblings) want to focus on being positive, empowering, and happy to accept the help. Here are some ideas for the types of preschooler chores you might include on your chore chart:

Preschooler Chores:

- Filling the water glasses at dinner: Fill up the water jug and be responsible for filling the water glasses. This is a great interactive activity that's done in the presence of other family members so the child can receive some positive affirmation while engaging in the chore. It's also a more difficult activity with room for her to grow and master it. Make sure the water pitcher isn't glass or fragile and that the water glasses are held down as the preschooler pours. It's fine for water to spill, but not for glass to break.

- Setting napkins on the table: Have cloth or paper napkins within easy reach and ask your preschooler to place one at each place setting. To turn it into a creative activity with paper napkins, challenge your child to find fun ways to fold and present the napkins.
- Putting folded laundry away: Make sure your child can safely reach drawers and shelves for his clothes and hand him a basket of clean, folded clothes. Challenge him to neatly put all his clothes—pajamas, shirts, pants, socks, and underwear—in the correct spot.
- Making her own bed: Start simple by showing her how to easily pull up the blanket or duvet cover and place the pillow and stuffed animals on top, and reinforce her bed making by asking her as she gets into bed each night, "Doesn't it feel good and cozy to climb into a neatly made bed?"
- Pouring out a pet's food: Show your preschooler how to pour dry food, scoop out wet food, and pour water for their pets' feeding areas. Their animals will naturally reaffirm your preschooler's act of help and kindness, as well as build his sense of responsibility, as your pets will come to know to go to your child for food.

Angela's Clues

Helping is a strong learning tool and it can become an invaluable part of your handy dandy parent notebook as you promote kindness, empathy, responsibility, and cooperation through modeling, asking for help, and in the media you choose to feed your kids. We want to be there for our kids to help them with their feelings and decision making while also nurturing in them a strong sense of intrinsic motivation, desire to help themselves, and the empowerment to know they can help others. We can do this in many different, and simple, ways—showing gratitude on Thanksgiving, helping around the house, and having empathy in times of need.

At the same time, we're also letting our preschoolers know we're there to help them, keep them safe, and teach them the skills they need in order to grow and learn. When we *look for the helpers*, as Fred did, we're reinforcing the powerful message that it takes a village . . . or a neighborhood.

- **Be Involved** and point out acts of kindness you see in the world around you.
- **Ask Questions,** especially this powerful one: *Will you help me?*
- **See the Spark** to notice your child engaging in acts of kindness and give them opportunities to be in a "giving role."

YOUR MEDIA "YES" LIST

☑ The characters demonstrate kindness toward themselves and each other.

☑ The majority of the show isn't modeling the "problem" (negative behaviors).

☑ My preschooler is inclined to be more helpful after watching the show.

Clue Takeaways

○ Helping supports our preschoolers to develop empathy.

○ Kids naturally *want* to help—it's how they're wired.

○ Asking children to help leads them to feel capable, confident, and smart.

○ Getting kids involved in helping builds their empathy.

○ Helping can be used to promote cognitive development and boost a sense of responsibility.

CLUE #8: MODEL

Modeling Shapes Our Preschooler's Behaviors and Experience

After Fred Rogers died in 2003, my heart literally hurt, and I knew I wanted to be part of promoting his legacy for future generations. So, when the Fred Rogers Company asked if I had any ideas as to what kind of show I could create that would do just that, I was ready.

Daniel Tiger's Neighborhood is an animated preschool series based on *Mister Rogers' Neighborhood*, where all the characters have grown up and have preschoolers of their own. Daniel Tiger wears a little red sweater and sneakers, and speaks directly to the home viewer. The show is based on Fred's curriculum, inspired by his music, and if you look closely, there are a ton of "nods of love," as we call them, to the original *Mister Rogers' Neighborhood*. Before we premiered, fans of the original show were understandably wary, but I promised that, as Fred's number one fan, I wouldn't let them down. Today, we still receive thank-you letters from people who appreciate the care we took in honoring Fred's legacy through our show. I even got a dream letter from Fred's wife, Joanne Rogers, saying, "When I hear from friends about how much Daniel Tiger is helping them in their lives, I can't help but feel proud. I am thrilled that all our hopes for *Daniel Tiger's Neighborhood* have come true AND THEN SOME!!! I know Fred would have been really proud of the show and of you, Angela."

Swoon.

THANK YOU FOR EVERYTHING YOU DO . . .

One such thank-you letter moved us to tears when we realized the far-reaching impact of what we were doing. "We've spent thousands of dollars on therapies, and countless hours at trial-and-error play dates. In spite of all that, I know just where the credit lies for my high-functioning autistic son's newfound ability to connect with others: Daniel Tiger." In July 2015, *The New York Times* printed Rasha Madkour's article, "Daniel Tiger Becomes a Boy with Autism's Guide to Social Life."[1] In it, Rasha writes about watching her son the first time she saw our show's "magic" in action.

As she describes it, her son was playing with a train set in the waiting room at their occupational therapist's office, oblivious to the fact that a nearby baby was crying out of desire for one of the trains. Rasha suggested her son share the trains, which he wasn't interested in doing until she sang him a strategy from Daniel Tiger: "Think about how someone else is feeling; maybe you can help them feel better." The next thing she knew, Rasha's son passed a train to the crying baby, who immediately settled down. Explains Rasha, "You could see the understanding dawn on my son's face as he watched the transformation. Then he smiled."

PRESCHOOLERS AS SPONGES

Preschoolers are commonly referred to as "sponges," as they seem to absorb all information and insight within arms' reach. In many ways, the analogy of a sponge is spot on: preschoolers soak up and learn from *everything* in their environment, whether new vocabulary words, the alphabet, or the lyrics to sing-along songs. In fact—and what's especially important for parents, caregivers, and teachers to realize— *everything* preschoolers see is fair game. They soak up what they see on television shows, advertisements, in games, and on websites, as well as what they see their family, friends, and teachers do. And they imitate what is modeled.

CLUE #8: MODEL

The notion that children imitate the behavior they observe was explored by social theorist Albert Bandura from Stanford University, when he conducted a series of famous experiences between 1961 and 1963 known as the "Bobo Doll" experiments.[2] The Bobo doll was a toy with a weighted bottom that, when punched or kicked, would right itself back up. Preschoolers between the ages of three and six were placed into two groups: those who watched someone model violence toward the Bobo doll and those who watched someone who modeled nonaggressive behavior toward the toy. To break it down even further, different children were exposed to different role models. Some preschoolers watched a live actor, others a short film of a live actor, and others saw a "cartoon-like" film of a live actor wearing a cat costume.

After observing their respective models, the preschoolers were given an "aggression stimulus" of being placed in a room with toys but being told they couldn't play with them, a situation the researchers knew would result in elevating their level of frustration. Now fully frustrated, the preschoolers were placed in another room with the Bobo doll from the experiment, as well as other toys that were categorized as either "aggressive" (such as dart guns and pounding boards) or "nonaggressive" (tea party sets, dolls). The results were astounding. It didn't matter which group they were in. Where aggressive behavior was modeled (a live person, a live person on film, or a "cartoon-like" film), the kids imitated the aggressive behavior.

Interestingly, the kids not only modeled what they saw, they added their own aggressive acts, and in some cases even used the toys in the room to further act violently, as well as be more aggressive with the other toys. This shows that preschoolers not only imitated the behavior they saw, but even scarier, they internalized or "mastered" the behavior by making it their own and using other toys to be aggressive with.

The truth is, preschoolers imitate what they see every day in their real lives, *and* they are just as likely to imitate what they see on screens, whether it be a live-action show or an animated cartoon. This realization brings cause for both concern and joy for creators of children's media, as well as parents and caregivers who choose media for their kids.

And because so many shows for young children are animated, it's even more important that adults realize the potential impact of the programs their children are watching. Since cartoons show situations and actions that we as adults know are pretend, many parents and caregivers assume there can't be any real consequences for their kids, good or bad. But preschoolers have a hard time differentiating between fantasy and reality. In actuality, animated preschool shows rooted in make-believe are just as influential to them as what they see happening in real life. In the end, *content matters*—what they see, how much they see it, and in what context.

PARENTS ARE THE STARS OF THEIR KIDS' WORLD

The good news is that preschoolers model who and what they love most. And who do they love the most? Who are they watching with the utmost interest? Who is the "star" of their lives?

Well, *we* are.

As parents, everything we say and do influences them—our words, what we eat, how we behave, how we talk to them, and what media we let them watch. And right behind us are our preschooler's friends— both real and animated. And these "peer models" can be both a godsend and a detriment to their learning about the world.

Though the common metaphor is that preschoolers are sponges, more accurate would be relating them to a sieve. Preschoolers are active in their process of modeling and learning. Like a sieve, they will take in information, use what is relevant to them through repeated exposure or positive feedback, and discard the rest. When they model behavior, they're taking cues from everyone around them and don't differentiate between behavior that's relevant, funny, interesting, or inappropriate. With gentle guidance in the form of social scaffolding, our preschoolers will learn how to best absorb and learn what's important information and discard the rest.

Case in point, when my daughter Hope was five, she announced to my husband, Greg, and me, "I would like to have a family meeting." She picked up our family meeting journal, sat herself down at the kitchen table, and gestured for us to join her. Like a judge, she nodded, opened the journal, and wrote a few letters and words, as if dictating her thoughts. Then in a slightly accusatory tone, she looked us in the eyes and calmly said, "We need to talk about what *happens* after Ella and I go to sleep. It seems that the parents are having some sort of snack party after we're in bed." Cue a loud gasp from her three-year-old sister.

Hope nodded to Ella in a "sisters unite" kind of way, and continued. "Yes, I saw both of you come upstairs with *cookies on a plate* and *mugs of tea*. And . . . the *television was on!*" Another gasp escaped from Ella, this time with the added drama of her little hands covering her mouth in shock.

Hope leaned in, stared fixedly at the two of us, and asked, "Were you having a snack party and watching television?! Without us?!"

Busted! We slowly nodded yes.

"Well, I'm not sure that is allowed during bedtime," she continued. "Let's discuss."

So, we discussed. We took this opportunity to talk about how adults have different privileges than kids, and that as adults, we have "adult time" after they go to bed, and sometimes that means we watch a little TV with a snack (or a glass of wine). Well, their minds were equally blown.

Hope was modeling how Greg and I broached important subjects we wanted to "discuss" with the kids. And as I'm sure you've experienced, watching your kids "act" like you, whether with a positive or negative portrayal, is eye-opening.

INTERACTIVE MODELING

Modeling in and of itself is effective when it comes to short-term learning. We see this on exhibit every day in the way our preschoolers take cues from the world around them. But in order for a behavior to stick and be mastered, it needs to be *interactively modeled*. In other words, our kids need to embrace it and interact with it.

The equation for a behavior to stick, long-term, takes into consideration the preschool child and what exactly is being modeled, by whom, and for how long. In the classroom, "interactive modeling" is preferred over traditional modeling because it shows kids why a skill they're learning is important, involves them in the process of learning by interacting with the teacher, enables them to watch their peers model the skill and practice the skill themselves, and provides them with feedback. As a result, preschoolers achieve greater, faster, and longer-lasting success.

We can replicate this same approach at home and get similar results. For example, we can model cleaning up our workspace after spending time working on a craft project. By talking with our child about what we're doing and enlisting her help, we're interacting with her in a way that activates her learning. Each time we finish working on our own craft projects, we continue to model putting things back where they belong, while simultaneously working with our child to encourage her to put her own craft supplies away. And all of this is done while offering positive, effort-focused feedback: "I like the way you chose to organize the crayons in the box. That is a very colorful pile of paper you've assembled there." Over time, this interactive modeling will lead to competency and confidence and learning the positive behaviors we're looking for.

The same goes for when we want to "un-stick" a *negative* behavior, such as aggression or sassy talk. We need to use the same model, but with a special focus on reinforcing the *positive* behaviors we want to see instead—in real life, through play, or by introducing a more positive media role model. For example, my friend's daughter was going through a particularly sassy phase, and so every time she said something sassy, my friend would lightheartedly pick up a pretend remote control to "rewind" the situation, giving her daughter the chance to try again in a more appropriate and respectful way. Then they would repeat the exchange, only this time her daughter would have dropped the sass, and my friend would say. "Oh, that feels so much better! I love responding to you when to talk to me so respectfully. High five!"

HAZARDOUS MODELING

One of the primary reasons why television has gotten a bad rap over the years is because of the awful stories splashed across the headlines about preschoolers imitating what they've seen on television with harmful and sometimes deadly results. One such tragic incident occurred in 2008, when a couple found their four-year-old daughter hanging by her hair band because, it was believed, she was trying to copy a stunt from her favorite series. Of course, there are many contributing factors to heartbreaking accidents like this one, but this story does shed light on just how worrisome the modeling of media can be. As parents, we must not only be aware of what our preschoolers are watching, but know how to guide them when they're inspired to play out the experiences they see, so they can do so in a safe way. Although this is hard story to write about, it is these types of stories that have motivated me—as a mother and as a creator—to make positive media for kids.

Superhero Violence

Some of the violence preschoolers encounter on television and in apps is superhero play. Superheroes are the best of the best in our preschoolers' eyes—they are revered by their peers, they save the day, *and* they wear cool costumes! Most preschoolers love to dress up like their favorite superheroes, and regularly interact with them via toys, books, music, and potentially even visits to their world, in real life, through amusement parks. Talk about *sticky* content. When a superhero uses a violent act on a "bad guy," he or she "wins the day" and is celebrated, over and over again.

Though we, as adults, understand that these superheroes are using their powers for good and that they engage in violence only in order to defeat the "bad guy," help someone, or fix a problem, preschoolers don't make this distinction. What they're seeing is the *behavior*. Behavior their admired, popular, charismatic heroes are acting out. And so it's both the good and the bad behavior that young viewers will absorb and model.

DIFFERENT KINDS OF HEROES

Introducing your preschoolers to "other" kinds of heroes, as well as looking at the idea of "superheroes" from different perspectives, will expand their definition of superhero and also give them plenty of positive role-models to emulate. Here are a few ideas:

- Get creative: Ask your preschooler to create their own superhero—one who can solve problems only through positive superpowers and actions.
- Find positive superheroes in the media: *Wild Kratts* ("superheroes" who save animals), *Super Why* (has the power to read), *WordGirl* (defeats bad guys through vocabulary).
- Introduce real-life heroes: Read biographies on presidents, innovators, sports heroes, music heroes, and others.
- Help your child identify *his or her* superpower: Encourage your preschooler to think about the things they do really well that can be helpful to them and other people (super-fast runner, super block constructor, super singer, super animal lover, super helper).

CLUE #8: MODEL

Long-term Effects of Violence in Media

Understanding and being mindful of the level of aggression our children encounter in their media becomes increasingly important as they get older. About 90 percent of movies include some depictions of violence, as do 68 percent of video games, 60 percent of TV shows, and 15 percent of music videos.[3] So how does the accumulation of all this violence affect our kids over the long term?

As cited in Common Sense Media's "Media and Violence" report, a study following children ages eight to nineteen showed that boys who viewed TV violence heavily at age six were more likely to manifest violent behavior at age nineteen.[4] The researchers revisited the same participants years later when they were thirty years old and found a correlation between early exposure to TV violence and self-reports of adult aggression,[5] including criminal behavior. It should be noted that this study controlled for the participants' initial aggressiveness, social class, and IQ but did not control for children's exposure to violence in the home, another variable thought to be a key contributor to violent behavior.[6] But despite this, the findings of this study are notable enough to give us reason to Pause and think critically about the content we're serving our preschoolers on a day-to-day basis.

Violence and Background Television

Even background television, or any screens that are left on and constantly playing, acting as the "background noise" to a child's life—has an effect on our preschoolers, even when they don't seem to be paying attention. In fact, children between eight and twenty-four months old are exposed to an average 5.5 hours of background TV per day, mostly adult television and the news. Preschoolers between two and four are exposed to an average of 4.4 hours. That's a lot of inappropriate content. Whether they're actively watching or not, preschoolers are affected via modeling.

Peer Modeling

As a creator of children's media, I take the responsibility for the content we put on the air very seriously. And because I studied (and have been scared by) the research on violence in the media, I've been inspired to take this influential nature of the media and the way kids model what they see in the media and use it to teach.

The characters in our preschoolers' favorite shows become our children's *peer models*. Everything they say and do becomes fodder for our kids to imitate. Peer models are aspirational, exciting, interesting, relevant to our kids' lives, and often very funny. Add in the interactive model of television, and our children become truly bonded and invested in these peer models as trusted friends and guides. And that's great, because our preschoolers' best friends in their favorite shows can become part of our parenting notebook for navigating tough situations with our kids.

Case in point, when Sesame Workshop put a sticker of their iconic character Elmo on an apple, researchers at Cornell University found that children ages eight to eleven were 65 percent more likely to add an apple to their lunch as compared to when the apples had no stickers.[7] One can only assume the numbers would have been even higher among preschoolers, the target audience for *Sesame Street*. Either way, the study proved that beloved characters can help to model behaviors—in this case, choosing healthy food.

The same year that the Elmo sticker study was released, we tapped into the power of positive food modeling for *Daniel Tiger's Neighborhood*. We had decided to write an episode dealing with the issue of *waiting*, and in trying to come up with a preschool appropriate context they could relate to, we thought, *What better spot to have our characters wait than at a restaurant?* As we were brainstorming in our script meeting about what Daniel should eat at the restaurant, we deliberated over choosing what preschoolers might typically choose (for example, chicken fingers and French fries) or featuring an aspirational choice (read: healthy and positive) for our preschool viewers to model.

Believe it or not, the topic of what Daniel Tiger should eat was hotly debated. Did we want preschoolers to feel like Daniel is "like them" and eats what they eat? Or did we want to use the influential nature of Daniel as our strong preschool "peer model" to raise the bar? We ended up going with the aspirational choice and, in the episode, Daniel Tiger orders a kid's meal of grilled chicken and broccoli. Our hope was that it would inspire our preschool viewers to make similar healthy choices. In fact, everywhere we can, we choose the "healthier" options for Daniel—his favorite breakfast is oatmeal with blueberries, and his favorite dessert is "banana swirl" (frozen banana smashed into an "ice cream" treat . . . so good!). For our Halloween episode, we even had our Neighbors in the Neighborhood of Make-Believe give out stickers instead of candy. We've been applauded for these efforts because kids are following in Daniel's footsteps.

Modeling Positive Anger Strategies

Preschoolers, of course, get frustrated or angry from time to time. (Can we say meltdown?) Luckily, our preschoolers' favorite characters as peer models are one of the clues we can pull out of our notebook to help temper those difficult situations. In one study, researcher Eric Ramussen of Texas Tech explored some of the *Daniel Tiger's Neighborhood* strategies to see if the skills like anger management, empathy, and conflict resolution that we depicted on the show did in fact *teach* those skills. What he found is that, yes, they do, and even more so when combined with parental interaction and reinforcement of the concepts.[8]

- -

MOM GETS MAD SOMETIMES, TOO

Daniel Tiger's strategies have been known to help parents, too. In our "Daniel Is Mad" episode, we showed Mom Tiger get angry. Showing Mom use the strategy was particularly powerful to our preschool audience. Case in point: my friend's preschool son, noticing his parents in a particularly heated conversation, proceeded to pull at his mom's shirt to get her attention. As she looked down, she noticed her son's wide, sad eyes as he sang Daniel's mad strategy song, hoping to diffuse the situation with his parents. Which it did.

. . . .

MODELING IN THE MEDIA

Understanding what types of modeling our preschoolers are learning in some of their favorite shows is important as we decide what behaviors we are comfortable with. Here is an example of the type of chart we would make for our characters when we create a show. We think about the type of humor we will model, how they will talk to the home viewer, what their favorite foods are, how they would role play our show, etc. Add your own shows and ask yourself these very same questions.

Character	Show	Conflict resolution	Humor approach	How they talk to kids	Play
Steve	*Blue's Clues*	Finds clues	Hide and seek	Respectful	Games
Daniel Tiger	*Daniel Tiger's Neighborhood*	Sings strategies	Imagination	Best friend	Dramatic play
Super Why	*Super Why!*	Reading power	Finding book characters	Smart	Superhero
WordGirl	*WordGirl*	Vocabulary	Wordplay / slapstick	Confident	Superhero
Curious George	*Curious George*	Investigating	Slapstick	Silly	Monkey play
Arty	*Creative Galaxy*	Art	Epiphany	As an artist	Crafts
Bianca	*Wishenpoof*	Executive functioning	Wish magic	Problem solver	Fairy play
Odd Squad	*Odd Squad*	Math	Slapstick	Friend	Detective

SO WHAT DO WE DO? MODELING, IN REAL LIFE

So, how do we use what we know about modeling in our real, everyday parenting lives? In addition to citing our preschoolers' "friends" on television and using what they do to reinforce the behaviors we like, we can also examine our own behaviors and see what we are modeling for our kids versus what we are saying.

What We Say Versus What We Do

o Effectively modeling is a very visual and iterative process. When we scream "Don't YELL!" while yelling, we are modeling—you guessed it—*yelling.*

o When we say, "Eat healthy," while we chow down a bag of chips and a soda for a snack, we are modeling eating junk food.

o When we say, "Be kind to your sister," while simultaneously lashing out at a family member, we are modeling the exact opposite behavior we want to see in our child.

So, as the "star" of our preschoolers' lives, it's imperative to be clear on this point: it's what we do and not what we say that has a lasting impact on our children.

PARENTING PRODUCTION NOTES
Use Modeling as a Tool to Encourage Positive Behavior

Modeling is one of the most powerful clues in our handy dandy parent notebook. But in order to use this tool effectively, we need to take into consideration *how* we model behaviors, with what *content*—morals and values we agree with, or violent/aggressive content—and in what *context* our preschoolers are learning from modeling, both at home and through the media.

Positive Behavior	Ideas for Positive Modeling for Parents
Kindness	• Pick something up off the floor when you see it there. • Say please and thank you. • Look strangers in the eye. • Talk positively about people. • Deliver groceries to a sick friend or neighbor.
Healthy Eating	• Eat what you want your kids to eat. • Drink water instead of soda. • Model a healthy plate. • Don't eat in front of the TV.
Conflict Resolution	• When upset, taking a deep breath. • Take a walk to calm down. • Talk about what happened. • Apologize and take responsibility for your emotions. • Model debating without judgment, shame, or blame.
Talking About Feelings	• Talk about how you're feeling in a preschool appropriate way • Label your feelings, using a variety of rich words to describe how you feel (exhausted, famished, overjoyed, etc.). • If appropriate, express why you are feeling the way you are.

Positive Behavior	Ideas for Positive Modeling for Parents
Talking and Listening	• Interact and talk with your child about preschool-appropriate topics. • Listen with your full attention (active listening) and encourage your child to share thoughts openly. • Respond non-judgmentally to your preschooler's thoughts and ideas.
Independence	• Give them some ownership of things around the house (chores). • Regularly show them you are capable, and independent (let them see you work, write thank-you notes, cook, read). • Trust your preschooler ("I know you can do it" versus "Don't drop your plate!").
Failure	• Acknowledge that you don't know everything and show them it's okay to ask for help or find out the answers you need to know. • Let them see you fail and remind them that this is how you learn. • Be transparent with your difficult emotions such as disappointment, frustration, and sadness. • Get back up, and try again.

Angela's Clues

As "sponges" and "sieves," our kids interact with what's around them as they form their own opinions about what's appropriate behavior and what is not. As their parents and caregivers, we are a critical part of that iterative, interactive process that will help cement our preschoolers' ideas and ideals as they grow. At this important time in their lives when we have the most influence, we are planting seeds and setting the stage for the teen years and beyond. If we do the work now, we will reap what we sow with positive, engaged, kind, open, interested and involved kids who are bonded to us and our family.

Since we are our preschoolers' biggest influencers, modeling through interactive family bonding activities can lead to mastery of those behaviors we deem most important. For example, when we do a family craft, our children are learning interactively on so many levels. We're modeling the value of being together, laughing, and letting go of stress. Even better, we're creating a space to talk about and model our hopes, wishes, morals, values, and future goals for our family. Instead of lecturing or pounding kids over the head with what we believe, making the time for fun family activities creates the perfect opportunity to learn more about how our child sees the world while giving us the space to talk about own feelings and views of the world. Here are some my family's favorites:

Wish Jar

1. Everyone in the family has their own jar for collecting wishes (we use Mason jars, but any sort of jar or even a small box will do).
2. Everyone writes or draws a "wish" for each member of the family and places it in their jar (including themselves). Some of our best wishes have been: always have Sunday dinners; go on a family beach vacation; learn Italian; write a song; learn how to sew.
3. Everyone reads the wishes in their jar aloud!

Thankful Tree

1. Buy a small pine tree (the kind you can find in a supermarket).
2. Have everyone write at least one thing they are "thankful for" on small pieces of paper (the more the better!).
3. Fold the notes and tape them to the branches.
4. At a special dinner, read them aloud!

Vision Board

1. Get one or more pieces of large poster board.
2. Gather some old magazines, copies of favorite photos, construction paper, markers, crayons, pencils, and glue or glue sticks.
3. Have everyone cut out or draw pictures that represent their "vision" and make individual vision board collages (or make a giant family collage). "Visions" are for a specific time frame: the upcoming school year, for vacation time, who they want to be when they grow up, etc.
4 Have everyone share their boards.

• •

- **Be Involved** and know that everything we do is modeling for our child.
- **Ask Questions** to discover your child's innate sense of values.
- **See the Spark** to notice the behaviors your child is modeling.

• •

YOUR MEDIA "YES" LIST

☑ The characters model positive behaviors (and don't engage in sassy talk).

☑ My child models positive behaviors after viewing (i.e., cleaning up, sharing, applying coping strategies, using expressive language, etc).

☑ My child wants to emulate their favorite characters (and I'm okay with that!)

☑ The theme of the show reflects my family's values and dreams.

• •

Clue Takeaways

○ What we do is more influential than what we say, and our preschoolers are always watching.

○ Modeling is a powerful tool for promoting kindness, healthy eating, positive conflict-resolution strategies, social-emotional literacy, and independence, as well as how to handle failure and setbacks (by grown-ups modeling positive anger management).

○ Engaging in family activities is a great way to consciously model your family's values, morals, hopes, and dreams.

CLUE #9: OBSERVE

Finding the Extraordinary in the Ordinary
Can Spark Our Preschoolers' Passion

As overzealous parents living in New York City, Greg and I couldn't wait to share the Macy's Thanksgiving Day Parade with our daughter Hope when she was three years old. This was doubly special for me, as I was bringing my daughter for the first time to see the giant balloon of our favorite puppy, Blue, beyond a lifelong dream come true. We bundled her up to protect her from the chilly November breeze and maneuvered our way to the front of the huge mass of people who came, as they do every year, to watch the balloons and floats slowly make their way down Broadway. We were so excited to have front-row "seats" as we sat on the cold ground with Hope in our laps. I'm honestly not sure who was more excited—me, my husband, or our little girl— as we clapped and swayed to the music. I got misty-eyed when Blue floated by as a huge balloon, and I pointed and cheered to make sure Hope felt like she was a part of our excitement.

When the parade was over, we asked Hope what she liked best about the parade. Seeing all the balloons? The floats? The marching? Blue as a balloon? So, what did my daughter tell me she liked best? In classic form, embracing the literalness that is a preschooler, Hope responded, "The cold!"

What?! My two-year-old was most excited about being out in the cold? She smiled and continued, "And when I was cold, you would hold me tight-tight-tight and I would get warm!" To Hope, it wasn't about the parade, it was about the ordinary, everyday idea that we were together.

Another time was when we were leaving for our very first family vacation with both Hope, then five, and Ella, three. We woke them up at five in the morning to head to the airport in the comfy clothes they had slept in (exciting in its own right—sleeping in your *clothes*?!). We carried them to the car and gently placed them in the backseat, where we'd already set up a cozy blanket and a yummy early-morning snack. It was still dark out as my three-year-old, snuggling up to me in the backseat (Mom in the backseat? Exciting, too!), said with a huge smile on her face, "This is the best vacation EVER!" We hadn't even pulled out of the driveway yet.

The world is anything but ordinary to preschoolers. That fallen leaf we just walked by? *Extraordinary!* That annoying orange light flashing on the dashboard? *Amazing!* The sound of Velcro being ripped apart we didn't even notice? *Incredible!* The truth is, preschoolers don't need a big Macy's Thanksgiving Day Parade or a fancy vacation. They are happy to just be hugged by you to "stay warm" or even just to sit comfy cozy in the backseat of the car. What's mundane to an adult is anything but to a preschooler.

EVERYTHING IS A FIRST

So what is it about the ordinary that makes it so extraordinary to our preschoolers? The simple answer is that the world is one enormous set of "firsts" to our preschoolers. Just as babies learn by touching, feeling, and putting everything in their mouths, preschoolers need to explore, touch, play, and ask questions in order to fully absorb and learn. Amy Dombro, friend and author of *The Ordinary Is Extraordinary*, compares this to watching a new baby discover he has hands for the first time. Because, come on . . . hands are fascinating! Babies spend an exorbitant amount of time exploring with their hands—looking at them, turning them into little fists, sucking on them, and then ultimately discovering, through trial and error, that they can soothe themselves by sucking on their fists. The ordinary of little hands is extraordinary to babies discovering them for the first time.

Though they've learned a lot about their bodies and the world in their first two years of life, preschoolers are still very much little explorers. And while they learned through the trial and error of discovery as babies, they now have their minds set on learning by *doing*. Preschoolers learn best through active play and meaningful experiences during which they have the time and space for hands-on explorations and the opportunity to ask questions of us.

What makes up a meaningful experience? Dombro states that "everyday life" is the most valued time with the best opportunities for learning. That means that the small things, the routines, and the mundane tasks, are actually the ones filled with the most learning opportunities. (And by the way, this type of learning doesn't end in preschool!) Things we do every day—things we do mindlessly as part of a routine and things we simply take for granted—are new for preschoolers and give them important information about how to act and be a part of the world outside of themselves. This means that everyday activities such as going to the store, answering the phone, writing, working from home, doing the laundry, and cleaning up around the house, are all chock-full of educational opportunities. As Dombro says, "The mundane is new, unclassified territory and it's magical."[1]

Making the most of every day is the cornerstone of a child-centered, "ordinary is extraordinary" preschool philosophy. What's interesting to me is that we see this in the plethora of popular YouTube videos. Think about it—many of the most popular videos found online are also the most mundane. For example, "un-boxing" videos (watching someone take apart the box of a new toy or game), how-to videos on applying makeup or hairstyling or cooking, gaming videos showing someone play a video game, and even videos where people show what's inside their beach bag or give a tour of the products they use in the shower. Even as we age, we are still explorers at heart, wanting to get a glimpse inside other people's everyday lives—and it's still a valuable learning experience.

THE CHILD-CENTERED APPROACH

As adults we may take much of what we see and experience in our daily lives for granted. The philosophy of "the ordinary is extraordinary" and a child-centered approach sees the value of observing our preschoolers and being in tune with who they are, so we can be a better support and guide. Similar to attachment parenting and a child-centered approach to a preschool classroom, this "ordinary is extraordinary" philosophy places an importance on understanding the individual nature of each child.

Child development theory gives us the foundation for understanding preschoolers at this stage of development. We know the universal aspects of the way preschoolers think, the way they learn, and the lens through which they see the world. Yet observing our preschoolers opens the door to understanding their individual differences that will shape, color, and determine who they will become and how they will make their mark on the world.

Understanding that the preschool years form the foundation of human development, our child-centered approach is focused on understanding the main tenets of our child-centered preschool philosophy:

- o Understanding the way preschoolers *think*: literally, concretely, and actively.
- o Understanding the way preschoolers *learn*: through play and meaningful experiences.
- o Seeing what makes preschoolers *excited*: with awe, wonder, and curiosity.

Literal Preschoolers

When adults and caregivers remember that preschoolers think differently than we do, and when we respect the fact that they are *always* thinking, we can better understand what makes them tick and why certain aspects of logic don't work on them.

Understanding how incredibly literal preschoolers are made the challenge of figuring out what to name our characters on *Blue's Clues* much simpler. Rooted in this idea, we named our mailbox Mailbox. And the side table drawer? She was named Side Table Drawer. We had a clock named Tickety Tock, salt and pepper shakers named Mr. Salt and Mrs. Pepper, a bar of soap named Slippery Soap, a shovel and pail named . . . you guessed it. And of course, there was Blue, a blue puppy. Let's just say that preschoolers knew the names of our characters after just one viewing.

The literalness of preschoolers has its obvious drawbacks. Preschoolers may sometimes come across as stubborn, but there's a reason for that. Many times, it's because they are still working out the cognitive connections between what we're saying, what they need to do, and how to articulate it. It's hard and active work.

Since much of what we say is both literal and figurative, preschoolers just learning language tend to focus on the true, literal meaning of words and have a hard time seeing this second layer of meaning. For instance, the first time we suggest to our preschooler that they "hop in the bathtub" or "jump into their PJs," many will stop in their tracks to think about it. Yes, they know how to "hop," so do we actually want them to "hop" in the tub? To make matters worse, if they *did* hop in the tub, we'd be upset and worried about their safety. Of course, once they know what these figurative statements mean, they will definitely want to be in on the joke—having them attempt to actually "jump" into their PJs or even "hop" in the tub will be so funny. Understanding their concrete view of the world helps us ensure that the words and vocabulary we use are direct, specific, and comprehensible by preschoolers.

PARENTING PRODUCTION NOTES

Get Literal with Your Language

What Not to Say	What to Say
"Throw it in the garbage."	"Please put your wrapper in the garbage."
"Run to the store."	"Let's get in the car to go to the store."
"I have an upset stomach."	"I'm not feeling well and my tummy hurts."
"Jump into bed."	"Get into bed and snuggle under the covers."

OH, THOSE LITERAL PRESCHOOLERS!

Misinterpreted Phrases, Said to Kids

Let's carpool!	→	Pool in a car?
Potty training	→	Is it a potty train?
The band is coming to play!	→	With my toys?
Jump to it.	→	Jump?
Hop on in.	→	Hop?
Making me crazy	→	Crazy?
Patience is draining.	→	Draining how?

Keeping Preschoolers Preschoolers

Sounds ordinary, right? But this idea of keeping kids young for as long as possible is *extraordinary*, since fully embracing and experiencing this once-in-a-lifetime moment reveals what intrinsically motivates our preschoolers as they hop and skip from one play to another. As preschoolers, they innately take in information they're hungry for, and we can recognize their level of comprehension and their thirst for more information in the way they play. But when we push for our preschoolers to be older than they are—emotionally *or* cognitively—we're taking away this critical period of self-exploration. Instead, we can savor this time by staying cognizant of the media we offer so we can keep them in play mode and not thrust them into a harsher reality. A silly analogy, but one I've definitely used on numerous occasions with my own girls: just because they can *fit* their feet into my shoes doesn't mean they should be *wearing* them. Four-inch heels at thirteen years old!

As an educational media advocate, I feel strongly that preschoolers should stay preschoolers, especially with the media they consume. Certain television shows, movies, books, games, and background television featuring news and adult-oriented shows will only confuse and emotionally upset our little ones. In following a child-centered philosophy, we want to open up the world to our kids a little bit at a time *and* ensure that they're emotionally, physically, and cognitively ready for everything we're exposing them to. And by the way, this is a philosophy well worth sticking with all the way up through adulthood. For instance, when my daughter Hope was ten years old, there was a lot of pressure among her friends to read *The Hunger Games*. I personally devoured the book and knew Hope had the *ability* to read it, but I also knew that *emotionally* she wasn't ready for the dark subject matter. So, we held off for a few years.

Of course, no parent would be lulling their preschooler to sleep with Katniss Everdeen bedtime stories, but this example speaks to a bigger issue: the idea that pushing more mature subject matter on our kids at younger and younger ages has somehow become in vogue and is treated as if it's a signifier of just how smart a child is. Interestingly, I've even noticed an uptick in this type of pressure from teachers and other parents, which I find peculiar considering the fact a child's future success isn't determined by their intelligence, but rather how robust their level of grit and passion.

What's Extraordinary About Everyday Life

During the preschool years, one of our more important jobs is building a foundation of "ordinary" behaviors—such as sleeping, eating, and play—that have a profound impact on our child's development. For example, preschoolers need between eleven and thirteen hours of sleep each night. Although an ordinary activity, its importance is extraordinary. Getting enough sleep is critical for optimal brain growth and a child's healthy mental and physical development, while lack of sleep may contribute to behavioral issues. The research on healthy eating shows a similarly important role in a child's optimal growth and development.

To help preschoolers discover the extraordinary aspect of this ordinary part of life, Ellyn Satter, in her book *How to Get Your Kid to Eat: But Not Too Much*, suggests stocking the refrigerator and snack drawer with only "yes" foods so preschoolers can tap into their innate sense of exploration by trying different foods and making their own choices.[2] We can apply the same approach to clothes by filling drawers and closets only with "yes" clothes options, and fill our DVRs with only "yes" programs so our preschoolers can explore their own tastes and styles, independently.

THE PASSIONATE PRESCHOOLER

When considering the most intelligent thinkers in history, many people conjure up an image of Albert Einstein. And while, yes, Einstein was known for his high intellect, what drove him to be the influential scientist he was wasn't actually his IQ—it was his *passion*. In fact, as a child and student, Einstein didn't appear to be remarkable at all; his teachers reportedly said he was "mentally slow" and always "lost in thought." A 1985 study entitled "On the Brain of a Scientist: Albert Einstein" described how a dissection of Einstein's brain showed he was essentially the same as any other person. But what differentiated his brain from others was a higher than usual number of glial cells, which are the cells that form synaptic connections. These connections resulted from meaningful experiences that were grounded in his passion for learning and his out-of-the-box thinking.[3] What's so fascinating about these results is the knowledge that we too can strengthen our brain development through hard work and intrinsic motivation fueled by *passion*.

And so can our children. In fact, the preschool years are the best time to incite, foster, and nourish a passion. For these impressionable children, the high level of development and focus on play, sets the stage. And for many of us, personal experience would confirm this. How many of us had passion experiences or "a-ha!" moments as young children only to continue exploring that passion today? As parents, we need to be on the lookout for these "a-ha" moments and then be there to affirm, nurture, and support by providing ample time to play, materials, and experiences that can deepen the learning.

Research on the long-lasting effects of interests and passions culti-vated in childhood points to the possibility that such experiences, es-pecially when fostered by others, may in fact affect a child's decisions for life.[4] One of the key factors is the presence of an "anchor relation-ship," which is defined as a person who affirms and supports a child's passion. These anchor relationships are an important and influential contributor to helping a child foster that desirable trait—intrinsic mo-tivation.[5]

Play as a Tool for Exploring Passion

One of the most powerful and simplest ways to encourage our pre-school children's exploration of their passion is to allow for adequate amounts of free play. Play is the work of the child, not to mention a fantastic tool for us as parents and caregivers. Giving our preschool-ers time to play and ourselves time to observe them in their play helps us understand what makes them tick, what problems they're grap-pling with, what vocabulary they have, what they're interested in, and their level of creativity. It can also give us fantastic clues as to areas where they are sparked. When our preschoolers are highly engaged in an area of play, we can use scaffolding to fully awaken their sense of passion and build their intrinsic motivation. To do this, we take what our preschoolers love and provide more and more levels of play through providing materials and additional resources to continue fu-eling the fire.

PARENTING PRODUCTION NOTES
Look for the Passion Stages and Creatively Support Their Passion

- A-Ha!: Keep an eye out for the "a-ha" moment, which is that moment the interest is first "sparked" and the excitement and intrinsically-motivated play begins.
- Nurture: Affirm the interest and support and nurture through materials, new experiences, education, and time.
- Play: Support and affirm a preschooler's continuing of their passion play on their own, because of their internal drive and motivation and enjoyment in doing it.

Here are some ideas for how to take a preschooler's area of interest and support their passion around it through experiences and projects:

Your Preschooler's Interest	Experiences	Projects
Nature	Walks	Make a nature journal; collect leaves and glue them in a construction paper homemade book or make leaf prints.
Math	Sculpture gardens	Count, do tallies, charts, and tabulations of what you see in a sculpture park.
Drawing	Museums	Create your own museum artwork using crayons, markers, paints, illustrations, etc.
Reading	Library outings	Make a book, read books, write about books.
Dress-up	Children's theater or dance performances	Make costumes, have a costume parade, write scripts for superhero play, firefighter play, doctor play, house play, mystery play, etc.

PASSION THAT LASTS A LIFETIME

Interestingly, many adults who discovered their passion early on report they weren't very good at it initially, but because of how much they loved it, they continued to work at it and develop their skills. As parents, we want to provide support but be careful not to cross the line and turn the passion into "work"—with extrinsic consequences and extrinsic motivation. An extreme example of this would be a child who loves dramatic play and acting being pushed into work as a child actor; or a child who shows real passion and talent for sports pressured to be the best and become highly competitive. No surprise here: responses like these are often a fast-track pass to blowing out the spark of the passion.

On the other hand, support and guidance without pressure can yield a much better result. Take Eric Carle for example, world-renowned writer and illustrator (*The Very Hungry Caterpillar* and many others), who found his passion in kindergarten. Carle's teacher was so impressed by his talent that she displayed his signed artwork all around the classroom. When he was just five years old, she encouraged him to keep drawing and asked his mother to nurture and respect his interest and talent. In interviews, Carle has said that his parents provided him with art materials, encouraged him, and "showed off" his work whenever possible, support he considers to be the most important "door" that opened for his future career as one of the most influential and successful children's book authors and illustrators.[6]

Perhaps my favorite story of passion sparked young is about Gillian Lynne, one of the most accomplished choreographers of our time, choreographing *Cats* and *Phantom of the Opera*. When Gillian was eight years old in the 1930s, her teachers contacted her mother because they were concerned about her inability to turn in homework on time, her poor test scores, and her constant fidgeting and need to move. Her teachers believed she had a learning disability, so her mother brought her to a psychologist for testing. The psychologist asked a lot of questions of Gillian's mother and then simply observed the young girl.

The psychologist had a hunch as to what was going on, so he let Gillian know he needed speak to her mother privately outside the room. Before he stepped out, he turned on the radio. As soon as they were in the hallway, the psychologist asked Gillian's mother to watch her daughter. Almost immediately, Gillian began moving around the room to the music, an expression of pure pleasure on her face. The doctor turned to the mother, saying, "Gillian isn't sick. She's a dancer. Take her to dance school." Once there, Gillian was thrilled to be around people like her, people who had to move to think. Eventually, Gillian went to the Royal Ballet School in London before going on to collaborate with Andrew Lloyd Webber on some of the most successful musical theater shows of all time. As an eight-year-old girl, Gillian may not have realized that dancing was her passion, but someone took the time to look into her eyes and read the signs.

Michael Phelps, the most decorated Olympian of all time with twenty-eight medals, has ADHD and hyperactivity. His mother, Debbie Phelps, has been a strong advocate of her son's educational nurturing, supporting, and affirming his needs and passions. She says, "ADHD kids have great passion—it just needs to be funneled." Smartly, she saw the signs and made a conscious decision to harness her child's passion in the pool. When Michael didn't like getting his face wet, she turned him over and showed him the backstroke, and his swimming career took off. And the rest, as they say, is history.

EXTEND THE LEARNING

Staying true to the interactive nature of how preschoolers learn through play, we want to extend the learning by offering materials and media that interests them. Our goal is to spark our kids, but how?

Conversations

Conversations centered on our preschooler's interests continue their exploration as they grow and, as such, their interests widen and deepen. For instance, if our preschooler is collecting leaves, we can help ignite a spark by affirming their interest, asking questions about them, showing an interest ourselves, and brainstorming ideas with them for extending the learning with leaves. Igniting the spark of their interests will lead to more conversations, more learning, and will ignite a passion, perhaps in this example, for environmental science.

Meaningful Experiences

Taking note of how interesting preschoolers find the world, we can turn ordinary everyday outings into meaningful excursions. A walk around the block or a hike through the woods could be a nature walk; a trip to the local farm could evolve into a rich conversation about how food gets onto our plates; a trip to the bakery could spark a conversation about how bread is made; a trip to the post office could incite curiosity about how mail gets sent. We can take our musically inclined child to a recital or performance or our outer-space-obsessed child to peek through a neighbor's telescope to spark them.

When we go somewhere . . . *anywhere*, really . . . with a preschooler, it's always more about the journey itself than the destination. Making the most of even the simplest experiences by being present, asking (and answering!) questions, and initiating conversations with our preschoolers creates valuable learning time and grows their brains, hearts, and feelings of self-respect. Think of it as the new the recipe for happiness. As Steve Jobs said: "The journey is the reward."

In addition to leaning into the magic of simple yet meaningful experiences, we can also proactively embrace the power of the ordinary is extraordinary to help our preschoolers when they're having a hard day or are emotionally dysregulated. When her son was a feisty, differently wired preschooler grappling with very big and intense emotions, my coauthor Debbie used to regularly take him to spots in nature to play the "senses game." Together, they'd focus on one sense at a time and see what they could observe (sounds, smells, sights) as a mindful meditation of sorts. By noticing and connecting with what was *extraor-*

dinary all around them, she also helped her son develop self-calming skills and feel more grounded and less anxious. Plus, it created special bonding moments for the two of them.

Make Time for Nothing!

When we Pause to let our preschoolers make time for ordinary everyday activities, like coloring, dramatic play, or picking up rocks, we are giving them room to figure things out through trial and error. When our preschoolers are taking part in imaginative play they are, in a sense, visualizing what they want to create. And according to creativity and motivation expert Daniel Pink, visualizing something makes it much more likely that it will be created. By combining play and visualization, creative thoughts and imagination join forces in a vivid way, and the results for our children can be powerful. This is especially because creative pursuits, such as the right brain's artistry, empathy, inventiveness, and big-picture thinking, are just as important as left brain's logical, linear abilities. When preschoolers play, they're naturally engaging both sides of their brain while creating and imagining their way to future success.

Chris and Martin Kratt (a.k.a. the Kratt Brothers), who create the popular PBS Kids shows *Kratts Creatures* and *Wild Kratts*, said their favorite activity growing up was exploring animals in nature in their backyard in New Jersey! Now, they've made a life of exploring animals all over the world and sharing them with preschoolers through their shows. Their spark turned into a passion and their passion is contagious!

Take a Moment to Observe

As parents, taking a moment to *observe* what our preschoolers are seeing through their eyes will give us great insight into their interests, which will, of course, incite their passion in life. We can observe what sparks them, what they're doing (think of Gillian and her dancing or Michael and his swimming), what words they use, what props they play with (Eric Carle's drawings), what makes them laugh, and what excites them. We can extend the learning by affirming their interests and providing opportunities to further what excites them—with books, dance classes, paints, dress-up clothes, or even the pool!

On my shows, we've modeled each of these areas of extending the learning through the way our characters communicate with each other (and the viewer), have meaningful experiences, make time for playing and exploring, and observe to get more information. By modeling this in different ways, we're hoping to spark a passion for something new and inspire kids to go out and find their own passions.

On *Creative Galaxy*, our main character, Arty, is innately empathetic and extremely observant of his friends. For example, in one episode he notices how much his friend Annie loves flowers and his friend Juju loves rainbows, but when Annie finds out that flowers make her sneeze and that Juju keeps missing the rainbows in nature, he wants to help. Arty searches the Creative Galaxy to find out how he can make flowers out of paper that won't make Annie sneeze and a huge rainbow for hanging in a window that will catch the light and reflect a beautiful myriad of color for Juju. Observing and noticing will help evoke empathy, creatively solve a problem, and incite a passion.

In one *Wishenpoof* episode, we tackled self-directed learning, one of the seven executive function skills kids need in life. Miss Bridget, Bianca's teacher, tells the class that she wants them to explore their own "Passion Project"—discover what excites them, research it, and create something to showcase their passion. Armed with this mission, Bianca, who is enamored with space, researches what she could create. She then resorts to play, and using her wish magic, wishes up a rocket that takes her and her sidekick Bob to space to visit the planets. She takes a rocket ship ride, slides down Saturn's rings, and notices the red dust on Mars, along the way learning why it's red. Further inspired, Bianca looks up on a tablet how to make a bottle rocket that will blast off using baking soda, and then models asking for guidance from her dad to actually make it. Once she makes her rocket, Bianca proudly shares her passion project with the class, singing her anthem "What's Your Passion?" while also showcasing the other kids' passions—ant colonies, volcanoes, and even pickle electricity! Every little detail of this episode was created to show how to delve deeper and learn more about a passion—using books and computers, playing and exploring, asking for help from an adult, and hands-on creating.

· ·

NO OBVIOUS PASSION? NO PROBLEM

Don't panic if you haven't yet "seen the spark" in your preschooler. Sometimes it's just a small spark. It's subtle. It's about what they love to do. It's noticing how much they love to play with baby dolls or cars or sing or kick a ball or cook with you. Adding props or materials and providing ample time to do what they love will extend the learning and add to the spark.

· ·

EVERYDAY ACTIVITIES THAT SPARK

If everyday experiences are valuable, what *exactly* can we do to make them meaningful? We can make a "game" out of the *ordinary* like going to the grocery store and make it *extraordinary* by giving them a list of three things they need to find (while in the cart with us). Like our interactive games on my shows, we can ask them to point to the milk when they see it, or have them look for more challenging objects like kale or avocadoes. We can even challenge them to match the words for items they may not know visually, encouraging them to carefully "read" and search for the items: olives, pickles, carrots, celery. Other fun learning games you could try at the grocery store include letting them handle the money at the register (math), guessing how much money all the groceries will cost (estimation, understanding about money), or ordering the lunch meat or cheese at the deli counter (vocabulary, public speaking).

We can use this same type of approach with so many everyday activities—going to the bank (estimating how long the wait in line will be, trying to walk only on a certain style of floor tile, asking them to "help" fill in a deposit slip), taking public transport (reading transit maps, counting how many stops, playing I Spy with the advertisements), taking the recyclables out (separating glass, plastic, and paper; sorting or depositing in the right bins; returning bottles to the store in exchange for change or credit; talking about the environment), and so much more. When you think about it, as long as we have things to do and errands to run, the possibilities for maximizing engagement in everyday activities are endless.

PARENTING PRODUCTION NOTES
Look for the Learning on Everyday Activities

Activity		Learning
Folding laundry	→	matching, sorting
Putting dishes in dishwasher	→	math, categorizing
Grocery shopping	→	math, literacy, planning, predicting
Computer work	→	writing, drawing, learning games
Cooking	→	math, literacy, measuring, science
Walking the dog	→	relationship between animals and people
Dusting	→	science, where does dust come from
Watering the garden	→	nature, plants, botany
Depositing a check	→	economics, budgets
Putting on sunscreen	→	solar energy, outer space, light and heat

Channeling the "ordinary is extraordinary" helps us write successful shows for preschoolers, ensuring that the storylines, characters, dialogue, and humor are specifically written *just for them*. We write and create to empower and challenge preschoolers to widen their world and see what excites them. As the saying goes, media is a "window into the world"—it is opening the door to different cultures, characters, and storylines. But in media, we're not only looking to model different curricular areas—we're also hoping to set a foundation for future learning, mastery, and passion for the budding scientists, innovators, problem solvers, leaders, and future presidents we know are in our audience. For example, by having Daniel Tiger use his imagination in every episode, our goal is to provide examples of a passion for creative thinking, storytelling, and curiosity. When he learns how to ride a bike, we're showcasing resilience and asking questions with curiosity and passion.

On *Super Why*, Whyatt transforms into a superhero with the "Power to Read" because of his awe, wonder, and insatiable desire to know "Why." Arty on *Creative Galaxy* is passionate about art and shows his excitement by learning from art masters—such as Kandinsky, Seurat, and Van Gogh—and applying that knowledge to creating artworks and "masterpieces!" in his real life that solve problems. We know that passion is contagious, and sparking passion in our preschoolers at home, through our characters, is one of our goals in every show and episode.

Angela's Clues

There is nothing I love more than seeing a preschooler's face light up when something sparks them. When they have a question or make an observation, it's like a window into their minds. Affirming our preschoolers' thinking and ideas will engage our kids and entice them to explore their passions, preschool-style, and continue to play, try new things, and practice failing and trying again. These abilities are, in the long run, even more important than natural talent.

When it comes to embracing the "ordinary is extraordinary" aspect of childhood as a clue in our handy dandy parenting notebook, our end game is to nurture children to be intrinsically motivated. When our preschoolers find joy in learning, being curious, and feeling connected to their areas of passion, they'll be fueling their own fulfilling, successful future (and they'll never stop learning).

CLUE #9: OBSERVE

- **Be Involved** to observe your preschooler in everyday situations.
- **Ask Questions** to find out what they are excited about.
- **See the Spark** to witness the extraordinary and deepen the learning of what they love.

YOUR MEDIA "YES" LIST

- ☑ The storylines, characters, dialogue, and humor are written specifically for preschoolers.
- ☑ The themes and characters regularly offer a "window to the world."
- ☑ The show presents a variety of interests, activities, and possibilities.
- ☑ My child is "sparked" by some aspect of the show.

Clue Takeaways

- ○ There's tremendous value in letting preschoolers be preschoolers.
- ○ Providing materials and opportunities based on your preschooler's interests encourages open-ended, imaginative, and hands-on deeper learning and play.
- ○ Talking with our preschoolers about the little things as we go about our day respects their preschool perspective and experience.
- ○ We can parent in a child-centric way by embracing new experiences, modeling curiosity, discovery, novelty, risk taking, and trial and error.
- ○ We can spark our preschoolers' passion by tapping into his natural excitement that comes through with awe, wonder, and curiosity.

Laugh, Sing, Celebrate

CLUE #10: ENJOY

Singing and Laughing Makes Parenting Easier

Hope, age three: "Knock-knock."
Me: "Who's there?"
Hope: "Wendy."
Me: "Wendy who?"
Hope: "Wendy, my friend!" Erupts into hysterical laughter.

Do you get it? No? Well, that's because it's preschool humor at its finest. You see, Wendy is Hope's *friend*. My three-year-old thought this was so funny because Wendy is an *adult* and Hope *knew* this information and thought we didn't know it ourselves (even though of course we actually did). Yup. That's it. Are you laughing yet?

Humor, as well as music, is a big part of any preschooler's life, and you can recognize this by the way both are generously used in preschool television shows, not to mention in the classroom. But the value of humor and music goes well beyond simply being playful and entertaining. When we understand *what it is* that makes our preschoolers laugh or sparks them to sing, these clues can become an invaluable part of our handy dandy parenting notebook, because these ingredients are the ultimate access pass to open minds and open hearts, and that leads to engaged learning. When we learn how to use humor and music effectively, we gain entry to their world and can powerfully influence and teach them, because we are connecting with and enjoying preschoolers on *their* level.

THE MAGIC OF HUMOR FOR PRESCHOOLERS

Here's another silly moment, this one from *Blue's Clues*. Joe enters the frame looking for Steve. He looks into the camera and asks the home viewer, "Where's Steve?"

The preschoolers point off-screen and say "That way!"

Joe (looks at camera): "He went that way? Okay, thanks."

Joe exits camera left. Then Steve enters camera right.

Steve: "Where's Joe?"

The preschoolers laugh, point, and scream: "HE JUST WENT THAT WAY!"

Steve: "He did? He went that way? Okay, thanks."

Steve exits camera left. Joe re-enters camera right.

Joe: "I can't find Steve anywhere!"

By this point, preschoolers are holding their bellies laughing, the universal sign for the funniest thing *ever* in preschool terms. They can't even get the words out as they scream, "THAT WAY!!"

Why is this so incredibly funny? Because the preschoolers are the ones in control. *They* know which way Steve went, and *they* know which way Joe went. And the fact that *they* know but Steve and Joe, who are adults, *don't* know? *Hysterical.* Even funnier, we included this particular gag in *Blue's Clues* over and over again and, I swear, it just got funnier every time. Truth is, we could do it all day long and get the same holding-the-belly-laughter results.

At its most basic level, preschool humor is all about *knowing information* that someone else doesn't know—and being in on the joke. Therefore, much of preschool humor is concrete, literal, and downright silly. Salt and Pepper shakers aren't alive, right? But what if they were? We know that shoes belong on your feet. But what if we put shoes on your—wait for it—head?! How about a good old-fashioned booty dance? Other sillies include grass that giggles when you walk on it because it's ticklish, crayons that come to life when you're not looking, a bar of soap that has a face and can't wait to slip and slide in the sink while making bubbles. Sensing a pattern here? Inanimate objects coming to life is the epitome of preschool of humor. It's funny and fantastical and imaginative all at the same time. And it happens to be my favorite kind of preschool humor.

WHY HUMOR?

Of course, when we're talking about humor, there is plenty of science speaking to the physical and emotional benefits to laughing, not just for preschoolers but for any person of any age. Laughing delivers pleasure-inducing dopamine and boosts endorphins, while neurons called spindle cells assist by transmitting the delighted emotion across the brain. In fact, the physical act of laughing releases endorphins similar to those that are released during a serious workout. It's also been proven that laughter decreases stress, beefs up immune responses, boosts memory levels, lowers cortisol levels, and protects against heart disease.

Great, right? But while these are fantastic benefits, the primary reason humor is so effective for preschoolers is because it fosters a climate of joy, love, and openness that has long-term, positive repercussions for their social-emotional growth. Humor can instantly make us fluent in a preschooler's universal language of play, putting us on the same level and wavelength, which gives us an advantage when helping them work through problems.

Humor is also a great bonding tool. Think about it: when we adults laugh together, we're sharing a mutual experience and the ability to laugh at ourselves. The same goes for laughing with our little ones. When we use humor with our preschoolers, we're doing so on their level, and they love us for it. It connects us in a way that few other experiences can. Bonding with humor says, "I get you." It shows how in-tune we are with what's going on and how much we understand each other. When we create inside jokes with our children, it shows them how much we remember and treasure the things we've done together.

Bonding with humor can be a self-deprecating type of humor. It's taking a situation and turning it on its head. It's your preschooler accidentally spilling water, and then you spilling it, too. It's playing along with hide and seek and pretending to not be able to find your preschooler even when she's hiding in plain sight. It's your preschooler deciding to eat his pizza backward, and you joining right along.

The power of a good sense of humor and its ability to enhance relationships is shown by the correlation between humor and positive marital satisfaction.[1] If humor can help with a marriage, surely it can do wonders for parent-child relationships! I'm a big believer in the power of bonding with our preschoolers, as having a solid bonded and positive relationship with our children as they grow into tweens and teens can't be underestimated. Humor itself, and using humor as a tool, garners good results, period.

FINDING THE SILLY IN THE EVERYDAY

Knowing what makes our preschoolers laugh and finding little moments during our day to tap into those catalysts is a great way to bond, diffuse with humor, and show closeness and love. Little examples of day-to-day dabbling in humor include:

Changing Up Routines

Preschoolers love the little surprises rooted in everyday, predictable, and familiar routines. Even the smallest things are funny. Put a ridiculous picture in your preschooler's lunchbox to bring on some unexpected sillies. Have an impromptu breakfast for dinner while donning your silliest pajamas. Now, you're killing it! And my husband's favorite, arranging food on the plate in the form of a smiley face. Works every time.

Exaggeration

Exaggeration is THE MOST UNDERUSED HUMOR TOOL IN THE UNIVERSE! Seriously, though, we can use exaggeration in different ways to get our point across in a humorous way. For example, exaggerated facial expressions are a simple and fun way to let our preschooler in on what we're feeling. Overly silly and sometimes made-up words are funny, no matter how much we overuse or abuse them. (On *Blue's Clues* we had a character named Ooglah Booglah who made a repeat performance because of how silly his name was.) Of course, really loud and exaggerated snoring never fails to bring on the giggles, and overdramatic reactions to random situations are also really funny ("Waaaaah!"). A good rule of thumb? The sillier and the more visual, the better.

In our first episode of *Super Why!*, entitled "The Three Little Pigs," we asked the Big Bad Wolf why he was so big and bad. His response? "Because it says so in my story, see?" And as the wolf looked down, we revealed his sentence in the book, where it indeed stated that he was "the Big Bad Wolf." So, using Super Why's power to read, we changed the story! We interacted with the home viewer to figure out the opposite of big (small!) and changed the sentence to read, "The small bad wolf." Well, of course, the wolf, now tiny, was still running around blowing things down.

The kids at home found this pretty funny, but the story still wasn't right. So Super Why and the viewers went back to the drawing board to truly solve the problem and figure out the word that means the opposite of "bad" instead. *Now* the new sentence reads, "The Big Good Wolf." At this, the wolf burst into big, exaggerated sobs, "WAAAAAHHHHH! WAAAAAHHHH!"

Kids watching were now rolling in laughter at the thought of a big, scary wolf crying in this overdramatic and ridiculous way. In the end, the wolf admitted to acting horribly because he has no friends. We promised to play with him and be his friend, and we saved the day. Hip hip hooray!

Visual Slapstick Humor

Slapstick gets a bad name because back in the day it was defined by dangerous and scary physical stunts—axes falling on someone's head or characters getting run over by a car or hit with a bat. Young preschoolers are actually concerned by these actions and don't find them funny at all, except in cases of nervous laughter. On the other hand, to preschoolers, obviously non-hurtful (preschoolers are innately empathetic), super-visual, overdramatic pratfalls are funny with a capital *F*. Falling down because you're surprised? Hysterical.

Rule-Breaking Humor

Breaking the rules on a preschool level might include anything from bathroom humor (oh, the noises!) and sock puppets (wearing socks, with faces, on your *hands*! Funny stuff!) to mixing-up routines (wearing bathing suits inside in the winter!). On our shows, we've had our share of silly upside-down tea parties, backwards days, as well as more fantastical silliness of going underground and dancing with inchworms or having lizard dance parties.

DIFFUSING WITH HUMOR

Through humor, adults can help preschoolers engage and learn. But humor has an even more powerful application that can make an immediate, positive change in your world: the power to diffuse difficult or tough moments. In fact, diffusing with humor is my go-to strategy for dealing with conflict, not only with my kids, but with my husband and in work. If you can keep your sense of humor, this strategy is golden, because humor is a proven, powerful strategy for tackling difficult situations, conquering fears or challenges, or simply breaking the tension and diffusing in the moment. Not only do I regularly use this strategy in real life—I use it on all my shows. I find it's a strategy most underused by my parent friends.

I like to say that diffusing with humor is the "snack" of strategies. It's always good to have on hand because you never know when you're going to need it. And when you do use it, it works so fast and so well (really and truly), you don't know why you didn't think of using it earlier.

Tips for Diffusing with Humor

To use humor as a tool during a conflict, following these rules will help you be the most successful. It can be a little tricky; we don't want to make any situation worse. We want to strike the right balance and diffuse quickly and efficiently.

o Start by affirming the problem: For example, "Oh no! Your ice cream dropped on the floor!"
o Show an understanding of the problem: Restate the problem in a respectful and serious way. For example, "You look so upset. I can see how your ice cream falling on the floor is so upsetting."
o Laugh *with* the other person: Whether it's your preschooler, your spouse, or your best friend, the humor needs to be *inclusive*, not exclusive. Laughing *at* someone will have the opposite effect than what you're going for. Never point or state something negative or derogatory and laugh ("Is that a new haircut? Hahaha, it's a joke!"). It's *never* a joke unless both people are laughing.
o Think about the timing: Is it funny yet? How about now? Knowing *when* to make the joke is as important as *how* you make it.
o Know your audience: Learn what kind of humor is going to get at your kid right away and use that. You don't want to make an inappropriate joke or say something they won't understand.
o Use inside jokes: If there was ever a good time to use an inside joke, it's now! Using an inside joke is a great way to break the ice and diffuse with humor. Jokes about personal experiences that you can pull from increase the bonding and help you cut through the stress even faster. For instance, "Remember when Daddy's ice cream fell and he caught it with his shoe? He still couldn't eat it!"

Of course, the main challenge with employing humor to diffuse is that it can be hard for us as parents and caregivers to stay calm enough in the moment to remember to use it. When my girls were younger and my own emotions would get away from me, sometimes I'd find myself falling into a negative spiral—*they* had a meltdown, *I* had a meltdown, and round and round we went. To get out of that spiral, I've worked hard to tap into humor as a strategy to not only help me with my children (and my husband), but also help me with *myself*! In fact, I've talked about this strategy so much that a friend of mine recently asked me to speak about it at her wedding as a "virtue of marriage." The funniest part? The wedding was a room full of stand-up comedians and comedy writers!

PARENTING PRODUCTION NOTES
Use the Funny Stuff to Deal with Challenges Big and Small
Think about a time when you used humor or could use humor to:

Desired Result	Example	Your Example
Break the tension	"No one is talking; do you think everyone fell asleep at the dinner table?" Add some snores for good measure.	
Reduce anger	"I'm so angry I'm like the giant in Jack and the Beanstalk. Fee Fi Foe FUM!"	
Reduce stress	"I'm so stressed I think I need some silly dancing." Turn on pop music and dance it out!	
Reframe a problem	Repeat the problem in an exaggerated way: "So, you're sad that it's raining. And you said that it's going to rain forever. Does that mean forever forever? Like there will be so much water we will have to take a boat to school? And swim instead of walk around the block?"	

Desired Result	Example	Your Example
Put a situation in perspective	Similar to reframing a problem, but you can be more specific. "Is this like the time when I dropped our entire turkey dinner on the floor and we had nothing to eat? I mean, it was ON THE FLOOR! ALL OVER! THE FLOOR!"	
Bond with a greater connection	Silly sock puppet play! Make salt and pepper shakers talk during dinner. Talk with a funny voice and expect them to talk back to you in their own funny voice.	

REDUCING STRESS

When my girls were preschoolers, they each had their own "song." Whenever "our song" was on ("You Belong to Me" by Taylor Swift and "Bubbly" by Colbie Callait), no matter what we were doing at the time or where we were, we had to dance together. This was bonding and funny, released stress, and in the long run, created so many loving memories.

SOMETIMES WE DON'T GET IT RIGHT

Of course, sometimes the media gets it wrong when trying to make preschoolers laugh. I've even crashed and burned with one particular episode we were working on for *Super Why!* Since the focus of *Super Why!* is solving problems by jumping into books and stories, we often feature public domain fairytales or folktales, as was the case with one episode we wrote called "The Foolish Wishes." In the story, based on the Swedish folktale by Dianne de Las Casas, a woman and a man get three wishes, along with the advice to use them wisely. For the first wish, the husband asks for a sausage. Well, the wife is aghast. After all, he could wish for anything in the world and he chooses a sausage? The husband gets so angry about his wife's disapproval that he wishes the sausage was stuck to her nose! Of course, as it does in fables like this, the wish came true.

Now, seeing a sausage at the end of someone's nose is silly, right? I mean, a long, bulbous, silly looking sausage on the END OF YOUR NOSE! Hysterical, right?!

WRONG.

The preschoolers *were not* laughing. Why not? Because they were *concerned,* and some were even upset that there was a sausage on the end of someone's nose. And when you think about it that way, it wasn't comedy at all—it was pure drama! Of course, in the end, the man used his last wish to get the sausage off his wife's nose. Phew. Crisis averted—but of course such a waste of magical wishes! The kids listening to the story were relieved and we learned a lesson on preschool humor and what is *not* funny after all.

Paying careful attention to how humor is used in the media your preschoolers engage with will help you determine if a show or app should make it onto your "Yes" list. Is the humor offensive? Negative? Does it involve making fun of or laughing at someone? Or is it shown as a conflict-resolution and bonding mechanism? Preschoolers will pick up on these cues as they watch and model what they see with us and their friends.

SING! IT DOES A BODY GOOD

Music is as effective as humor when it comes to inspiring, diffusing, and setting a tone or feeling. In fact, studies find that music and music experiences play a significant role in supporting the formation of important brain connections that are established in the first three years.[2] From my time in the classroom, I know that music inspires creative movement. It calms at rest time. It fosters listening skills. Through music, kids can learn about patterns. Through singing, kids can learn rhymes and new vocabulary. It's fair to say that music ignites pretty much all areas of child development, some of them at the same time:

○ Intellectual and language development and literacy are sparked as preschoolers learn sounds in music and the meaning of words.
○ Social and emotional development are sparked by the nature of the songs, the closeness of being rocked during a lullaby, and the bond that occurs when songs are sung by preschoolers, teachers, and parents alike.
○ Motor development is sparked from innate movements and dancing during music. Moving and dancing to music helps the body and the mind work together.

It's incredible to realize that the simple act of singing while rocking a baby can have so many positive outcomes: it stimulates early language development, promotes attachment and bonding, and supports an infant's growing spatial awareness as the child experiences her body moving in space. Powerful.

MUSIC AS AN EDUCATIONAL TOOL

While creating the concept for *Daniel Tiger's Neighborhood*, I was wracking my brain trying to figure out how to make sure the social-emotional skills in the show were being conveyed as clearly as the cognitive skills we taught on *Blue's Clues* were. I knew that, in the past, shows with a social-emotional curriculum have often been defined and recognized by the inclusion of a good, moral story with a point of view on an important topic, such as bullying or making a new friend. But I wanted to do more than that. I wanted to make sure our messages were actual strategies, and that these strategies were easy for both parents and preschoolers to use. Since we were using the tried-and-true curriculum created by Fred Rogers, we knew how strong these messages were going to be. So, how could we make sure they were inherently useful, straightforward, and couldn't be missed when you watched the show? How could we make them as sticky as *Blue's Clues* was?

The answer came to us when we were studying Fred's use of music. He wrote all the songs on *Mister Rogers' Neighborhood*, and they were all poignant stories and strategies from a child development perspective. He was like the Billy Joel of preschool music. So, to honor his legacy, and using what we knew about research and child development, we created musical jingles for each of the themes and strategies we used throughout the series. We then repeated them, purposefully, to show Daniel mastering the strategies as well as to show different and distinct uses for them. We also honored Fred's original songs by including covers of some of his songs, as well as some new songs inspired by his work, at the end of every episode. *Daniel Tiger's Neighborhood* is infused with music, and music is what makes the learning stick.

SONGS HAVE POWER

Music and lyrics have an influential power to motivate, inspire, set a tone, solve a problem, give an insight, and plant a seed in your mind. I believe in harnessing the power of music to further reinforce my messages. For *Wishenpoof,* our song "Believe in Me" written by the brilliant Blain Morris and performed by the talented Hope Cassandra (also my daughter!), gives reasons for preschoolers to know why they need to believe in themselves, to make a difference, to make a change in the world, to be a good friend.[3] What could be a better way to use music? On *Blue's Clues*, I wanted preschoolers to work hard and believe in themselves, so we created the lyric "If we use our minds and take a step at a time, we can do anything that we want to do." And we repeated it in every episode.

Back when I was an assistant preschool teacher at Catholic University, one of my head teachers in the preschool classroom used to say, "If you sing it, they will do it!" And she put her money where her mouth was by incorporating singing into every aspect of her child-centered preschool curriculum. We would sing each child's name as a hello in the morning. We would sing as we transitioned to another activity. We would sing to clean up. We would sing a loving song, using the children's names, as they went down for a nap. These weren't complicated ballads or great operatic tunes—they were simple, straightforward, and literal mini-songs. And they worked like magic. One of my preschool students Doug's favorite ditty before naptime was, "Time to sleep, oh yes, it is, time to sleep, let's not hear a peep 'cause it's time to sleeeeep!"

There's perhaps no clearer example of the power of a simple melody and lyrics to instill action than the infamous clean-up song featured on *Barney* and used in preschool classrooms everywhere. It's simple, it tells preschoolers what they need to know and what they need to do, and it's inherently repetitive: "Clean up, clean up, everybody do their share."

MUSIC FOR TRANSITIONS AND ROUTINES

Music is incredibly helpful for preschoolers when transitioning from one activity to another. That's because it helps put these transitions into context, using literal words and repetition in a sticky, bouncy, happy song. We can see these types of transition songs at work when Steve sings "We are looking for Blue's Clues," a short ditty of a song that is just what it says. We sing it when we transition from one room of the house to the next or from one activity to another. As we move through the house, we are reminded of our overall goal—finding Blue's Clues to figure out what Blue needs. We use the ditty to remind preschoolers of what we need to do. Simple, catchy, sticky, and useful. Kids knew what to do.

On *Daniel Tiger's Neighborhood*, we've used these types of simple songs in our strategies to make rules of "what to do" easier to remember. Everything from our potty song to a morning and bedtime routine are all conveyed through simple, chanty music.

PARENTING PRODUCTION NOTES
Make Up Your Own Song!

If you haven't already tapped into the power of music in your world, why not try making up your own little ditties to help you and your preschooler with transitions, routines, and any other areas where you regularly find yourself repeating yourself, feeling flabbergasted, getting impatient, or noticing that your preschooler is having trouble remembering the steps they need to take? I kid you not—they work like *magic*. And don't worry about musical talent or songwriting skills. When it comes to preschool songs, the more straightforward, repeatable, and easy to sing, the better. Can't get your preschooler out of the house? Sing it! Can't remember to put her shoes on? Sing it!

Here are some examples to get you thinking of the scenarios where a little music could go a long way:

- Getting dressed for preschool or putting on pajamas
- Remembering to flush the toilet and wash hands after going to the bathroom
- Taking off shoes when coming in the house (or putting them on when it's time to leave!)
- Hanging up coat and backpack on their hooks
- Brushing teeth: top, bottom, front, back
- Getting strapped into the car seat
- Picking up toys after playtime
- Nighttime routine (saying good night to favorite stuffed animals and toys)

MUSIC TO TEACH COGNITIVE SKILLS

Music has been proven to help with memory for both adults and pre-schoolers, so it only makes sense that setting more challenging con-cepts to music can be a great tool when used correctly. For instance, when we wanted to teach the names, attributes, and order of the plan-ets in the solar system, we sang it. When we wanted preschoolers to understand the rules of the *Blue's Clues* game, we sang it. When we wanted preschoolers to have coping skills they could pull out and use when they need them, we sang them.

However, one of the rules of putting information to music is that the lyrics need to be reinforced with visuals and the concepts have to be broken down enough to ensure that preschoolers not only know how to sing the words but actually *comprehend* what they're singing. Otherwise, this musical strategy may not actually work as well as one would expect. For example, Dr. Sandy Calvert studied the impact of learning via music on media when she studied *Schoolhouse Rock*, a hugely popular short-form animated series from the 1970s that taught concepts of history, literacy, and science entirely through song. What she found was that while *Schoolhouse Rock* had educational merit via short-term verbatim memory of the lyrics, it wasn't necessarily achiev-ing the deeper level of learning it was striving for.[4]

I think we can all relate to this finding. Think about it. Have you ever found yourself singing a song over and over without even realizing the meaning of the words? It's happened to me, many times. In one instance, my daughters and I were singing Carrie Underwood's song "Before He Cheats" around the house like a broken record until we took a closer look at the lyrics and realized what the song was actually about. Sud-denly our boppy, fun sing-along song wasn't so fun anymore.

Because, as is the case with all the strategies I'm sharing in this book, our goal is mastery and learning on the deepest level, Calvert's *Schoolhouse Rock* study offers us useful guidance on how to use songs to teach, on a deeper, more effective level. In order to fully ensure com-prehension, we need to slow down and break apart the information, state it as well as sing it, and even show the lyrics, both visually (words on the screen) and through the action if possible. At home, we can take a moment to Pause and ask for comprehension when our kids are singing a song.

. . . .

So is it okay to sing the Beatles?

Of course, you can. There's nothing wrong with sharing your favorite songs and developing your preschooler's taste in music. My husband shared the Ramones with our girls, as well as Ella Fitzgerald and Harry Belafonte, before they could talk. But they could move . . . and they did! The goal here, of course, is not comprehension or education with regard to lyrics, it's about the *feeling* that music gives you—and the bonding of sharing your favorite Spotify lists with your kids. Once they start asking about the lyrics, that's when it's time to begin those discussions (and depending on the lyrics, maybe make some different choices, at least for now).

. . . .

MUSIC TO SET A TONE

A 2013 study in the *Journal of Positive Psychology* found that people who listened to upbeat music could improve their moods almost immediately and that only twenty-five minutes a day can boost overall happiness in just two weeks.[5] Interestingly, the results are even stronger when you engage with the music by singing, playing an instrument, or dancing. Interaction is always key. Music can be incredibly powerful when it comes to changing a mood, in yourself, in your preschooler, or in your whole family. For example, putting on calming music when a preschooler comes home from school offers a cue to relax, just like dance or pop music can boost energy, lift spirits, and infuse some instant musical joy.

If you've ever watched a scary movie and turned down the volume to get through a particularly frightening scene, you've recognized the power of music to set a tone and create a mood. With our preschoolers, we can use this capacity for music in a positive way, by setting a tone that will help them appropriately experience what's happening in their world. For instance, we can use soft music to lull our preschoolers to sleep, calming music to help them relax, and upbeat music to celebrate. As a media literacy tool, just as we might mute the television during a scary scene, we can help our preschoolers learn about the power of music by turning down the volume when something seems upsetting or sad and asking them if they feel any different when watching the same scene without sound.

We use music as part of our social-emotional curriculum on both *Daniel Tiger's Neighborhood* and *Wishenpoof*. For example, when we want preschoolers to identify with Daniel or Bianca, we use music to set the tone. Excited, frustrated, sad, angry—it can all be felt with music.

Angela's Clues

Humor and music are powerful clues I use in every single episode of preschool television I write. Knowing preschoolers and how much they love to learn, play, be silly, and move, tapping into the power of these two ingredients makes it easy to offer them a plethora of opportunities to do all of these in every show!

When I broke the clues of humor and music apart, I realized how much they play a role in my everyday life, too, both for me and for my kids. Perhaps what I love most about them as clues in parenting is that they are bonding, and these family bonds are what I hold on to as my girls get older. Bonding us as a family is one of my most important goals. If humor and music can help to get me there, I'm hooked.

We've made homemade "music videos" by setting pictures and video footage of our girls to favorite songs that now will forever remind us of a specific moment in time, vacation, or event. We often rely on self-deprecating humor to help us get through times of conflict. My girls even remind us, using humor, of some of the strategies they've learned over the years. Having my kids remind me of what to do through songs and humor? It feels like my shows are kicking me in the butt saying, "Remember, adults can learn from kids' TV, too!"

- **Be Involved** and look for moments to diffuse with humor.
- **Ask Questions** and enlist your preschooler's help to make up new songs to remember things.
- **See the Spark** and remember that preschoolers will do anything if you sing it!

YOUR MEDIA "YES" LIST

☑ The humor is preschool appropriate and not mean-spirited.
☑ The humor and music deepens the bond with my child.
☑ The song lyrics are positive, inspirational, uplifting, and/or educational.
☑ My child understands the words in the songs and often sings them after the show is over.

Clue Takeaways

o Humor gives us entry into a preschooler's world and helps us connect with them on their level.
o Fostering a climate of joy, love, and openness contributes to a preschooler's healthy social-emotional growth.

CLUE #10: ENJOY

- Diffusing with humor can ease conflicts, stress, and tension (if used carefully).
- Music can set a new tone or shift a preschooler's energy. Does your preschooler need to calm down or be energized?
- Musical strategies are perfect for cleaning up, for transitions, for routines.

CLUE #11: CELEBRATE

Celebrating the Small Things Grows Preschoolers' Sense of Optimism and Intrinsic Motivation

Like many little kids, when Ella was little, she loved to count. She would count to ten over and over again: "One, two, three, four, five, six, seven, eight, nine, ten." When she got to ten, she would clap, and we would celebrate. "Yay!" We did this over and over again. "One, two, three, four, five, six, seven, eight, nine, ten . . . YAY!" One day, I Paused and asked, "Ella, what comes after ten?"

After thinking about it for a moment, she replied enthusiastically, "Yay!" Apparently, little celebrations are great, but perhaps we were overdoing it since "Yay!" had somehow become another word for eleven. Mom fail.

When you're a preschooler, no accomplishment is too small for some recognition. I'm not saying our children should get a "trophy for everything," but rather I'm suggesting we prioritize positive *affirmation, acknowledgment,* and *encouragement.* The truth is, the little things mean a lot to a preschooler because, for the most part, they are *firsts!* Remember the first time you moved into your own apartment or house? I bet you celebrated! How about landing your first job? A cause for celebration. Remember when you got married? Chances are your DJ spun a little bit of Kool and the Gang's "Celebration" at some point during the reception (even if you didn't want him to).

My point is, it's important that we don't lose sight of what's important to our preschoolers. And even though our preschoolers' firsts may seem small or insignificant to us, to them they are *big* accomplishments. Recognizing this is another way of respecting them by getting on their level and understanding the world according to who they are. Once we launch into their world of play, one where we are the stars of their shows, we can't help but want to play along while teaching them invaluable lessons about loving life, empathy, and making the most of our time together.

So what things are worth celebrating to a preschooler? How about when the mail comes (seriously, there's a whole celebratory song!)? How about a lost tooth? A first plane ride? A first successful hop across the playground? These are all big deals to our little ones and deserve to be called out and celebrated. By doing so, we're making a conscious point to stop, smell the roses, and celebrate life with our children. And what more could we really want as parents? And for our children? Giving them the clues and wherewithal to be in the moment and celebrate what *is* will do wonders for their sense of self-worth, both now and in the future.

FINDING THE REASON TO CELEBRATE

I've written many different "celebration episodes" for my preschool shows over the years, but the one I'm most proud of is one where I really had to dig deep to find the positive (which is exactly the point I'm making in this chapter). I'm talking about perhaps the most difficult episode I've ever had to write—when our host Steve Burns announced he wanted to leave *Blue's Clues* for good. Time for a celebration episode? It didn't feel like it at the time—I was a puddle of tears.

When he first told us about his decision, I flashed back to that day many years earlier in the conference room with Traci when we heard Blue couldn't be a kitten and felt that same kick in the gut. My immediate thought once again: *Our show was done.* Tears were streaming down my face. Traci and I felt an overwhelming sense of loss, because we had so many more things we wanted to say to kids through our show. We also had eighty staff members, many with young families, and we couldn't just pull the plug. It wasn't time. We weren't ready to leave. So, after a Pause (not to mention a teeny tiny pity party and perhaps a chocolate chip cookie or two), I started to write. Just as Traci drew our new puppy in our time of need, this time, I scripted and scripted and scripted. I wrote the saddest script I'd ever written—a heartbreaking, tear-filled story.

But then it hit me. How would we want a preschooler to react to this news? After all, we had the power, in the way we dealt with the story, to model a positive, happy transition. And even though I wasn't feeling so positive about it, I did feel motivated and inspired to model it as something positive for preschoolers. So, I threw out my sad script and wrote a new aspirational story. I knew the only way our audience would feel good about Steve saying good-bye to Blue (and them) would be for him to leave for something important. And what's more important than leaving to go to college? The more I wrote, the more excited I became. And I actually grew to love the idea that, since so many kids were watching our show, Steve's departure was giving us a unique opportunity to show them what college looked like and be sparked by Steve's pride. Ultimately our goal was to motivate our viewers to grow up wanting to go to college, just like Steve did. In the end, we remembered to celebrate, and that made all of the difference, both for our viewers, and our crew. And, of course, I also wrote in someone to take care of Blue—Steve's younger brother Joe. And our show could go on!

THE PSYCHOLOGY BEHIND POSITIVITY

Embracing the tool of celebration as a regular part of our preschoolers' lives has the power to imbue their world with healthy doses of positivity, which is no small benefit. We know that children who have a positive outlook on life are more motivated, do better in school, feel they have more control of their lives, are less likely to be depressed as adults, and live longer.[1] That's because these optimistic kids have a different, more positive way of viewing the causes of events in their lives. Much like higher-order thinkers, they feel empowered because they've learned how to make sense of the world. They know how to see possibilities and make positive changes. In fact, many people consider optimism to be the single most important factor in determining resilience, above intelligence and genetics.[2] As we know, many theorists believe that resilience and grit are what's behind success in life. To me, the most exciting aspect of this idea is that mindsets are flexible— they have the ability to change. So just like higher-order learning, an optimistic mindset can be taught.

To demonstrate this, Dr. Martin Seligman at the University of Pennsylvania began the Penn Resiliency Project (PRP), whereby he and his staff taught young children how to identify pessimistic explanations, as well as how to generate more optimistic and realistic explanations, for the problems they encounter. The Penn Resiliency Project proved that children with a pessimistic outlook were in fact able to *change* to being more optimistic, which ultimately decreases their chances for depression. And these results weren't a fluke, either. The success of Dr. Seligman's project has since been validated in thirteen different controlled research studies involving two thousand children, ages eight to fifteen.[3] The best news? The clues behind this transformation, known as *learned optimism,* can be used successfully with our own kids, just as I've used them on my shows to teach optimism through media.

FOSTERING "LEARNED OPTIMISM"

The skills needed to learn optimism are similar to those required for resolving conflicts. Both begin with a problem and both call for looking at the problem in an active, positive way. The difference is that in the case of learned optimism, we want to help our child learn to recognize the thoughts that are creating their inner monologue. Because it's this inner monologue that we want to change or strengthen to be more optimistic.

But how do we define the concept to preschoolers in the first place? We can say that optimism is "looking for the good parts" of something or someone, or that it's "seeing the happiness" in everything, or even that it means to "find something good" in a bad situation. While we don't want to brush our children's sad, or frustrated, or uncomfortable feelings under the rug, we do want preschoolers to understand that sad feelings and disappointments won't last forever. As one optimistic preschooler once said to us during a research session on a particularly rainy morning, "The sun will come out tomorrow!" Then, as if on cue, she launched into the signature song from *Annie*, "Tomorrow," for us. Optimism at its best.

The Role of the Inner Monologue:
Wiring the Brain to Be Positive

Like it or not, it's our voice and the words we say to our children that will form the foundation of their inner monologue. And that very same inner monologue will ultimately become their guiding force as they move away from us and into the world beyond. It's the voice they'll hear in a tough situation or when facing a challenging decision. It's the voice that will shape how they perceive themselves during the tween and teen years and beyond, as they think about their weaknesses, strengths, and capabilities. That's why it's so important that our voice is positive, kind, and keeps them safe by helping them make good choices. But above all, we want to do what we can to ensure their inner voice is an optimist.

Now that my girls are teenagers, my husband, Greg, and I are trusting and hoping that we've ingrained in them enough of our thoughts, points of view, positive outlook, and critical thinking skills in their younger years so that as their friends become more influential, they have a healthy, optimistic foundation to work from. In order to help give our preschoolers an inner voice that is realistic, positive, and empathetic, we need to model it ourselves. This is what I love so much about preschoolers—they are there, listening to us, with an open mind and an open heart, taking everything in.

PARENTING PRODUCTION NOTES
Foster Your Children's Learned Optimism

Using the same strategies we tapped into for resolving conflicts, we can foster the trait of learned optimism in our children by pausing, empowering, and interacting.

- Pause: When a problem arises, it's important that we Pause to give our preschoolers space to collect their thoughts as opposed to jumping right in and telling them what to think. We want our children to discover what they're feeling and how they're feeling *on their own*. Sure, we can probe, nudge, and scaffold, but ultimately our job is to teach them how to do it for themselves. When we Pause, we're also pausing to acknowledge our child's feelings. We lean in, give a hug, empathize, and take a moment to be *present* with our child. This underscores that they are important to us and that their feelings are important.

- Empower: We want to empower and guide our preschoolers so they can think of new ways to look at any situation, as well as teach them feeling words and offer an acknowledgment of their feelings. Lastly, we want to empower them to understand what an optimistic view looks and feels like.

- Interact: We interact with our preschoolers by actively encouraging them to brainstorm new ways to look at a situation. To do this, we ask questions, we probe, we scaffold, and we guide, all the time encouraging new positive, optimistic ideas.

LEARNED OPTIMISM WITH A FOUR-YEAR-OLD:
GABRIELLA AND PETER

My friend Gabriella and her four-year-old son Peter had made plans to play at the park one morning. He was beyond excited to go to this particular park and had talked about it all night before bed the day before. When he woke up, Peter rushed to the window, as preschoolers do, excited to start his day, only to see the huge, torrential rainstorm happening outside. Understanding that the stormy weather meant he couldn't go to the park as planned, he burst into tears. When Gabriella entered his room, she saw the circumstance as an ideal opportunity to help Peter foster learned optimism.

First things first, she sat down next to him on his bed and gave him a hug, *Pausing* to let him express his feelings:

Peter (angrily): "It always rains when I want to play outside! I never get to go out and play!"

Gabriella empowered her son by *acknowledging* his feelings and letting him know they were important while giving him a loving squeeze:

Gabriella: "You seem angry and sad."

Peter nodded, tears streaming down his sweet little face. Gabriella *empowered* him to *share his internal dialogue*, one she knew had the potential to become a negative spiral or thought pattern if not affirmed and reversed:

Gabriella: "What are you saying in your head that is making you so sad?"

Peter: "I wanted to play with my friend. I *never* get to play with him. He goes to another school. I miss him."

And with that admission, he crumpled into Gabriella's lap with huge tears. Gabriella gently *interacted* with him, asking him if he could come up with a new way to look at the situation and solve the problem.

Gabriella: "I know it feels like you never get to play with Jack anymore. But remember when we went trick or treating with him? That was fun."

Peter nodded. Gabriella continued to interact until they could come up with an optimistic solution together:

Gabriella: "What do you think we could do to make you feel better?"

Peter (angrily): "Nothing. Nothing will make me feel better."

She took another *Pause* so Peter could think. If he had continued to be angry, she might have offered him a coping strategy and asked him to take a deep breath and count to four so he could be calm and think of a solution. But as it happened, Peter Paused and then looked up at his mom and said:

Peter: "Since it's raining, maybe Jack could come here to play instead of the playground? And next time, when it's sunny out, we can slide down the slide."

Gabriella (smiling): "Good idea! Let me call his mom now."

. . . .

The Three Ps

Through his work developing the clues in the relatively new field of positive psychology, Dr. Seligman has identified what he calls the Three Ps of Learned Optimism—permanence, pervasiveness, and personalization—that we should look for and work to nurture in our kids. Here's a breakdown of what these Three Ps look like in action, as well as how to look for these "clues" when our kids talk, using Gabriella and Peter's story as an example:

The "P"	What It Is	Pessimistic View	Optimistic View
Permanence	An understanding of how long the problem will last.	Using restricting language: "I'll *never* get to play!"	"It's raining today, but it won't rain every day. What was the weather like yesterday?"
Pervasiveness	How far-reaching and dire the problem is.	Looking at the problem in broad, exaggerated strokes: "We can't play!"	"We can't play outside, but maybe we can still play."
Personalization	Who or what is responsible for the setback.	Believing they are personally responsible: "This always happens to me."	"Remember when we went trick or treating together?"

SELF-WORTH AND PRESCHOOLERS

We hear a lot about the importance of self-worth, which is defined as feeling good about ourselves and recognizing our inherent value and worth as we are. I very much believe in the value of acknowledging and affirming a preschooler's self-worth, but, as is the case with everything when it comes to parenting choices, the clue to doing this well can be found in *how* we do it. It's important that while trying to boost our children up and strengthen their sense of self, we pay close attention to what's developmentally appropriate for their young age. We don't want to "throw them into the real world" yet just to teach them a lesson, and they are still too young to learn that "life isn't fair." When it comes to self-worth, preschoolers need to learn about trust through feeling *safe and nurtured.*

Looking back, it's hard to imagine there was a time when research stated parents were spoiling their baby by picking her up every time she cried and that a newborn baby could be manipulating its parents. The truth is, *everything we know about human beings tells us that we want to be listened to.* Babies, especially, need to understand they are safe, secure, and heard. It's why we swaddle them. It's why we baby-wear them. They come out of the womb—a safe, contained, cozy place—into this huge world, and we need to let them know we're near, with comfort and security.

When we pick our babies up and understand their cries, they grow up being "attached" to us—they know we are there for them. As they become toddlers, these attached little ones will continue to look at us, as they stretch themselves to go further and further away and try new things. And as long as they know we're there, with just a little bit of eye contact and a smile, they know they're okay. And so it goes. As they age up, they continue to open the door wider, knowing we are on their side and believing in them, as we give them larger and larger boundaries—a fenced-in backyard to keep them safe, then more freedom in the neighborhood, and eventually, the world. Our job is to teach our children how to learn, grow, and cope, independently.

FOSTERING INTRINSICALLY MOTIVATED SELF-WORTH

Self-worth has its roots in intrinsic motivation which, as I wrote earlier, is at the foundation of the work we do as parents. We want our preschoolers to want to learn about something *from within*. We want our preschoolers to feel a sense of accomplishment *from within*. We want our preschoolers to have a sense of themselves and a sense of self-worth *from within* and not from outside sources. And this is the problem with false accolades, celebrations with no meaning, and trophies where, instead of celebrating an actual accomplishment, we are celebrating something that took no effort and is therefore undermining our child's intrinsic motivation.

· ·

THE PROBLEM WITH EFFORTLESS TROPHIES

As parents and caregivers, we want our preschoolers to have high self-worth and feel good about themselves, in large part because children with high self-worth do better in school and ultimately in life, as do kids who are optimistic and those who can tap into their higher-order thinking skills. When we make efforts to boost our child's self-worth, we're doing so with the hope that we'll encourage them to walk taller, try harder, and achieve more because we know they're capable of doing so. However, according to Dr. Leonard Sax, a physician and author of numerous books including *The Collapse of Parenting*, in an attempt to ensure their child reaps all the benefits of having high self-worth, many parents attempt to boost their child's esteem in everything they do, which may actually result in a negative outcome.[4]

As parents, we often commend the effort and accomplishments of our preschoolers, such as saying "Good job" when they learn how to tie their shoes or (in my case) saying "Yay!" after they count to ten. But then, according to Dr. Sax, many of us take it too far, praising our kids for just showing up, a.k.a. something they had no control over, whatsoever. It's like saying "Good job!" as a reaction to their waking up in the morning.

Dr. Sax says, "In the 2000s, when psychologists such as Dr. Roy Baumeister and Jean Twenge took a closer look at it all, it became clear that simply inflating self-worth, without kids actually earning the trophy (i.e., without trying), doesn't lead to better outcomes. It leads to narcissism and a bloated sense of entitlement."

Just as we nurture a growth mindset, building self-worth in a healthy way with the ultimate goal of mastery and independence happens through acknowledging the effort. Oh, and in case you're wondering, I do not equate saying "thank you" to our kids when they do things like help to clean up after dinner with giving them a "trophy" just for doing what they need to do. In my view, by saying thank you in this circumstance, I'm acknowledging the positive, just as I would if a friend came to dinner and helped out. They both deserve the same response— a smile and a thank you.

- -

CELEBRATING OUR PRESCHOOLER THROUGH OUR ACTIONS

When celebrating our preschooler, we want to acknowledge her effort and encourage her sense of intrinsic motivation by emphasizing her actions and hard work. Instead of making general statements, it's better to make specific, detailed statements that show we're listening, paying attention, and focusing on our kids. We want to be as specific as possible, using descriptive language. Instead of "I love your painting," we talk about what we love *about* the painting. "I love your use of color and the size of those snowflakes!"

Our actions speak volumes as well. When we remember to make their favorite snack after school without them asking or we're on time to pick them up from a playdate, we are celebrating them. When we sit down to have a meal with them and give them our focused attention, we are celebrating them. When we give them a hug or take them with us on an errand and include them in what we are doing, we are celebrating them. Our actions *and* our words are equally important in boosting their self-worth.

We can do this every day, in little ways, by:

o showing them unconditional support;
o showing them how much we love them with our actions (what we remember, what we do, how much we listen, how we look at them, how we talk with respect);
o letting them learn by allowing them to try, fail, and try again;
o supporting their efforts unconditionally;
o celebrating their accomplishments; and
o acknowledging their hard work.

PARENTING PRODUCTION NOTES
Celebrate Your Preschooler in a Way That Reinforces
His Self-Worth and a Growth Mindset

As you read through these examples, think about the words you can use in celebrating your child.

What Not to Say	What to Say
"Woohoo! You got a book out of the library!"	"Tell me about what you read in the book! What did you like, not like, or love? Let's make the banana swirl they talked about in the book!" (Type of celebration)
"That's okay . . . you don't have to go to soccer."	"You made a commitment and need to follow it through." (Responsibility)
"You scored a basket!"	"You really tried hard today! How does it feel?" (Getting at intrinsic motivation)

What Not to Say	What to Say
"You're the best one on the team!"	"You helped a teammate to score—I noticed what a team player you are." (Collaboration)
"You're so smart!"	"I really like how hard you're working." (Work ethic)
"I love that drawing!"	"Tell me more about your picture. I love how wavy those lines are." (Paying attention to detail makes them feel good)
"I love the tie you sewed for me!"	Wearing the tie proudly speaks volumes without saying a word. (Pride in work)
"That painting is beautiful!"	"I love your use of color and how you are combining and mixing colors to make something new!"

TALKING EYE TO EYE WITH YOUR PRESCHOOLER IS A CELEBRATION

In "interactive" television, where we are breaking the fourth wall and our hosts or characters are looking *directly* at the preschoolers at home—eye to eye—we're creating a bond. This "interactive" format also gives preschoolers a way to practice active *listening* by looking into the eyes of our host. But beyond that, this bond can form the basis for our characters to reach out and guide the preschoolers at home and celebrate them for who they are, remind them that there is no one in the world exactly like them, and reinforce the message that they are special.

Powerful messages like these were the cornerstone of *Mister Rogers' Neighborhood*. And actually, Fred's frequent use of the word *special* in relation to his audience has gotten lots of flack in recent years. Critics say he used the word indiscriminately, neglecting to tie it to any sort of effort, and that as a result, a whole generation of kids grew up feeling entitled.[5]

But what Fred was actually doing was modeling the way we want to boost self-worth in our own kids. If you go back and look at old episodes, you'll see that he first *Pauses* as he talks directly to the camera, emulating active listening. He *empowers* the preschool audience by being the calm, kind, and trusted guide who spends time and "visits" with his preschool friends every day. And he *interacts* with the home audience by speaking to them with respect, explaining things to them, and asking for their point of view. Fred believed that if he looked through the camera directly, he could make a difference in at least one child's life by letting them know they are "special" and have value and worth just the way they are. In today's terms, he was saying "You be you."

Because preschoolers don't differentiate between media and real life, Mister Rogers was being at least one person in their lives who believed in them. For me, personally? He told me just what I needed to hear as a preschooler. And in reality, the generation raised on Mister Rogers is *my* generation—today's parents. A generation that the *Wall Street Journal* article referred to as the "most educated and the most child-centered." So, we don't need to *blame* Mister Rogers—we need to *thank* him for helping raise a generation of smart parents who respect kids as much as he did.

On my shows—which, as you know, have been deeply inspired by Mister Rogers—I create many opportunities for our characters to say kind, empathetic, and loving words to their "friends" on the other side of the camera. For instance, to acknowledge the audience's interactions in our games and their help in finding and solving Blue's Clues, Steve, and later Joe, lean in, look directly at the preschooler at home, and say, "You sure are smart!" By doing so, we are not only celebrating— we're praising their effort as they practice their problem-solving skills.

Likewise, Daniel Tiger looks directly into the camera and gives the home viewer an Eskimo kiss, saying "ugga mugga" at the end of every episode (which means, "I love you"). Super Why celebrates at the end of every show by singing our song, "Hip Hip Hurray! The Super Readers saved the day!"

On our episodes, we've celebrated everything from losing a tooth, riding a bicycle for the first time, and jumping in a puddle to making a snowman, learning how to ice skate, baking a cake, and even drawing a picture to make Dad happy. Celebrating these small events shows how little things can have a big impact and reinforce the idea that what our preschoolers do is important and meaningful.

CANCEL THE MARCHING BAND! BUT, HOW DO WE CELEBRATE?

So . . . the big question for parents becomes: How do we celebrate our preschooler's accomplishments without going overboard? We can do so through celebrating milestones, transitions, and family traditions in our own unique, fun, preschool-appropriate way.

Celebrate Milestones

When we're raising children, we hear a lot about the idea of "milestones," or significant stages in the lives of our children. But when you think about it, milestones are really just an optimist's version of transitions. And all transitions—going back to school, losing a tooth, learning to read, going on vacation for the first time, even the first snowfall—can be embraced and celebrated in different ways. As I wrote earlier, transitioning from Steve to Joe was a transition for *us*, but it was also a transition and a milestone for our preschool home viewers. The key was handling it with optimism and positivity.

Here are a few other examples of milestones and transitions that might resonate with you and your family:

○ **A New Baby:** Because preschoolers are inherently curious, when it comes to big events or changes in our families, they want to be in the know. To celebrate and acknowledge our preschoolers' experience, we can lean into their natural curiosity by giving them some control and power over their world. For example, when a new baby is born, we can have our preschoolers help set up the baby's room, go through their personal "baby" things and make a pile for the new baby, and even help to name him or her. Of course we, as the adults and caregivers, ultimately maintain all the control, but making our children feel a part of the process will help them with this transition that is definitely cause for celebration—a new baby in the family!

○ **A New Babysitter:** In many ways, when Joe replaced Steve on *Blue's Clues*, he essentially became a new "babysitter" in Blue's life, and we treated the transition as such, with a celebratory flair. We can do the same at home when we invite someone new into our lives to take care of and spend time with our preschoolers. We want to ensure our children feel comfortable, safe, and secure with them, show them the new babysitter knows how to play (a.k.a. that they speak fluent "preschool"), and make sure they see that we, as their parents and caregivers, trust this new presence in their lives.

○ **Going Back to School:** There are many opportunities for little celebrations tied to this rite of passage. Even the simple act of going to the store to pick out school supplies can be a celebration in and of itself, as most preschoolers love to do it. We can also get them actively involved and build up the excitement surrounding this annual celebration by having them pack their own backpack, pack their own lunch, make a new school schedule, and/or set up a special "schoolwork" area. Pro Tip: To help with angst over what to wear on the first day, I used to set out two outfits, giving my girls the choice between the two—control and choice, but with boundaries.

○ **Losing a Tooth:** While we all know that losing teeth is a *big deal*, no matter when it happens, the truth is, preschoolers can sometimes feel "out of control" when a tooth is lost. They may even worry that *all* of their teeth will come tumbling out. I remember that my girls felt funny about giving away their first tooth to the Tooth Fairy— after all, it was part of them, and so they wanted to keep it. We let that be their choice, and so they wrote a letter to the Tooth Fairy explaining that they wanted to keep their tiny baby tooth.

In my family, we had a silly, celebratory tradition whereby we gave names to our girls' two front teeth when they came out, based on where we were when the big event happened. We started this tradition due to the circumstances surrounding Hope's first lost tooth. We were on our way for our first big family vacation when her front tooth was suddenly *very* loose. She had been playing with it for so long, we weren't thinking it was actually going to come out anytime soon. But there, while waiting on the check-in line for Jet Blue with tickets in hand and luggage half-checked, was Hope's bloody smile as she grinned from ear to ear holding her first lost tooth. A milestone! A mess! A wrong time! How could we mark this moment and quickly? We all smiled, cheered (even the woman checking us in; Jet Blue is so great!), and we named her tooth as I wrapped it up in a tissue (and cleaned her mouth). We appointed it Turks! Funnily enough, she ended up losing Caicos! after biting into a hamburger at lunch the next day. Little Ella loved this aspect of the milestone, and like any little sister, couldn't wait for her turn. So, at five (a year earlier than Hope; sisters can be so competitive!), Ella lost New York! Two days later, out came New Jersey! (Less exotic, but exciting nonetheless.)

Celebrate with Traditions

Celebrations can also come into play as our family traditions. Ours range from heart-shaped pizza on Valentine's Day, Sunday-night family pasta dinners, and fondue on birthdays to impromptu pajama days and biscuits on Christmas morning. But what the traditions are about isn't what matters—it's the fact that they are repeated and that they are *yours*. They don't even have to be repeated over and over—we just want to mark them as special. Here are a few ideas to add to your mix:

○ Family game nights
○ Meatball throw-down

o   Home movie nights
o   Making a family project (quilt, scrapbook, vision boards, craft projects)
o   Buying a small trinket to collect from every vacation
o   Making hot chocolate on the first day of winter

Angela's Clues

There is a reason that every one of my preschool shows ends in a celebration of sorts. From closing celebration songs like "We Just Figured Out Blue's Clues" and "Hip Hip Hooray, the Super Readers Saved the Day," to a celebratory "Ugga Mugga" Eskimo kiss, I believe in celebrating the accomplishments of our preschoolers as they learn, grow, and actively help my characters. Again, I'm not suggesting kids get a trophy just for showing up, but I am saying that a hug and an affirming smile or a song will go a long way in building our preschoolers' self-worth as they explore, discover, and learn.

We families are so busy juggling work, family, school, and our kids' activities, that sometimes we forget to slow down and celebrate. I've found myself rushing out the door on a holiday only to forget to stop for a moment to take a family photo—a small way to celebrate and capture a milestone forever. Taking a Pause to do so says that this moment in time is *important*—important enough to document as a celebration of your family—even if it means you are a few minutes late to the Thanksgiving dinner.

At the end of the day, we want our family to be a "circle of trust"— the one place where our kids know they can go for understanding, caring, kindness, and a big celebratory hug. Even if no one else is excited about their mastering the piano piece they've been working on or finishing reading their very first chapter book, our children will know that their family is always there to Pause, ask questions, empower, and celebrate.

- **Be Involved** and Pause, empower, and interact to support your child's development of learned optimism.
- **Ask Questions** about your preschooler's work and accomplishments versus praising the outcome.
- **See the Spark** and watch your preschooler's eyes light up when you include them and celebrate the little things.

YOUR MEDIA "YES" LIST

☑ The storylines and characters celebrate and affirm preschoolers' self-worth.

☑ The celebrations aren't overly "big" or lavish.

☑ The show models acknowledging effort, not outcome.

☑ My child feels celebrated and feels good about herself after watching the show.

Clue Takeaways

○ Our preschoolers' firsts may seem small or insignificant to us, but to them they are *big* accomplishments.

○ We can help children develop learned optimism by teaching them how to "focus on the good parts."

○ Our goal is to foster our child's self-worth in a way that also builds his intrinsic motivation (in other words, celebrate their effort).

○ We can celebrate preschoolers every day by showing them we're listening, paying attention, and focused on them.

○ There is much to be gained by celebrating the little things every day, embracing our preschoolers' milestones, and starting (and keeping) fun family traditions.

EPILOGUE

Picking up her son from preschool, Katie smiles as she sees his sweet little cherub face. Upon seeing his mom, Liam runs to her and she gives him a welcoming, *celebratory* hug. *Observing* that her son has a sad expression on his face, she ushers him into the car and as they drive, she *plays* a made-up game called "Guess how I'm feeling?"

Diffusing with *humor*, Katie starts the game and makes a super-excited face. Liam laughs and guesses that his mom is feeling excited because she picked him up from school. Katie smiles and nods.

Liam says, "My turn! Guess how I'm feeling?"

Katie starts to label Liam's face. "Well, you're frowning a little, and your eyes are watery. Are you feeling . . . sad?"

Liam gulps back a few tears and nods slowly. *Pausing*, Katie *affirms*, "It looks like you feel *really* sad." Liam slowly nods again. After another *Pause*, Katie probes by *asking a question*, "Can you tell me what happened that made you sad?"

Liam nods his head and opens up about his hard day at preschool. It seems Liam wouldn't share his truck today with his friend, Spencer. Spencer forgot his truck and wanted to play with Liam's. Liam made his point, emphatically crying, "But it's *my* truck! *Mine!* And *I* wanted to play with it!"

After a brief *Pause*, Katie nods, *affirming* his feelings. "It is your toy truck." She then carefully *scaffolds*, *asking* him another *question*. "How did that make you feel?"

He sobs again and says simply, "Not good."

EPILOGUE

Katie *Pauses* and then *models* a *conflict-resolution* strategy, asking, "What do you think you could do about it?"

Liam shakes his head and says he doesn't know. Katie leaves it at that, wanting him to have time to process and *learn how to think* and attempt to *solve his own problem.*

Back at home, Katie asks Liam if he will *help* her make a snack. He happily agrees, goes to the refrigerator, and picks out some green apples and cheese, his favorite. Katie cuts up the snack and lets Liam make his own plate, choosing how much of the snack he wants. Feeling proud, Liam wants to know how else he can help. Katie asks if he can pull out the veggies he wants for dinner and put them on the counter—that would be a big help. Liam does, with a smile on his face.

Modeling eating healthily, and *caring* to spend time with her son, Katie sits down with Liam for a few minutes and they eat their snack together. At the table, Liam tells her about how silly Spencer is, and then his face turns red as he seems to remember his issue with his good friend. Katie shares something silly that happened to her today, too, and they *laugh* and *bond* together.

Katie confides in Liam that she has some work to do in her home office and asks him how he could *help her.* Liam thinks hard and comes up with a plan: How about he gets to watch his favorite show—*Daniel Tiger's Neighborhood*—and she can do her work? Katie agrees that it sounds like a plan!

Remembering Liam's issue from preschool, she flips through her Media "Yes" list and calls up the episodes of Daniel Tiger on her streaming video on demand channel. She finds the one where Daniel Tiger has a problem sharing his toy car. Perfect. She knows that Daniel Tiger's *peer modeling* will be a help as he figures out how to solve his own problem.

Nearby, Katie goes to her emails, finishing up the work she needs to do. As she does, she can hear the Daniel Tiger sharing strategy being sung (and repeated ad nauseam!), "You can take a turn, then I'll get it back." Clutching his own truck as he watches Daniel Tiger clutch

266

his car, Liam looks at the show with big saucer eyes, drinking in the strategy.

After the show, Katie turns off the TV and nudges Liam toward his toys so he can play for a bit as she goes back to her emails. Liam starts to play with his toy car, zooming it all around the house, up and over Katie and back again. After about the third time of this, Katie realizes he needs some attention and decides that her work is done for now—forty-five minutes was a good chunk of time, anyway!

She sits on the floor with Liam and *plays*—asking for a turn with his car. Liam, at first, recoils. Katie starts to hum the *musical* jingle, and picking up on it, Liam sings, "You can take a turn, and then I'll get it back!" and hands Katie the car, all the while watching her. Katie plays with the car for a bit and then gives it back. Liam takes his turn and then lets his mom have another turn. They *repeat* this game a few times (repetition is the key to learning!), and soon it's time to go pick up Liam's sister.

As they walk out the door, Liam looks up at Katie and says, "I think I know what to do about Spencer."

Katie asks, "What will you do?"

Liam takes a deep breath. "Tomorrow I will give him a turn with my car. But then I will get it back."

Katie smiles, gives him a little Eskimo kiss in *celebration*, and says that it sounds like a good plan.

In this small slice of an ordinary day with a preschooler, Katie has used each one of the eleven Preschool Clues, as well as used healthy media as a parenting tool. Hurray! Like Katie, I hope you've recognized how powerful preschool media can be for enhancing your preschooler's social, emotional, and cognitive growth. I hope you feel confident about the healthy media diet you're choosing for your child—a green smoothie that's full of educational, interactive, and engaging content that sparks them. But most of all, I hope that after reading this book, you feel empowered and inspired to tap into powerful clues like play, the intentional Pause, repetition, modeling, respectful communication, asking for help, celebrations, and more, to help your preschooler develop as an engaged, smart, and kind person, but also to create a more deeply bonded, connected family.

So, please . . . ditch the guilt, grab the remote, and find all of the Preschool Clues inside high-quality preschool TV, for both your child *and* for you.

Angela C. Santomero

NOTES

FOREWORD

1. D. R. Anderson, A. C. Huston, K. L. Schmitt, D. L. Linebarger, and J. C. Wright, "Early Childhood Television Viewing and Adolescent Behavior," *Monographs of the Society for Research in Child Development,* 68(1), serial no. 264 (2001): 1–143.
2. M. Gladwell, *The Tipping Point: How Little Things Can Make a Big Difference* (New York: Little Brown and Company, 2000).
3. A. M. Crawley, D. R. Anderson, A. Wilder, M. Williams, and A. Santomero, "Effects of Repeated Exposures to a Single Episode of the Television Program *Blue's Clues* on the Viewing Behaviors and Comprehension of Preschool Children," *Journal of Educational Psychology,* 91 (1999), 630–37.
4. A. M. Crawley, D. R. Anderson, A. Santomero, A. Wilder, M. Williams, M. K. Evans, and J. Bryant, "Do Children Learn How to Watch Television? The Impact of Extensive Experience with *Blue's Clues* on Preschool Children's Television Viewing Behavior," *Journal of Communication,* 52 (2002), 264–80.

WATCH, LEARN, KNOW

Watch

1. Robert Mays, Sune Nordwall, et al., "Frequently Asked Questions: What Is the Philosophy Behind Waldorf Education?," Waldorf Answers, accessed March 15, 2017, www.waldorfanswers.org/WaldorfFAQ.htm#6.
2. American Academy of Pediatrics, Committee on Public Education, "Children, Adolescents, and Television," *Pediatrics* 107, no. 2 (February 1, 2001): 423–26, doi: 10.1542/peds.107.2.423.
3. Victoria J. Rideout, MA, Ulla G. Foehr, PhD, and Donald F. Roberts, PhD, *Generation M2: Media in the Lives of 8- to 18-Year-Olds—A Kaiser Founda-*

tion Study (Menlo Park, CA: Henry J. Kaiser Family Foundation, January 2010), http://files.eric.ed.gov/fulltext/ED527859.pdf.

4. Jenny S. Radesky, Jayna Schumacher, and Barry Zuckerman, "Mobile and Interactive Media Use by Young Children: The Good, the Bad, and the Unknown," *Pediatrics* 135, no. 1 (January 1, 2015), doi: 10.1542/peds.2014 -2251.

5. Anya Kamenetz, "American Academy of Pediatrics Lifts 'No Screens Under 2' Rule," NPR online, October 21, 2016, www.npr.org/sections /ed/2016/10/21/498550475/american-academy-of-pediatrics-lifts-no -screens-under-2-rule.

6. R. A. Reiser, M. A. Tessmer, and P. C. Phelps, *Educational Technology Research and Development (ECTJ)* 32 (1984): 217, doi:10.1007/BF02768893.

7. Richard C. Anderson, Paul T. Wilson, and Linda G. Fielding, "Growth in Reading and How Children Spend Their Time Outside of School," *Reading Research Quarterly* 23, no. 3 (1988): 285–303, doi:10.1598/rrq.23.3.2.

Learn

1. Jordan Brunson, "Teaching Through Big Bird: The Woman Behind Sesame Street," AAUW online, May 9, 2016, www.aauw.org/2016/05/09/how -she-got-to-sesame-street.

2. Malcolm Gladwell, *The Tipping Point: How Little Things Can Make a Big Difference* (London: Abacus, 2015).

3. Angeline S. Lillard and Jennifer Peterson, "The Immediate Impact of Different Types of Television on Young Children's Executive Function," *Pediatrics* 128, no. 4 (October 2011): http://pediatrics.aappublications.org /content/early/2011/09/08/peds.2010-1919.

4. Elizabeth Jensen, "A New Heroine's Fighting Words," *New York Times* online, September 1, 2007, www.nytimes.com/2007/09/02/arts/television /02jens.html.

Know

1. Jean Piaget, "Piaget's Theory of Cognitive Development," chap. 2 in *Childhood Cognitive Development: The Essential Readings,* ed. Kang Lee (Malden, MA: Blackwell, 2000), 33–48.

2. Ellen Galinsky, *Mind in the Making: The Seven Essential Life Skills Every Child Needs* (New York: Avon Books, 2010).

3. "Executive Function & Self-Regulation," Center on the Developing Child at Harvard University online, accessed March 19, 2017, http://developing child.harvard.edu/science/key-concepts/executive-function.

NOTES

4. Louise Bates Ames and Frances L. Ilg, *Your Three-Year-Old: Friend or Enemy* (New York: Dell Trade Paperback, 1987).
5. Erik H. Erikson and Joan M. Erikson, *The Life Cycle Completed (Extended Version)* (New York: W. W. Norton, 1998).
6. Deborah Reber, *Differently Wired: Raising an Exceptional Child in a Conventional World* (New York: Workman, 2018).

PLAY, PAUSE, REPEAT

Clue #1: Play

1. Rachel E. White, *The Power of Play: A Research Summary on Play and Learning* (Saint Paul, MN: Minnesota Children's Museum, 2012).
2. Dorothy G. Singer, Roberta Michnick Golinkoff, and Kathy Hirsh-Pasek, eds., *Play = Learning: How Play Motivates and Enhances Children's Cognitive and Social-Emotional Growth* (New York: Oxford University Press, 2006).
3. Iain Lancaster, "The Importance of Intrinsic Motivation in Transforming Learning," TeachThought online, accessed March 19, 2017, www.teach thought.com/learning/the-importance-of-intrinsic-motivation-in-trans forming-learning.
4. Daniel H. Pink, *Drive: The Surprising Truth About What Motivates Us* (New York: Riverhead Books, 2012).
5. Meghan Dombrink-Green, "A Conversation with Vivian Gussin Paley," *Young Children* 66, no. 5 (September 2011): 90–93, www.naeyc.org/con tent/conversation-vivian-gussin-paley.

Clue #2: Pause

1. Mary Budd Rowe, "Wait Time: Slowing Down May Be a Way of Speeding Up!," *Journal of Teacher Education* 37, no. 1 (1986): 43–50, doi:10.1177/002 248718603700110.
2. "Serve and Return," Center on the Developing Child at Harvard University online, accessed March 6, 2017, http://developingchild.harvard.edu /science/key-concepts/serve-and-return.
3. S. L. Calvert et al., "Interaction and Participation for Young Hispanic and Caucasian Children's Learning of Media Content," *Media Psychology* 9, no. 2 (2007): 431–45.
4. Daniel R. Anderson et al., "Researching Blue's Clues: Viewing Behavior and Impact," *Media Psychology* 2, no. 2 (2000): 179–94, doi:10.1207/s1532785 xmep0202_4.

NOTES

5. Julie A. Ross, *Practical Parenting for the 21st Century: The Manual You Wish Had Come with Your Child* (New York: Excalibur, 1993).
6. Jessica Lahey, *The Gift of Failure: How the Best Parents Learn to Let Go So Their Children Can Succeed* (New York: Harper, 2016).
7. G. J. Whitehurst et al., "Accelerating Language Development Through Picture Book Reading," *Developmental Psychology* 24, no. 4 (1988): 552–59. doi:10.1037//0012-1649.24.4.552.

Clue #3: Repeat

1. Lawrie Mifflin, "The Joy of Repetition, Repetition, Repetition," *New York Times* online, August 2, 1997, www.nytimes.com/1997/08/03/tv/the-joy -of-repetition-repetition-repetition.html.
2. "Five Numbers to Remember About Early Childhood Development," Center on the Developing Child at Harvard University online, accessed March 6, 2017, http://developingchild.harvard.edu/resources/five-num bers-to-remember-about-early-childhood-development.
3. Malcolm Gladwell, *Outliers: The Story of Success* (New York: Little, Brown, 2008).
4. Steve Wheeler, "Jerome Bruner on the Scaffolding of Learning," Teach-Thought online, accessed March 19, 2017, www.teachthought.com/learn ing/learning-theories-jerome-bruner-scaffolding-learning.
5. Alisha M. Crawley et al., "Effects of Repeated Exposures to a Single Episode of the Television Program Blue's Clues on the Viewing Behaviors and Comprehension of Preschool Children," *Journal of Educational Psychology* 91, no. 4 (1999): 630–37, doi:10.1037//0022-0663.91.4.630.
6. Carol S. Dweck, *Mindset: How You Can Fulfill Your Potential* (London: Robinson, 2017).

THINK, RESOLVE, RESPECT

Clue #4: Think

1. Michael Michalko, *Thinkertoys: A Handbook of Creative-Thinking Techniques*, 2nd ed. (New York: Ten Speed Press, 2006).
2. Aleszu Bajak, "Lectures Aren't Just Boring, They're Ineffective, Too, Study Finds," Science Insider, last modified May 12, 2014, www.sciencemag.org /news/2014/05/lectures-arent-just-boring-theyre-ineffective-too-study -finds.
3. Carol S. Dweck, "The Secret to Raising Smart Kids," *Scientific American*,

December 18, 2014, www.scientificamerican.com/article/the-secret-to
-raising-smart-kids1.

Clue #5: Resolve

1. Joseph A. Durlak et al., "The Impact of Enhancing Students' Social and Emotional Learning: A Meta-Analysis of School-Based Universal Interventions," *Child Development* 82, no. 1 (2011): 405–32, doi:10.1111/j.1467-8624.2010.01564.x.
2. Wesley H. Dotson et al., "Evaluating the Ability of the PBS Children's Show *Daniel Tiger's Neighborhood* to Teach Skills to Two Young Children with Autism Spectrum Disorder," *Behavior Analysis in Practice* 10, no. 1 (August 12, 2016): 67–71, doi:10.1007/s40617-016-0134-z.
3. Ross, *Practical Parenting for the 21st Century.*

Clue #6: Respect

1. Douglas Quenqua, "Quality of Words, Not Quantity, Is Crucial to Language Skills, Study Finds," *New York Times* online, October 16, 2014, www.nytimes.com/2014/10/17/us/quality-of-words-not-quantity-is-crucial-to-language-skills-study-finds.html?_r=0.
2. Roberta Schomburg, personal conversation.
3. Shuka Kalantari, "Why We Should Teach Empathy to Preschoolers," Greater Good, last modified June 29, 2016, http://greatergood.berkeley.edu/article/item/why_we_should_teach_empathy_preschoolers.

HELP, MODEL, OBSERVE

Clue #7: Help

1. Kristine Breese, "14 Little Ways to Encourage Kindness," *Parents* online, accessed March 6, 2017, www.parents.com/parenting/better-parenting/advice/14-little-ways-to-encourage-kindness.
2. David Brooks, "Nice Guys Finish First," *New York Times* online, May 16, 2011, www.nytimes.com/2011/05/17/opinion/17brooks.html.
3. Lara B. Aknin, Elizabeth W. Dunn, and Michael I. Norton, "Happiness Runs in a Circular Motion: Evidence for a Positive Feedback Loop Between Prosocial Spending and Happiness," *Journal of Happiness Studies* 13, no. 2 (2011): 347–55, doi:10.1007/s10902-011-9267-5.
4. Keely Lockhart, "Duchess of Cambridge: Teaching George and Charlotte Kindness and Respect Is as Important as Academic Success," *Lon-*

NOTES

don Telegraph, February 6, 2017, www.telegraph.co.uk/news/2017/02/06
/duchess-cambridge-teaching-george-charlotte-kindness-respect.

5. Daryl Cameron, Michael Inzlicht, and William A. Cunningham, "Empathy
   Is Actually a Choice," *New York Times* online. July 10, 2015, www.nytimes
   .com/2015/07/12/opinion/sunday/empathy-is-actually-a-choice.html?
   _r=0.

6. David A. Pizarro and Peter Salovey, "Being and Becoming a Good Person,"
   chap. 12 in *Improving Academic Achievement: Impact of Psychological Factors on Education*, ed. Joshua Aronson (San Diego: Academic Press, 2002):
   247–66, doi:10.1016/b978-012064455-1/50015-4.

7. Gwen Dewar, "Teaching Empathy: Evidence-Based Tips," Parenting Science, last modified September 2016, www.parentingscience.com/teach
   ing-empathy-tips.html.

8. Marty Rossmann, "Involving Children in Household Tasks: Is It Worth
   the Effort?," University of Minnesota, September 2002, http://ghk.h-cdn
   .co/assets/cm/15/12/55071e0298a05_-_Involving-children-in-house
   hold-tasks-U-of-M.pdf.

Clue #8: Model

1. Rasha Madkour, "Daniel Tiger Becomes a Boy with Autism's Guide to
   Social Life," *New York Times* online, July 12, 2015, https://parenting.blogs
   .nytimes.com/2015/07/12/daniel-tiger-becomes-a-boy-with-autisms
   -guide-to-social-life/?_r=0.

2. Albert Bandura, Dorothea Ross, and Sheila A. Ross, "Transmission of Aggression Through Imitation of Aggressive Models," *Journal of Abnormal
   and Social Psychology* 63, no. 3 (December 1961): 575–82, doi:10.1037/
   h0045925.

3. Barbara J. Wilson, "Media and Children's Aggression, Fear, and Altruism,"
   Future of Children 18, no. 1 (Spring 2008): 87–118, doi:10.1353/foc.0.0005.

4. Leonard D. Eron et al., "Does Television Violence Cause Aggression?,"
   American Psychologist 27, no. 4 (May 1972): 253–63, doi:10.1037/h0033721.

5. L. Rowell Huesmann and Laurie S. Miller, "Long-Term Effects of Repeated
   Exposure to Media Violence in Childhood," in *Aggressive Behavior: Current
   Perspectives*, ed. Huesmann, Plenum Series in Social/Clinical Psychology
   (New York: Plenum Press, 1994), 153–86, doi:10.1007/978-1-4757-9116-
   7_7.

6. Christopher J. Ferguson, "The School Shooting/Violent Video Game Link:
   Causal Relationship or Moral Panic?," *Journal of Investigative Psychology
   and Offender Profiling* 5, nos. 1–2 (2008): 25–37, doi:10.1002/jip.76.

7. Brian Wansink, David R. Just, and Collin R. Payne, "Can Branding Improve School Lunches?," *Archives of Pediatrics & Adolescent Medicine* 166, no. 10 (2012): 967, doi:10.1001/archpediatrics.2012.999.

8. Eric E. Rasmussen et al., "Relation Between Active Mediation, Exposure to *Daniel Tiger's Neighborhood*, and US Preschoolers' Social and Emotional Development," *Journal of Children and Media* 10, no. 4 (2016): 443–61, doi: 10.1080/17482798.2016.1203806.

Clue #9: Observe

1. Amy Laura Dombro and Leah Wallach, *The Ordinary Is Extraordinary: How Children Under Three Learn* (Lincoln, NE: iUniverse, 2001).

2. Ellyn Satter, *How to Get Your Kid to Eat: But Not Too Much* (Boulder, CO: Bull Publishing, 2012).

3. Marian C. Diamond et al., "On the Brain of a Scientist: Albert Einstein," *Experimental Neurology* 88, no. 1 (1985): 198–204, doi:10.1016/0014-4886 (85)90123-2.

4. Joanne F. Foster, "Intrinsic Versus Extrinsic Motivation," in *Encyclopedia of Giftedness, Creativity, and Talent*, ed. Barbara Kerr (Thousand Oaks, CA: Sage, 2009), doi:10.4135/9781412971959.n214.

5. Carrie Furrer and Ellen Skinner, "Sense of Relatedness as a Factor in Children's Academic Engagement and Performance," *Journal of Educational Psychology* 95, no. 1 (2003): 148–62, doi:10.1037//0022-0663.95.1.148.

6. Rawn Fulton, *Eric Carle: Picture Writer* (DVD video) (New York: Philomel Books/Scholastic, 1993).

LAUGH, SING, CELEBRATE

Clue #10: Enjoy

1. Avner Ziv and Orit Gadish, "Humor and Marital Satisfaction," *Journal of Social Psychology* 129, no. 6 (1989): 759–68, doi:10.1080/00224545.1989.97 12084.

2. Elizabeth B. Carlton, "Learning Through Music: The Support of Brain Research," *Child Care Information Exchange* 133 (May/June 2000): 53–56.

3. Wishenpoof Anthem, episode 101, music and lyrics by Blain Morris.

4. Sandra L. Calvert, "Impact of Televised Songs on Children's and Young Adults' Memory of Educational Content," *Media Psychology* 3, no. 4 (2001): 325–42.

5. Yuna L. Ferguson and Kennon M. Sheldon, "Trying to Be Happier Really Can Work: Two Experimental Studies," *Journal of Positive Psychology* 8, no. 1 (2013): 23–33, doi:10.1080/17439760.2012.747000.

NOTES

Clue #11: Celebrations

1. D. A. Snowdon et al., "Linguistic Ability in Early Life and Longevity: Findings from the Nun Study," in *The Paradoxes of Longevity*, eds. Jean-Marie Robine et al. (Berlin: Springer-Verlag, 1999), 103–13, doi:10.1007/978-3-642-60100-2_9.
2. Karen Reivich and Andrew Shatté, *The Resilience Factor: 7 Essential Skills for Overcoming Life's Inevitable Obstacles* (New York: Three Rivers Press, 2003).
3. "Resilience in Children," Positive Psychology Center, accessed March 7, 2017, https://ppc.sas.upenn.edu/research/resilience-children.
4. Leonard Sax, *The Collapse of Parenting: How We Hurt Our Kids When We Treat Them Like Grown-Ups* (New York: Basic Books, 2017).
5. Jeffrey Zaslow, "Blame It on Mr. Rogers: Why Young Adults Feel So Entitled," *Wall Street Journal* online, July 5, 2007, www.wsj.com/articles/SB118358476840657463.

ACKNOWLEDGMENTS

Thank You, For Everything You Do

What an honor and thrill it's been to have the opportunity to share the tools I so fiercely believe in with you in the form of a book. I've spent my life writing for preschoolers—and am honored to do so—but to turn my writing inside out and write for *you* has been a dream come true!

Truth be told, this book would not be possible were it not for the wonderful community of kids' media and the people I've been honored to work with. First and foremost, I need to tell you that *it really does take a village to make a show*. When I talk about my shows, I'm also acknowledging my *village*, and it's not just any village, but my smart, passionate, dedicated village that believes in the vision to make the world a better place for kids. I happen to have the very best village in all of children's media. Together we have thought hard, we've laughed, we've cried (and we may have even screamed a little). When I see our shows out there in the world, I think back and know that I am so proud of everything that we have done, together.

To the Co-Creator of our firstborn show, *Blue's Clues*—Traci Paige Johnson—what would I have done if you hadn't sent me your used pizza box? You amaze me with your level of creative genius and deep friendship. To my Extraordinary Executive Producer Wendy Harris— I followed you to the train station twenty years ago, and we've been together ever since! To Dr. (Aunt) Alice Wilder for always elevating what we do for kids each and every day and for being in my life for over twenty-five years! To my *BC* staff, I still tear up when I talk about you all—we will forever be family. Dave Palmer, Marcy Pritchard, and Jennifer Twomey for your creativity, friendship, undying loyalty, and squagels. For Steve Burns and Donovan Patton (Joe!), I'm forever grateful for your genius. For each animator, researcher, producer, musician, editor, and member of the production staff, including Sarah Landy, Claire Curley Rather, Amy Steinburg, Adam Peltzman, Jeff Borkin, Sascha Palladino, Jessica Lissy, Jeremy Slutskin, and Mason Rather. I'm so proud of what you have all created and continue to do for kids.

To my amazing Out of the Blue team who elevate what I do every day. Samantha Freeman—you have taught me so much. Becky Friedman Lowitt, you are a TRUE talent—thank you for writing, laughing, and rewriting with me until all hours of the night. Rachel Kalban, thank you for your passion, creativity, and smarts to heighten our work for kids. Sarah Wallendjack for your amazing creative and production instincts and savviness. Shevaun Grey for your creative eye. Alexandra Cassel for your ability to be an out-of-the-box thinker. Alex Breen for your genius. Steph, Gord, Aly, Daniel, Shivani, Noriko, Kyra, Chelsea, Taryn, Connor, Maddie—*you all* make it happen everyday! To Jen Hamburg—I dramatically fanatically adore you! And thank you to Josh and Jeff for believing in our little engine that could.

To my amazing Network partners—everyone at Nickelodeon who believed in this "research girl" and gave her a chance to make her dreams come true, especially Cyma Zarghami and Cathy Galleota. To everyone at PBS Kids, including Paula Kerger, Leslie Rottenburg, and Sara Dewitt, and most especially Linda Simensky, who told me I needed to write this book! The Fred Rogers Company with Paul Siefken, Kevin Morrison, Chris Loggins, Ellen Dougherty, and Bill Isler—thank you, *all*, for allowing me the honor to celebrate Fred's legacy—I will forever be grateful. To Amazon Kids, especially Tara Sorenson—you have been a wonderful visionary partner and your passion is contagious!

To 9 Story Media Group, who are leading the way to better content for kids: Vince Commisso—*you* are the real deal—Natalie, Tanya, Vadim, Julie. To Voo Doo Highway: Brian, Graeme, and the rest of the team for your Daniel Tiger creativity and passion to write and compose songs we can't get out of our heads—awesome songs and Daniel strategies that we keep singing. To DHX: Steven Denure, Anne Loi, and all of the creatives at DHX Hallifax—Phillip, Gilly, and Jay. To Blaine Morris for our beautiful *Wishenpoof* empowerment ballads that have changed lives.

To Dr. Rosemarie Truglio and Dr. Herb Ginsburg at Teachers College, Columbia University, for teaching me all I know about child development. To Dr. Dan Anderson for being my mentor, my friend, and an unbelievable source of inspiration. To Gerry Laybourne—you've inspired me from the first day I heard you speak. Changing the world for kids has always been our shared vision. To Kit Laybourne—you gave me my first "break." Interning for you was one of my greatest gifts. To Brown Johnson, Herb Scannell, Stacey Levin, Karen Hill Scott, Karen Flischel, Beth Young, Rande Price, and Julie Monahan. To my CUA family for showing me the way. To my friends in Anguilla, especially Peter and Anne Parles at Straw Hat. Maddie Kroll—research assistant on this book—extraordinaire! To Marc Chamlin—who makes me smarter; John Tishbe for your support; Susan Schulman—a fabulous literary agent. To Ellen Gallinsky, Melissa Wardy, Diane Tracy, Louise Chung. To Alexandra Venancio and my seventh-grade English teacher, Andy Walker, for inspiring me to write.

To my family: my parents, especially my mom, for teaching me how to be a strong, independent woman. My siblings—my brother, Robert, and sisters Jennifer, Alicia, Dawn, Julie, Francesca—you have my heart. My cousins and friends—Felicia, Christine, Lori, Julie, Gabriella, Elizabeth, Peter (my train buddy), Joyce, Rachel, Alyssa—for either watching or putting on plays with me in the basement. To the Santomeros, especially Vinny and Lauretta, for always believing in me. And to all the kids in my life who grew up on my shows: Morgan, Perry (from our very first *Blue's Clues* Mail Time letter!), Sabrina, Jenna (my Paprika and Muffin Pan!), Beau, Austin, Ryan, Grant, Will, Meri, Jack, Christopher, Calista, Landon, Aidan, Peter, Reese, Bennett, Vivian, and Meadow.

To Joanne Rogers for being my friend—you are a light in my life.

And of course, to Fred Rogers for being my mentor from afar. You started it all, and children's media thanks you for it.

To Cara Bedick, my editor, for sharing your genius, believing in us, and helping us find that North Star.

To everyone who has ever let their preschoolers watch one of my shows. Thank *you* for trusting us and allowing us into your homes.

To Deb Reber—thank you for your positivity, your love and support, your smarts, eloquence, goddamn beautiful writing, friendship, and all-around amazingness. When I met you almost twenty years ago I knew we would be doing wonderful things together. I couldn't have done this without you. Especially the charts. ;)

Finally, to my little family: my rock star husband, my anchor, my best friend—Greg Santomero—I would not be here if it wasn't for you. You are still the best decision I have ever made. I love you with all of my heart! And to my girls—Hope Cassandra and Ella Angelina—you are both amazing people, and I'm honored to be your mom. I can't wait to see what you do in this world!

FROM DEBORAH REBER

To our awesome editor, Cara Bedick—how fun to work with you on a book more than ten years after we first collaborated on a publishing project. It's been an honor!

To our agent, Susan Schulman—thank you for your belief in this book from the very beginning and helping us get it right where it needed to be.

To the most loving friends and family a gal could have: my sister Michele Reber, my folks, Dale and MaryLou, and my dearest friends, Alice Wilder and AnneMarie—I'm so grateful for your unwavering and continual support of my writing, parenting, and all the other stuff, big and small. And a special thanks to amazing friends who helped me balance a busy life while working on this book and showered me with support along the way: Simone Davies, Donna Bardsley, Emmy

ACKNOWLEDGMENTS

McCarthy, Jessika Lynch, Gia Duke, Lee Davis, and Daniel Afonso. And the best research assistant around, Maddie Kroll.

To the incredible guys I get to spend my life with—my uber supportive husband, Derin, and my brilliant boy, Asher—who cheered me on every day. I love you more than anything.

And of course to Angela Santomero—it's been such a joy to collaborate with you and help you share your vision with the world. From our midnight texting parties to our Skype work powwows, this has definitely been the most fun I've ever had working on a book. You are more than a dear friend—you are a mentor and someone who, oh so many years ago, helped me realize that I can do anything that I wanna do. Love you!

INDEX

Page numbers in *italics* refer to charts.

INDEX

INDEX

INDEX

INDEX

INDEX

INDEX

INDEX

William Taufic

ANGELA C. SANTOMERO, M.A., is the creator, executive producer, and writer for award-winning kids and family content/brands including *Daniel Tiger's Neighborhood* (PBS), *Blue's Clues* (Nick Jr.), *Super Why!* (PBS), *Creative Galaxy* (Amazon Studios), and *Wishenpoof* (Amazon Studios). Malcolm Gladwell referred to Angela's *Blue's Clues* as "One of the stickiest TV shows EVER made" in his book *The Tipping Point*.

Described by Joanne Rogers as "a modern-day Fred Rogers," and by Fatherly.com as "the driving force behind the best educational programming for children," Angela's work has won the prestigious Peabody award, two TCA awards, twenty-five-plus Emmy nominations, and numerous Parents' Choice Gold Awards. Angela's legacy is forever changing the way in which preschoolers watch television by presenting them with unique, challenging programs that enable them to learn through play, humor, and respect, changing the world one preschooler at a time!

Angela has a B.A. from the Catholic University of America, which awarded her a Young Alumni Merit Award, and her master's degree in child developmental psychology and instructional media and education from Columbia University (Teachers College), which awarded her its 1999 Early Career Award. Angela's children's education background coupled with her unique knowledge of kids' media and production allow her work to successfully integrate education, entertainment, and active participation to enable children to learn through play.

Angela likes to spend time with her daughters, her husband, and their puppies: Blue (just kidding!), Oreo, and Samoa. Angela loves to hear from YOU at angelasclues.com.

DEBORAH REBER, a bestselling author, life coach, and speaker, is a former children's television executive (Nickelodeon, Cartoon Network), as well as a writer and producer of educational media—books, online games, videos, CD-ROMs—for children ages two through eighteen. She is the founder of TiLT Parenting and the host of the TiLT Parenting Podcast, which is aimed at helping parents raising neurologically atypical kids do so from a place of confidence and peace. Debbie's latest book is *Differently Wired: Raising an Exceptional Child in a Conventional World* (Workman Publishing, 2018). She has a master's degree in media studies from the New School for Social Research.